Springer Texts in Business and Economics

Springer Texts in Business and Economics (STBE) delivers high-quality instructional content for undergraduates and graduates in all areas of Business/Management Science and Economics. The series is comprised of self-contained books with a broad and comprehensive coverage that are suitable for class as well as for individual self-study. All texts are authored by established experts in their fields and offer a solid methodological background, often accompanied by problems and exercises.

More information about this series at http://www.springer.com/series/10099

Hongmu Lee

Risk Management

Fundamentals, Theory, and Practice in Asia

Springer

Hongmu Lee
School of Commerce
Waseda University
Tokyo, Japan

ISSN 2192-4333 ISSN 2192-4341 (electronic)
Springer Texts in Business and Economics
ISBN 978-981-16-3467-3 ISBN 978-981-16-3468-0 (eBook)
https://doi.org/10.1007/978-981-16-3468-0

This Springer imprint is published by the registered company Springer Nature Singapore Pte Ltd.
The registered company address is: 152 Beach Road, #21-01/04 Gateway East, Singapore 189721, Singapore

Foreword

Enterprise risk management (ERM) has several applications, such as responding to changes in the environment and rational management to gain competitive advantage. The 9/11 terrorist attack on the United States has shown the industry the importance of ERM.

Furthermore, after the Enron scandal in December 2001 and WorldCom fraud in June 2002, several laws were enacted or revised throughout the world, such as the SOX Act in the United States and the Financial Instruments and Exchange Law and Companies Act in Japan, to prevent further corporate accounting frauds; this situation also led to the rapid spread of corporate risk management (RM). In this regard, the Committee of Sponsoring Organizations published its ERM framework, while the International Standards Organization published its RM framework. The author believes that the competition between these frameworks was an opportunity to systematize the RM theory and greatly develop it as a discipline.

Likewise, the Great East Japan Earthquake, which struck Japan on 11 March 2011, caused enormous losses. In order to cope with the effects of the earthquake, the Japanese government provided earthquake reinsurance, but this was not to compensate for the losses due to earthquakes, but rather to provide a limited amount of resources to improve the housing and financial situation of those affected by earthquakes and to ensure their safety. The Japanese government's earthquake reinsurance does not cover commercial properties and is not a corporate earthquake insurance measure.

In recent years, earthquakes as well as natural disasters such as floods and typhoons have been increasing in frequency along with climate changes. Companies thus need to adopt comprehensive and systematic countermeasures to safeguard their business activities from natural disasters. Environmental changes and increasing uncertainty have made ERM ever more important for business activities, with society increasingly demanding improvement and thorough application against the background of frequent corporate scandals and accidents.

In recent years, there has been a major reform of the industry due to the fourth industrial revolution, the technological innovation represented by Internet of Things (IOT) and Artificial Intelligence (AI). On the other hand, these changes have promoted the development of financial technology, Fintech or InsurTech, and have had a huge impact on the financial industry. For example, the virtual currency has no border and regulatory agencies, and complex financial products have exceeded the boundary of banks, insurance, and securities. In these circumstances, cyber risk has increased rapidly and is expected to continue to increase. In addition, the ongoing global pandemic demands a fundamental change in our way of working. Such situations increase uncertainty and increase risk.

ERM is seen differently depending on one's position. For accountants, it is a means for proper internal accounting control, whereas for financial institutions and others, it quantifies the risk that administrators can take to meet supervisory standards. Therefore, most of ERM outlines are written to suit the intended uses or topics such as risk financing, with no systematic RM overviews.

This book organizes the author's lecture notes while trying to create a systematic RM theory framework. I believe that the book can be used as an overview to help readers understand the systematic fundamentals of ERM from various perspectives.

School of Commerce, Waseda University Hongmu Lee
Tokyo, Japan

Acknowledgements

This book is an English version based on Principles of Risk Management (Japanese) (2019, Seibundo), revised and with Chaps. 16 and 17 added. The Principles of Risk Management (Japanese) was also published in Chinese and Korean by Hakueisha in 2020.

The publication of this book is supported by the Kano Foundation of Waseda University's Faculty of Commerce.

Contents

Abbreviations

AAA	American Accounting Association
ABS	Asset-backed security
AI	Artificial intelligence
AICPA	American Institute of Certified Public Accountants
AIG	American International Group
AIGFP	AIG Financial Products
ART	Alternative risk transfer
B/S	Balance sheet
BBA	British Bankers' Association
BCM	Business continuity management
BCP	Business continuity plan
BRM	Business risk management
CBO	Collateralized bond obligation
CBOT	Chicago Board of Trade
CBRNE	Chemical, biological, radiological, nuclear, and explosive
CCRIF	Caribbean Disaster Risk Insurance Organization
CD	Certificate of deposit
CDC	Centers for Disease Control and Prevention
CDD	Cooling degree day
CDO	Collateralized debt obligation
CDS	Credit default swap
CDS	Credit derivative swap
CDSCHQ	Central Disaster and Safety Countermeasures Headquarters
CEO	Chief executive officer
CFO	Chief financial officer
CLO	Collateralized loan obligation
CM	Crisis management
CMBS	Commercial mortgage-backed security
CME	Chicago Mercantile Exchange
CMI	CME Hurricane Index
CMP	Crisis management plan
COSO	Committee of Sponsoring Organizations
CP	Contingency plan

CRM	Comprehensive risk management
CSR	Corporate social responsibility
EAD	Exposure at default
EISS	Epidemic Investigation Support System
EL	Expected loss
ELF	Event link futures
EMS	Environmental management system
EPA	Environmental Protection Agency
ERM	Enterprise risk management
ETA	Event tree analysis
EWRM	Enterprise-wide risk management
FEI	Financial Executives International
FHLMC	Federal Home Loan Mortgage Corporation
FMEA	Failure mode and effects analysis
FRB	Federal Reserve Board
FT	Fault tree
FTA	Fault tree analysis
GCCI	Guy Carpenter Catastrophe Index
HDD	Heating degree day
HRM	Holistic risk management
HV	Historical volatility
IBRD	International Bank for Reconstruction and Development
IFEX	Insurance Futures Exchange
IIA	Institute of Internal Auditors
ILS	Insurance-linked security
ILW	Industry loss warranty
IMA	Institute of Management Accountants
IOT	Internet of Things
IR	Investor relations
IRM	Integrated risk management
ISMS	Information security management
ISO	International Organization for Standardization
IV	Implied volatility
JIS	Japanese Industrial Standards
JISC	Japan Industrial Standards Committee
KCDC	Korea Centers for Disease Control and Prevention
KDCA	Korea Disease Control and Prevention Agency
LGD	Loss given default
LIBOR	London Interbank Offered Rate
LMX	London Market Excess of Loss
MAC	Material adverse change
MBS	Mortgage-backed security
MERS	Middle East respiratory syndrome
NAIC	National Association of Insurance Commissioners
NBCR	Nuclear, biological, chemical and radiological

NCDC	National Climate Data Center
NGO	Non-government organization
NPO	Non-profit organization
OTC	Over-the-counter
P/L	Profit and loss
PCS	Property Claims Service
PD	Probability of default
PDCA	Plan-do-check-act
PHEIC	Public health emergency of international concern
PL	Product liability
PML	Probable maximum loss
REIT	Real estate investment trust
RM	Risk management
RMBS	Residential mortgage-backed security
RMS	Root mean square
SARS	Severe acute respiratory syndrome
SCM	Supply chain management
SD	Standard deviation
SEC	Securities and Exchange Commission
SPC	Special purpose company
SPE	Special purpose entity
SPI	Special purpose insurance company
SPV	Special purpose vehicle
SRM	Strategic risk management
TDL	Tokyo Disneyland
TIBOR	Tokyo Interbank Offered Rate
UL	Unexpected loss
US	United States
VaR	Value at risk
WHO	World Health Organization

List of Figures

List of Tables

Part I

The General Theory of Risk Management

1 The Concept of Risk and Corporate Risk

Risk is generally described as something dangerous with the potential to cause harm or damage. However, since "risk" does not have a generally acceptable definition, the concept takes on various meanings. This chapter outlines the concept of risk and its various forms.

1.1 The Concept of Risk

1.1.1 Risk in Insurance

Risk has traditionally been addressed by insurance as the probability of a loss or accident, limited to monetarily quantifiable losses. The concept of risk in insurance is as follows.

First, risk is a combination of hazards or risk factors. Hazards are the factors that contribute to the occurrence of damage, increasing either the frequency, severity, or size of the damage. For example, if cargo and gasoline are stored in a warehouse, gasoline by itself does not cause any damage, but can increase the probability of fires and the severity of damage. Thus, in this case, gasoline is hazardous. Hazards include physical perils, such as road surface freezing and sharp curves, and psychological perils, such as carelessness. The combination of these hazards is described as a risk. Second, risk refers to a peril, but peril in this case refers to the accident itself, such as a fire, explosion, or collision. Third, peril can result in a loss (or damage), and this potential loss can itself be considered a risk.

The relationship between hazards, perils, and losses is as follows:

As Fig. 1.1 shows, a "possibility" links hazards, perils, and losses. In insurance, risk represents the magnitude of peril (risk value) as the expected value of loss, a value obtained by multiplying the probability (frequency) of a peril and the magnitude (strength) of loss.

H. Lee, *Risk Management*, Springer Texts in Business and Economics,
https://doi.org/10.1007/978-981-16-3468-0_1

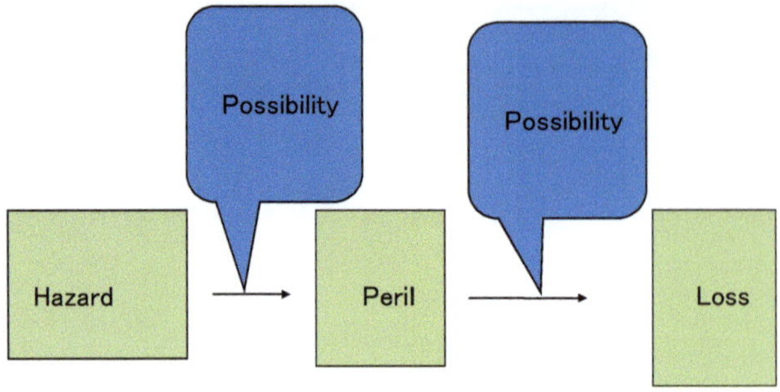

Fig. 1.1 Relationship between hazard and peril (*Source:* Created by the author)

$$\text{Risk value} = \text{probability of peril} \times \text{magnitude of loss}$$

This risk value includes the probability of peril occurring and the magnitude of loss expressed as a single value.

The term "damage" is often used when referring to an object or personal injury, while the term "loss" is often used when referring to money, as in "profit and loss". The term "damage" is widely used in insurance. In contrast, the term "loss" is often used in risk financing in Part II of this book. In this book, we use both terms as required.

1.1.2 Deviation from Expected Value

Risk is defined as a deviation from expected value, making it inversely proportional to the ability to predict expected value. Risk is the probability of the actual result differing from the expected one, expressed as "variance" or "standard deviation", to indicate the degree of dispersion of results.

Risk is also defined as "the effect of uncertainty on objectives" (ISO 31000).[1] Here, "effect" means a deviation from the expected target, both in desirable and undesirable directions. This definition of risk includes loss as well as the events that generate profit. For example, if the profit target is 500 million yen, a profit of 300 million yen and profit of 700 million yen are recognized as risks with the same magnitude. This definition is based on the fact that positive and negative values are inseparable in financial engineering and business strategy risks.

1.1.3 Black Swan

People in the West believed that swans could be only white. However, the discovery of a "black swan" in Australia in 1697 surprised the people at that time, breaking the

[1] See Chap. 5 for details.

commonly accepted idea of only white swans. Thus, the term "black swan" has come to mean the events that cannot be predicted from past experience and knowledge, and can cause unforeseen problems.

In his book *The Black Swan* published in 2006, Nassim Nicholas Taleb describes the features of a black swan as follows. First, it cannot be predicted. Second, it has a very large impact. Third, the event that occurs does not appear incidental, but as though it was planned.

1.2 Classification by Possibilty of Insurance Coverage

Traditionally, risk has been categorized by the likelihood of insurance. That is, some risks cannot be insured.

1.2.1 Pure Risk and Speculative Risk

This classification is based on the possibility of profit or loss, as proposed by Mowbray (1969).[2] A risk with no possibility of profit, and with the possibility of only loss, is a pure risk; it is also a "static risk", as described later. For example, fires, traffic accidents, natural disasters, personal risk, property risk, and liability risk are classified by the subject of risk, and are all pure risk models.

However, speculative risk generates either a profit or loss, such as price fluctuation risk and foreign exchange risk. Speculative risk is a "dynamic risk", which we will discuss later. This risk cannot be covered by insurance because the probability of its occurrence is difficult to measure statistically. However, pure risk can be covered by insurance because it allows for statistical measurement of its probability of occurrence.

1.2.2 Static Risk and Dynamic Risk

This classification of risk first appeared in Willet's (1951) *The Economic Theory of Risk and Insurance*. Static risk occurs in a stable society and economy. In other words, a static risk occurs in a state where the assumptions of risks, such as economic conditions, political conditions, legal regulations, technological conditions, business strategies, consumer preferences and trends, and other fundamentals, do not change. These can be natural risks, such as lightning, fires, death, etc., or man-made risks. Since static risks are pure risks, they can obtain insurance coverage.

In contrast, dynamic risk occurs when social and economic fundamentals change and develop. In other words, dynamic risk is a speculative risk occurring when the economic and political conditions, legal regulations, technological conditions,

[2]This is described in *Insurance* (sixth ed.) (1969).

business strategies, assumptions about risks such as consumer preferences and trends, and other fundamental basics change. Since dynamic risk has no regularity, it is difficult to understand statistically and unsuitable for insurance.

1.3 Corporate Risk Types

Companies face different types of risks.[3] In this book, we consider their market risks (e.g., interest rates and currencies), credit risks, and operational risks (Fig. 1.2).

Fig. 1.2 Corporate risk (*Source:* Various materials)

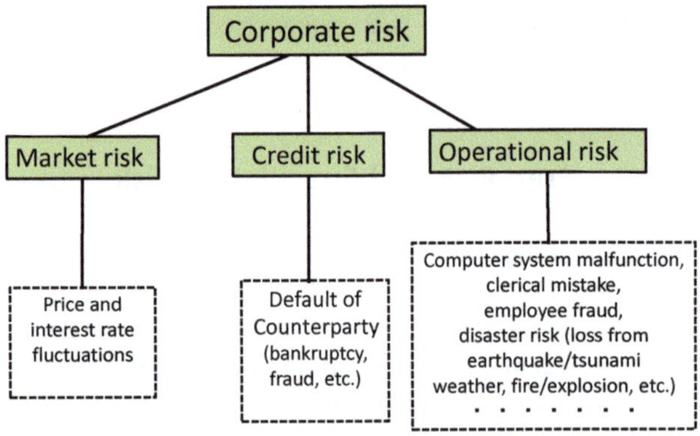

1.3.1 Market Risk

Market risk includes the risk of loss due to price fluctuations in interest rates, exchange rates, stock prices, and so on. However, a market risk arises in business from fluctuations in a product's demand or price. The market risks of firms vary depending on the type of business or company. Some examples of the market risk factors held by financial institutions are given in Table 1.1.

Table 1.1 Market risk factors

Risk	Description
Interest rate risk	The risk of interest rate changes affecting the present value (or periodic income) of assets and liabilities (including off-balance sheet). For example, deposits, loans, bonds, and derivatives have interest rate risk

(continued)

[3]The American Casualty Actuarial Society has classified the risks faced by businesses into four: (1) hazard risks, such as liability, property damage, and natural disasters; (2) financial risks, such as price risk, asset risk, currency risk, and liquidity risk; (3) operational risks, such as customer satisfaction, product defects, integrity, and reputation risk; and (4) strategic risks, such as competition, social trends, and capital availability.

Table 1.1 (continued)

Risk	Description
Exchange rate risk	The risk of exchange rate changes affecting the present value (or periodic income) of assets and liabilities (including off-balance sheet). For example, the assets and liabilities denominated in foreign currencies, foreign exchange transactions, and their derivatives (forwards, futures, swaps, options, etc.), and the assets and liabilities whose cash flows (redemption amounts, coupon rates, etc.) are determined by reference to exchange rates carry exchange rate risk
Equity risk	The risk of changes in stock index prices, etc., affecting the present value (or periodic income) of assets and liabilities (including off-balance sheet). For example, the assets and liabilities whose cash flows (redemption amount, coupon rate, etc.) are determined by referring to stocks, bonds with stock acquisition rights, derivative products (forwards, futures, swaps, options, etc.), stock prices, stock index prices, etc., carry equity risk
Commodity risk	The risk of product and product index price changes affecting the present value (or periodic income) of assets and liabilities (including off-balance sheet). For example, the assets and liabilities whose cash flows (redemption amount, coupon rate, etc.) are determined by referring to derivative products (forwards, futures, swaps, options, etc.), product prices, product index prices, etc., carry commodity risk
Other market risks	The correlations between multiple indicators in assets and liabilities (including off-balance sheet) whose cash flows are determined by referring to multiple indicators

Source: The *Financial Inspection Manual*

1.3.2 Credit Risk

Credit generally refers to delayed payment for goods and the like, but also to lending. Credit risk is the possibility of bad debts by business partners, delay in collection of payment, or delay in delivery. It can also be defined as the risk of losing receivables or loss of value (Financial Services Agency, *Financial Inspection Manual*). The risk related to collection of receivables is also referred to as default risk. Cash transactions do not involve credit risk because no "credit" is involved. However, "credit" is involved in the case of accounts receivables, financing, and bond investment, for example, with the possibility of not being able to collect receivables in the future, creating a credit risk.

As regards bond investment, the investor (creditor) has a credit risk in that the issuer (such as the country or company issuing the bond) can go bankrupt, making it impossible to collect the principal and interest. Depositors have a credit risk in that they would lose their deposits if the bank or other financial institution goes bankrupt. As for equity investment, the stock price of a company going bankrupt would fall sharply, with the investor having to carry the credit risk of the issuer (company). Furthermore, financial institutions are subject to credit risk when they lend (such as in mortgages and card loans), because the whole or some amount lent may not be repaid. The financial products inherent with credit risks include: loans; bonds, such as government bonds, corporate bonds, and financial bonds; stocks; and credit derivatives.

Fig. 1.3 depicts the concept of credit risk.

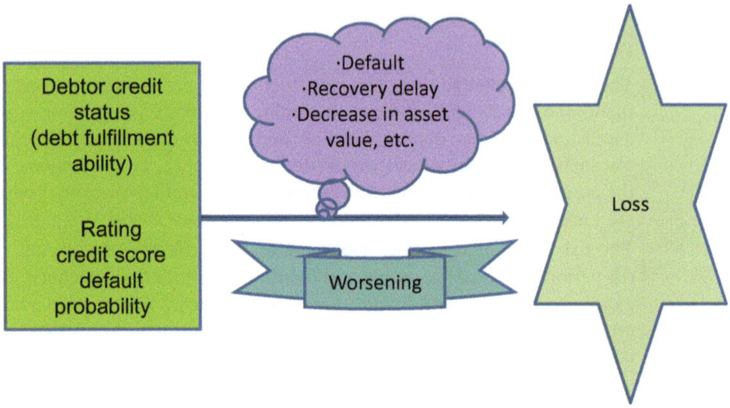

Fig. 1.3 Credit risk (concept figure) (*Source:* Various materials)

Creditors or investors suffer direct or indirect loss when a credit risk arises. Here, a direct loss occurs when the whole or part of the principal and interest, such as bonds, becomes irrecoverable from default. Indirect losses occur when one's credit-worthiness declines from an increase in default probability or decrease in bond prices reflecting such decline, and can be interpreted as a decrease in asset value due to an increase in default probability.

The perception of credit risk depends on the asset type. For loan receivables, credit risk refers to a loan not repaid due to borrower default. For traded financial instruments such as bonds or stocks, the decline in market prices due to changes in the issuer's creditworthiness is regarded as credit risk. For bonds, the interest rate reflects the magnitude of credit risk, with the interest rates of bonds of issuers with high credit risks set higher relative to their credit risk. In contrast, the bonds of issuers with low credit risk have lower interest rates. Therefore, if the credit risk of a certain company or country increases, the interest rate of the company's corporate bonds or country's government bonds will increase.

Similarly, country risk is the credit risk related to countries. In international investment, lending, and trade, changes in the political and economic situation of a partner's country might cause the debtor or counterparty in another country to default, making it impossible to collect any receivables. The risk of a government falling on account of wars with neighboring countries, civil war, revolutions, etc., causing limitations in lending and exchange to private companies in the partner country or the confiscation of goods by the government is known as "political risk". In transfer risk, the foreign currency reserves of a trading partner country become insufficient, external payments such as remittances are restricted or prohibited, and private companies default on debts. In addition, "sovereign risk" occurs when investments and loans to governments and government-affiliated institutions cannot be recovered. These risks are collectively known as country risks.

Furthermore, the other party in financial transactions is called "counterparty"; the credit risk of a counterparty is called "counterparty risk", or "counterparty credit risk". In trading on financial instruments exchanges, counterparties do not normally face a counterparty risk because a clearing house takes over the obligation to pay the settlement price on behalf of the direct counterparty. A clearing house adjusts and settles the payments and receipts of a large volume of transactions. However, over-the-counter trading has no clearing house, making it an "arm's length" transaction with counterparty risk in that the counterparty could become bankrupt and default in settlement.

Credit rating is a credit risk index for financial products such as bonds, and serves to evaluate the risk of a bond or stock issuer, such as a company or local government, going bankrupt. In particular, a country's credit risk rating is called its sovereign rating. This rating is carried out by rating agencies (also known as "rating firms"), the most notable being Moody's and Standard & Poor's in the United States and Fitch Ratings in England. The Japanese rating agencies include the Rating and Investment Information Center (R&I) and the Japan Credit Rating Agency (JCR). These agencies use the letters A to D to rate companies, countries, and municipalities.

Table 1.2 shows the rating symbols used by rating agencies.

Table 1.2 Rating symbols used by rating agency

Classification	Type	S&P	Moody's	R&I	Japan Rating Institute	Fitch
Investment grade	1	AAA	Aaa	AAA	AAA	AAA
	2	AA+	Aa1	AA+	AA+	AA+
	3	AA	Aa2	AA	AA	AA
	4	AA−	Aa3	AA−	AA−	AA−
	5	A+	A1	A+	A+	A+
	6	A	A2	A	A	A
	7	A−	A3	A−	A−	A−
	8	BBB+	Baa1	BBB+	BBB+	BBB+
	9	BBB	Baa2	BBB	BBB	BBB
	10	BBB−	Baa3	BBB−	BBB−	BBB−
Speculative grade	11	BB+	Ba1	BB+	BB+	BB+
	12	BB	Ba2	BB	BB	BB
	13	BB−	Ba3	BB−	BB−	BB−
	14	B+	B1	B+	B+	B+
	15	B	B2	B	B	B
	16	B−	B3	B−	B−	B−
	17	CCC+	Caa1	CCC+	CCC	CCC+
	18	CCC	Caa2	CCC	CC	CCC
	19	CCC−	Caa3	CCC−	C	CCC−
	20	CC	Ca	CC	D	CC
	21	C	C	C		C
	22	D		D		DDD
	23					DD
	24					D

Source: Rating agencies

Speculative grade bonds receive a rating lower than Ba or BB from Moody's, Standard & Poor's, or other rating agencies. These high-risk, high-return financial instruments are also known as "junk bonds", and have low creditworthiness with uncertain redemption of principal and interest. Highly rated bonds (at least Baa or BBB) are referred to as "investment grade bonds".

Rating companies provide investors with information on the probability of gaining funds from instruments such as bonds, but these companies receive rating fees from the said instruments' issuers. Thus, a conflict of interest exists between the rating agency and investor. However, measures have been taken to prevent analysts and sales departments from influencing each other.

1.3.3 Operational Risk

"Operation" refers to the operation of a business. Operational risk literally means the potential losses from business or operation. Operational risk is a general term for the risks arising during the course of daily business operations, and may include all the risks that a company faces, excepting credit and market risks. Currently, there is no consensus on the definition and scope of operational risk.

However, in recent years, operational risk management (RM) has been targeted for improvement, especially in banks. The Basel Committee on Banking Supervision (the Basel Committee) proposed Basel II,[4] which came into effect by the end of 2006, adding operational RM to the traditional credit and market risks. Basel II targeted the risks due to changes in bank operations, such as technology-related system failures or employee clerical errors.

Basel II focuses on the sources of risk, considering the operational risk of a financial institution as "the risk of direct or indirect loss resulting from inadequate or failed internal processes, people and systems, or external events".[5] Fig. 1.4 shows the operational risks as defined by the Basel Committee on Banking Supervision.

[4]The terms Basel I, II and III are part of the Basel Accords set by the Basel Committee on Banking Supervision for equity and follow a historic order. Basel I, also known as the Basel Capital Accord, was formed in 1988. It was created in response to the growing number of international banks and the increasing integration and interdependence of financial markets. Basel II was introduced in 2004. Basel II created a more comprehensive risk management framework. It did so by creating standardized measures for credit, operational, and market risk. The Basel III regulations were created in November 2010 after the financial crisis; however, they are yet to be implemented.

[5]The risk of direct or indirect loss resulting from inadequate or failed internal processes, people, and systems or from external events.

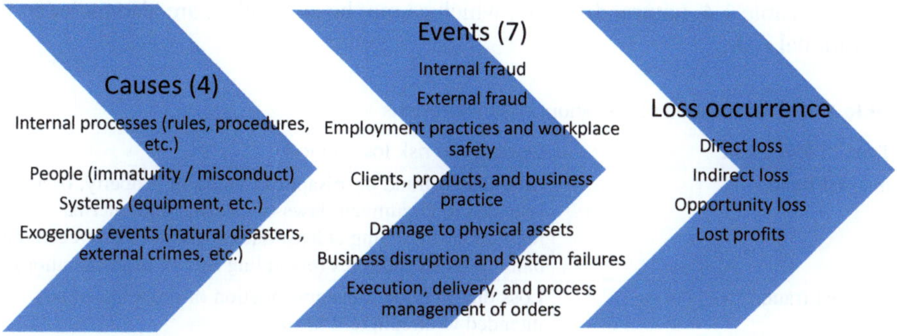

Fig. 1.4 Operational risks (Basel Committee) (*Source:* Basel Committee on Banking Supervision)

The definition of operational risk includes legal risk, but excludes strategic, reputational, and systemic risk. Systemic risk does not include the risk of an individual company or group; here, the bankruptcy of one financial institution or disruption of the system can have a cascading effect on other financial institutions or markets. The term "systemic" also means "generalized", in that it affects the entire financial system. In addition, supplemental direct losses have to be compensated, unlike indirect losses, opportunity losses, and lost profits.

The operational risks in Basel II are categorized by cause into the following four types (Table 1.3).

Table 1.3 Classification of operational risk (by cause) (Basel II)

Classification	Overview
Process risk	Risk of loss due to complex business processes and lack of standardization and systematization
Human risk	Risk of loss due to negligence or malice of executives and employees
System risk	Risk of loss due to system malfunction or downtime
External factor risk	Risk of loss due to external crime or natural disasters

Source: Basel Committee on Banking Supervision

Furthermore, the notice of Japan's Financial Services Agency (JFSA) to supervise financial institutions under internationally uniform standards specifies the following possible operational risk loss events for financial institutions (Table 1.4).

From Table 1.4, natural disasters, which cannot be controlled, are also included in operational risk.

Table 1.4 Classification of operational risk loss events

Type of loss event	Operational risk loss subject
Internal fraud	Loss due to fraud or misappropriation of property, or acts intended to circumvent laws or external and internal regulations involving at least one officer or employee of the bank or its subsidiaries (excluding acts of discrimination)
External fraud	Loss due to fraud, misappropriation of property, or acts intended to circumvent laws
Employment practices and workplace safety	Loss due to acts violating laws or agreements related to employment, health, safety, payment for personal injury, work accidents, or discrimination
Clients, products, and business practice	Loss due to breach of duties (fiduciary duty, suitability, etc.) related to a particular customer or nature or design of a product
Damage to physical assets	Loss from damage to tangible assets due to natural disasters and other events
Business disruption and system failure	Loss from interruption of business activities or system failure
Execution, delivery, process management of orders, etc.	Losses arising from relationships with business partners or suppliers, or from failure in transaction processing or process management

Source: JFSA Notification No 19, 27 March 2006, Appendix 2

Operational risk often includes business as well as compliance risk. Business risk is unavoidable in business operation since it includes management and strategy errors, competition between companies, trends in product markets, and so on. However, there is no consensus on its range. In particular, the boundaries between business and operational risk are not clear.

Compliance risk is the risk of loss due to employee behavior and business conduct, including adherence to laws and regulations. However, it is often included in operational risk. Here, "compliance" includes legal compliance, but takes on a broader sense to include internal and organizational rules as well as ethical behavior. Disaster risk includes natural disasters such as earthquakes, storms, heavy rains, floods, eruptions, and other abnormal natural phenomena, as well as human disasters such as man-made accidents.

Discussion Questions

1. Discuss the concept of risk. Also, give your opinion on whether the concept of risk can be unified.
2. It is said that speculative risk cannot be covered by insurance. Do you think that insurance will cover it in the future? Please present the basis for your opinion.
3. It is said that insurance cannot cover dynamic risks. Do you think that insurance will cover it in the future? Please explain your opinion, along with its grounds.
4. Discuss, with examples, the types of risks associated with corporate activities.

Enterprise Risk Management and Related Fields

2

Companies need to address the various challenges they face. This chapter outlines the relationship between RM and the various steps that companies take to address their corporate difficulties.

2.1 RM

RM is a systematic approach to maximize the positive, while controlling the negative, impacts of risk. The term "risk management" was first used in the 1950s,[1] but humans have recognized and addressed risk since the beginning of history. RM has several definitions.

The Committee of Sponsoring Organizations (COSO) (2004) defines enterprise risk management (ERM) as " a process effected by an entity's board of directors, management, and other personnel, applied in strategy setting and across the enterprise, designed to identify the events that may affect the entity, manage the risk within its appetite, and provide reasonable assurances on achieving the entity objectives".[2] In addition, the COSO ERM (2017) revised the definition of ERM as the "culture, capabilities, and practices, integrated with strategy-setting and performance, that organizations adopt to manage risk in creating, preserving, and realizing value".

In addition, ISO 31000 (2009) defines ERM as the "activities coordinated to direct and control an organization with regard to risk".

---

[1]The term "risk management" was used in Russell B. Gallagher, "Risk Management: A New Phase of Cost Control", *Harvard Business Review* (1956) (John Fraser, Betty J. Simkins, *Enterprise Risk Management* (John Wiley & Sons, Inc., 2010), pp. 22–29).

[2]COSO, *Enterprise Risk Management—Integrated Framework (Executive Summary Framework)* (September 2004), p. 4.

H. Lee, *Risk Management*, Springer Texts in Business and Economics,
https://doi.org/10.1007/978-981-16-3468-0_2

The main perceptions gained from these varying definitions of RM are as follows. (1) RM activity is coordinated to direct and control an organization.[3] (2) It appropriately manages various internal and external business-related risks in the company to maintain and increase its value.[4] (3) It consists of a series of actions (process) effected by an entity's board of directors, management, and other personnel in strategy setting and across the enterprise, designed to identify the events that may affect the entity, manage risk within its tolerance limit, and provide reasonable assurance regarding the achievement of entity objectives.[5]

2.2 Enterprise Risk Management

Integrated risk management (IRM) has been a focus of attention in the United States and Europe since the 1990s. This approach was developed by some advanced companies into a comprehensive RM method to address all risks they face and increase corporate value. Introduced during the first half of the 1990s, this approach has been called by different names, such as enterprise-wide risk management (EWRM), strategic risk management(SRM), business risk management (BRM), comprehensive risk management(CRM), holistic risk management, and total risk management.

Unlike the traditional insurance RM, IRM uses both non-insurance and insurance financial technologies,[6] and is commonly referred to as ERM. ERM targets all the risks that arise when managing a company as a whole.

Conventional RM mainly focuses on specific risks, such as credit risk and market risk, and vertically manages the risks related to each department. This RM model is called "siloed approach" RM. For example, credit risk is handled by the lending department, and market risk is managed by the department in charge of asset management. Furthermore, people in charge of finance or audit, or internal auditors, are usually in charge of this approach. Here, since the risk information remains within each department, the risks crossing departments or borders may not be handled properly in some cases. However, RM can be performed more efficiently and thoroughly in ERM through risk identification, risk evaluation, and risk response across the company.

In conventional RM, risk is a decrease in profit (loss) and therefore something to be avoided, but in ERM risk is a potential source of profit to be pursued. ERM deals with company-wide risks at the management level and across the company in an

---

[3]Coordinated activities to direct and control an organization with regard to risk (ISO Guide 73: 2009).

[4]Ministry of Economy, Trade and Industry, "Internal Control in the New Era of Risks: Guidelines for Internal Control Functioning together with Risk Management," Study Group on Risk Management and Internal Control (June 2003).

[5]COSO, *Enterprise Risk Management-Integrated Framework, Executive Summary Framework* (September 2004).

[6]Neil A. Doherty, *Integrated Risk Management* (2000), pp. 10–13.

integrated manner. Thus, in ERM, risk information is shared across the company, enabling the management to take cross-departmental or borderline risks. Compared to conventional RM, ERM moves from (1) avoiding to pursuing risk, (2) avoiding and reducing losses to maintaining and improving corporate value, (3) improving corporate profits to profiting society and stakeholders,[7] and (4) individual RM to comprehensive RM.

In addition, the traditional RM relied heavily on insurance RM by buying insurance. However, unlike the traditional insurance RM, recent ERM targets pure risks as well as speculative risks. For example, when considering the risks of automobile exports, insurance RM has traditionally targeted pure risks such as losses due to compensation for accidents in automobiles transportation. However, ERM targets pure risks as well as speculative risks (market risks), such as fluctuations in exchange rates and prices (Table 2.1).

Table 2.1 Conventional RM and ERM

Classification	Conventional RM	ERM
Target	Individual risks, such as operational risk and crisis management	Risks related to achieving strategies and financial targets
Risk definition	Possibility of future losses	Uncertainty of the future. Includes both profits and losses
Attitude to risk	Risks should be avoided	Risks should be managed
RM	A process that prevents the occurrence of losses and minimizes the impact (loss) of risk	A process ensuring the increase in value of the business as a whole, while recognizing that risks can lead to profits
Target risks	Pure risks	Pure risks Speculative risks (market risks)
Purpose and management system	A collection of individual RM systems; the objective is to reduce individual risks. Different systems for each company or site in the group	Integrated management of company or group risks. A unified approach with shared purpose and policy
Characteristics	There are also cases of risks being recognized in a single department, and not by a group at large. Lack of management and monitoring of profitable strategic risks	Cross-organizational risk awareness. Achieve business objectives, while controlling for risks within corporate risk tolerance

Source: Created by the author

[7]The term "stake" in "stakeholder" refers to "important things facing the risk of being lost" and show an interest in a company's activities. For companies, stakeholders are investors and creditors, shareholders, business partners, suppliers, employees, labor unions, users and consumers, and all other people or organizations having some interest in the company. Recent definitions tend to include local residents, industries, local governments, and related ministries.

2.3 Crisis Management

Crisis management (CM) targets the adverse effects of a crisis and efforts to recover from it when a company faces a threat to survival. CM is considered to be a part of RM. It is a relatively new academic branch based on the systematization of crisis countermeasures following the large-scale industrial or environmental disasters that occurred in the 1980s.[8]

A crisis refers to a serious risk threatening the existence of an organization, such as an earthquake, explosion, eruption, terrorism, scandal, or war. CM targets minimizing the impact of a crisis and early recovery.

The differences between RM and CM are as follows. In RM, the potential risks are identified before they are apparent, the risks are analyzed and evaluated, and the responses to those risks are implemented on a daily basis. Therefore, RM may include the preparation of manuals in the event of a crisis. In contrast, CM is a series of activities to prevent the spread of losses that follow a crisis, and deals with problems that have already arisen.

The relationship between RM and CM is shown in Fig. 2.1.

[8] P. Shrivastava, I.I. Mitroff, D. Miller, and A. Miglani, "Understanding Industrial Crises", *Journal of Management Studies* (1988), pp. 285–304.

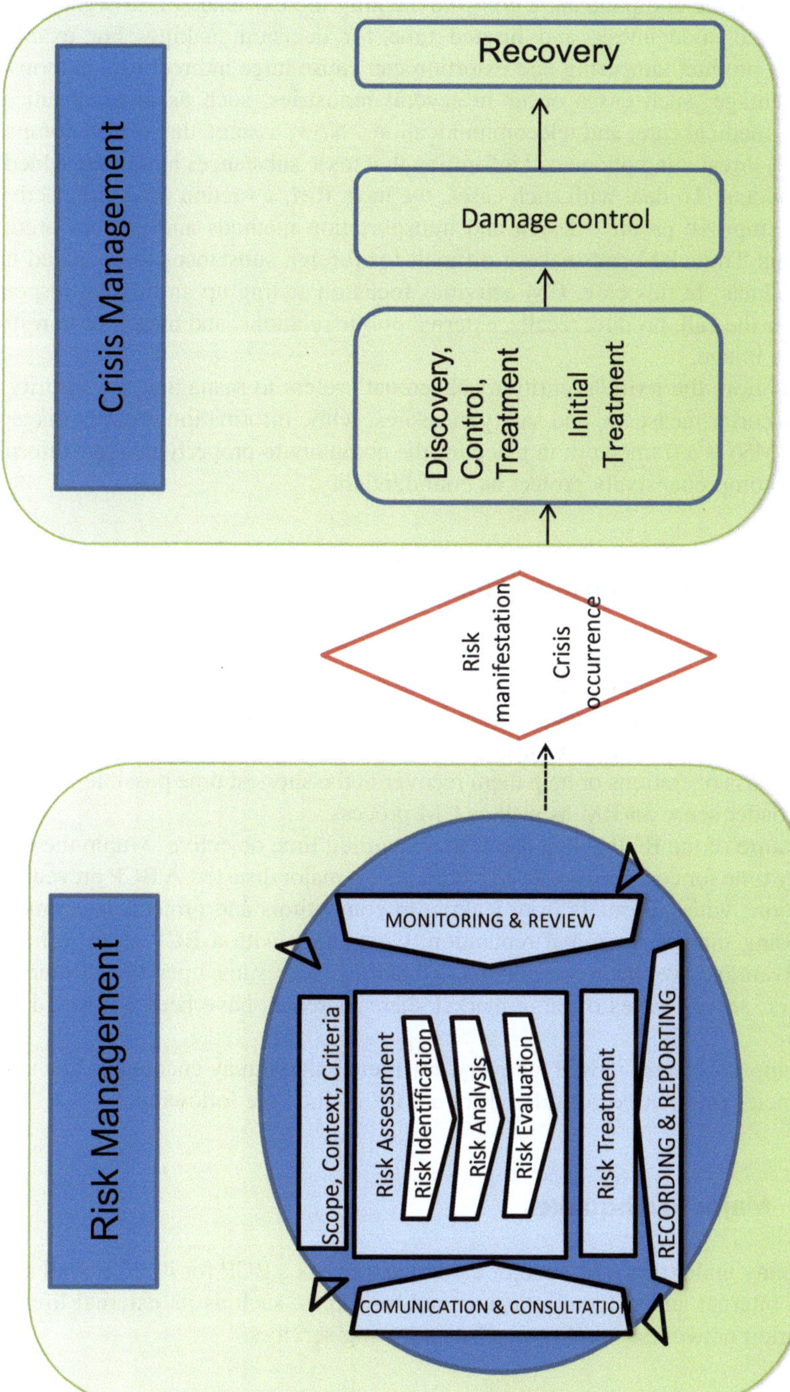

Fig. 2.1 Relationship between RM and CM (*Source:* Various materials, including the International Organization for Standardization (ISO) documentation)

CM has three components: a crisis threatening the existence of an organization, urgency and suddenness, and limited time for decision making. For example, malicious product tampering and extortion can cause huge indirect loss in terms of product image; such cases occur in several industries, such as pharmaceuticals, bedding, medical care, and telecommunications. Now, assume that a food company receives a threatening phone call informing that toxic substances have been added to their products. To deal with such cases, we have RM, a routine peacetime activity that can improve product design and transportation methods and prevent product tampering. Thus, RM can make it difficult for foreign substances to be added into food products. In this case, CM activities focus on setting up an internal response team after the call, product recalls, external public relations, and measures to restore corporate image.

In addition, the term "security management" refers to managing the security of assets, security measures, and safety measures, while information security management (ISMS) is a framework in place for the company to properly manage information and comprehensively protect its confidentiality.

2.4 Business Continuity Plan

Business continuity plan (BCP) refers to the "systems, procedures, plans, etc., designed to prevent unforeseen circumstances, such as natural disasters like large earthquakes, spread of infectious diseases, terrorism, major accidents, disruptions in supply chain (supply network), and sudden business environments that interrupt vital business operations or help them recover in the shortest time possible".[9] BCP is in its broader sense an RM as well as CM process.

A feature of the BCP is that it sets the "required time objective" within the target recovery time for core businesses to restart after a major disaster. A BCP prevents the transactions with customers from leaking to competitors and protects the company from losing market share and reputation. Companies with a BCP seem to have a great advantage over their competitors in that they can resume operations faster after a disaster; several cases of large market share increases have been reported in the literature.

A company creates a BCP for every emergency that it may encounter. The major emergencies that can be considered for a BCP include the following:

2.4.1 Major Earthquakes

A company under threat of a major earthquake needs a BCP for itself as well as for various internal and external management resources, such as its external lifelines, distribution networks, suppliers, and outsourcing services.

[9] "Business Continuity Guidelines, Third Edition" (subtitle: Strategies and responses to overcome any critical event), Cabinet Office Disaster Prevention Bureau, revised in August 2013.

2.4.2 Floods (Floods, Storms, Tsunamis)

Disaster prevention measures, such as against inundation, are necessary against floods, but if the floods are too large, such measures may not be adequate. Therefore, a BCP against floods needs to include measures for reprocurement and restoration, and adopt alternative measures when the company is damaged by a disaster or one of its remote suppliers or an affiliated company is damaged affecting the supply of important parts.

2.4.3 Infectious Diseases (New Influenza Strain Pandemic)

The term "pandemic" refers to an epidemic involving a large number of infected people and patients worldwide as well as the spread of diseases such as AIDS and Co. The COVID-19 pandemic, also known as the coronavirus pandemic, is an ongoing pandemic of coronavirus disease 2019 (COVID-19) as of March 2021. It was first identified in December 2019 in Wuhan, China.

Pandemics have repeatedly occurred throughout history, taking large number of lives every time. Normal influenza is an infection with symptoms of chills, high fever, muscle pain, and general malaise at a rate faster than in a cold. However, a new strain of influenza can be expected to spread explosively compared to normal influenza because most people would not be immune to it. If a highly virulent avian influenza pandemic occurs in Japan, hundreds of thousands or millions of deaths could occur, with schools closed for weeks to months to prevent the spread of infection. All outings, including those for school and work, would be restricted. Therefore, a BCP would be helpful in responding to telework and the potential human damage.

2.4.4 Ash Fall Due to Eruption of Volcano and Snow Fall Following Cold Wave

A BCP is useful to deal with disasters that hit the transportation network and lifelines, such as the Mount Fuji volcanic eruption in the Tokyo metropolitan area and unexpected snowfall in normally warm regions. If volcanic ash causes a power outage disrupting the distribution network, or snow fall paralyzes the traffic in temperate areas, employees will not be able to work. In addition, various natural disasters such as landslides, tornadoes, lightning, and hails can occur in different degrees depending on the area or location.

2.4.5 Indiscriminate Human-Made Disaster

Traditionally, disasters are categorized into natural and human-made, based on a wide variety of causes. Human-made disasters refer to the accidents caused by humans, such as power outages, large-scale accidents, nuclear accidents, terrorism, and wars; natural disasters are caused by pollution and environmental degradation. The disasters attributable to chemical, biological, radiological, nuclear, and explosive (CBRNE)[10] causes are special disasters.

Unexpected human-made disasters that do not specifically target any company, such as power outages due to power company troubles, large-scale factory fires, nuclear power plant radiation leaks, and armed attacks, are a threat similar to natural disasters. In particular, since large-scale accidents and nuclear power plant accidents can occur as secondary disasters after a large earthquake, it is necessary to take precautionary measures in advance, just as with natural disasters.

2.4.6 Disasters, Bankruptcy, and Scandals of Affiliated Suppliers

A BCP is also useful when a supplier manufacturing important parts is severely damaged by a natural disaster and shuts down, a supplier outsourcing core businesses suddenly goes bankrupt, or an affiliate or parent company is facing a scandal involving the company itself.

2.4.7 Intimidation/Theft/Cyber Attacks

A BCP is helpful in cases of excessive demand by customers, crime damages such as shoplifting or theft, and cyber-attacks (e.g., unauthorized access and falsification of information), depending on the type of business, intimidation, or business obstruction. In addition to the direct loss itself, these risks can have secondary negative consequences if no appropriate action is taken or knowledge of the mishandled crisis spreads through the Internet, social media, etc.

2.4.8 Information Leakage, Food Poisoning, Window Dressing

Internal scandals can jeopardize business continuity; for example, dressing up accounts, spoofing of production areas or expiration dates, leaking of personal information, illegal dumping, or violation of laws and regulations. Any risk to business continuity, whether it be from outside or inside the company, is a good case for BCP.

[10]Also referred to as nuclear, biological, chemical and radiological (NBCR).

2.4.9 Death, Hospitalization, Retirement, or Job Change of Important Person

Human resource events, such as the sudden death of a president with extensive duties, the hospitalization of the general affairs manager in charge of all back-office work, the retirement of craftsmen who form the source of competitiveness, and the withdrawal of competent sales staff may threaten the feasibility of a small and medium-sized business.

Fig. 2.2 illustrates the concept of BCP (sudden event type).

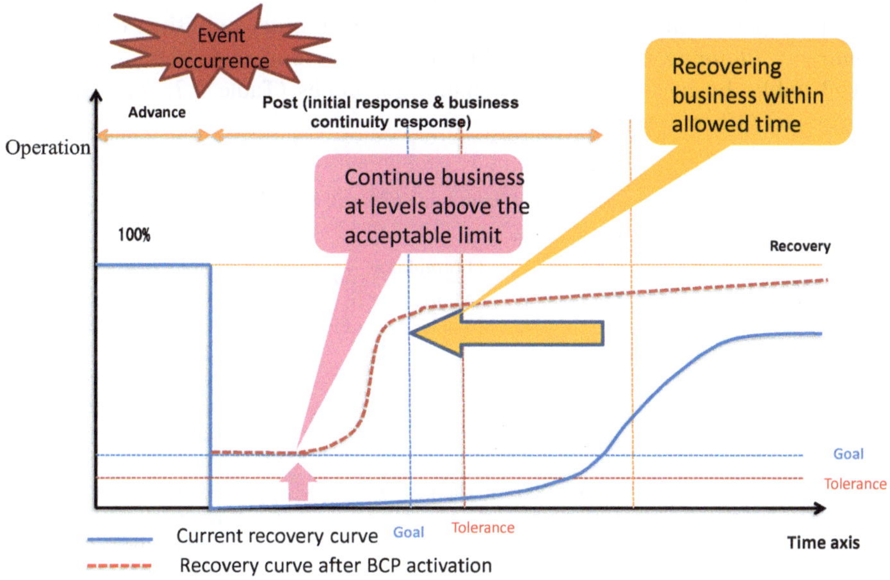

Fig. 2.2 BCP (sudden event type) (*Source:* Cabinet Office, *Business Continuity Guidelines* (3rd ed.))

In the absence of countermeasures, a company severely damaged by a disaster can take a long time to recover and the business may even be interrupted. Furthermore, if the resumption of business is delayed beyond a reasonable time, the business partners might want to leave and deepen their relationship with other business operators, thus making it difficult for the company to restore its transactions to the previous levels.

The most important BCP elements are as follows. (1) Identify the core businesses. Since human resources, facilities, and credits could be limited, the core businesses would have to be narrowed down in case of an emergency. (2) Set the recovery time. This is the time allowed for the core businesses to resume operation following an emergency; the business partners' viewpoints need to be considered while setting this target. (3) Discuss the core businesses and target recovery time with the business partners in advance. Quick contact with business partners is vital in an emergency. (4) For raw material and human resources, find the scale and procurement method, as well as an alternate method.

In addition, both the disaster prevention plan, or disaster response, and BCP assume natural disasters (earthquakes, storms, and flood damage), large-scale accidents, and emergency situations, such as pandemics. However, while a disaster prevention plan or disaster response protects human lives and property, a BCP is a management plan to promptly recover and resume high-priority operations, focusing on initial on-site response. The disaster prevention plan was inspired by the Great Hanshin-Awaji earthquake (1995), whereas the BCP concept began to spread after the 9/11 terrorist attacks on the United States.

After Japan's Ministry of Economy, Trade and Industry published the *Business Continuity Planning Guidelines* in March 2005, several ministries and agencies issued public business continuity planning guidelines (Table 2.2; for details, see the Cabinet Office website).

Table 2.2 BCP guidelines issued by different ministries and agencies

Name	Formulation date	Formulator	Target risks
BCP guidelines	March 2005	Ministry of Economy, Trade and Industry	Does not cover specific risks. Case studies illustrate large-scale system failures, security incidents, information leaks, and data tampering
BCP guidelines	August 2005	Cabinet Office	Guidelines for overall business continuity with no limit on possible target risks
Business continuity guidelines for disaster mitigation and improved disaster response of Japanese companies	October 2005	Central Disaster Management Council	Does not cover specific risks. It shows earthquakes as a serious disaster risk
SME BCP formulation and operation guidelines to overcome emergency situations	February 2006	Small and Medium Business Administration	Does not cover specific risks. It focuses on earthquakes as well as storms, floods, fires, and epidemics
Business continuity guides for a BCP for construction companies in the event of a disaster	December 2007	Ministry of Land, Infrastructure, Transport and Tourism Kanto Regional Development Bureau	Earthquakes near the capital. It is intended for construction companies
IT service continuity guidelines	September 2008	Ministry of Economy, Trade and Industry	Interruption/stop of IT services

(continued)

Table 2.2 (continued)

Name	Formulation date	Formulator	Target risks
New influenza control guidelines at business sites and workplaces	February 2009	Related ministries and agencies meeting on pandemic influenza and bird influenza	H1N1 influenza
Guidelines for continuation of obligations when a new coronavirus infection occurs in nursing care facilities and business establishments	December 2020	Ministry of Health, Labor and Welfare	Covid 19

Source: Cabinet Office documentation

In countries such as the United States and the United Kingdom, business continuity management (BCM) standards centered on ISO and such standards were issued at a steady pace.

2.5 Business Continuity Management

BCM is a management method to ensure business continuity. Business continuity allows companies to provide products and services to suppliers continually and regular employment for the local community. BCM and corporate social responsibility (CSR) are closely related to each other. BCM is not just a plan, but a standard operation management activity, formulating, maintaining, and updating BCP; it secures budget and resources to realize business continuity, implements precautionary measures, conducts education and training, audits, and continuously improves. ISO22301 was issued in 2012 as an international standard for BCP.

Division of labor and outsourcing have improved the production efficiency of companies and organizations in recent years. Thus, an accident to a materials or outsourced production, assembly, shipment, or sales provider can affect the whole supply chain and a large number of companies. For example, the Niigata-ken Chuetsu-oki earthquake that struck Japan on 16 July 2007, recording a seismic intensity as high as 6, damaged the production facilities of Riken Co Ltd., which has two factories in Kashiwazaki; these factories were shut down from 16 to 22 July of the same year. Piston rings are an important part of automobile engines, and Riken is the largest manufacturer of piston rings, accounting for 50% of the domestic market. Under these circumstances, when Riken, which was delivering piston rings to several car manufacturers, stopped operating, all eight domestic car manufacturers had to stop production. However, Riken resumed production 1 week after the disaster, and, with the assistance of the auto manufacturers' employees, managed to restore the entire production line 2 weeks later.

In contrast, supply chain management (SCM) is a business management tool in that all the constituent companies of a supply chain work together to pursue business efficiency. An interruption in the business operation of one company in the supply chain could interrupt the business of another company. Therefore, all the companies forming the supply chain should cooperate and build a BCP.

In addition, both the BCP and contingency plan (CP) require that the possible emergency situations be identified and a response plan be prepared in advance for an emergency. BCP specifies the core operations a business must maintain and the practical steps to be taken from the perspective of business continuity, while CP focuses on responding to emergencies and minimizing damage.

Both the crisis management plan (CMP) and BCP are responses to a crisis, but have differences. A BCP is an action plan designed to resume and continue a core business within target time in the event of a specific crisis. Here, the term "specific crisis" refers to cases such as "loss of transaction data due to an earthquake" or "less than 50% of staff able to operate for a week due to an epidemic of infectious disease". The BCP is created for a particular crisis, such as an earthquake or infectious disease.

However, the CMP is a plan created immediately after an emergency and continues until it is resolved, with minimum damage to the organization. It is rarely limited to a specific crisis or action plan at a specific point in time, and is generally an action plan with a broader view on various crises and wider time axis. It is a plan targeting any generic crisis that an organization might face, including situations not covered under a specific BCP.

Discussion Questions

1. Describe the differences between enterprise risk management and traditional risk management.
2. Compare and explain crisis management and risk management.
3. Compare and explain your business continuity plan and business continuity management. Give your view on the relationship between these and risk management.

Accounting Fraud and Internal Control 3

The SOX Act was enacted in the United States to prevent frequent occurrences of accounting fraud.[1] This Act also affected Japan with the enactment of a Japanese version (the Financial Instruments and Exchange Law). Furthermore, the Company Law called for the development of an internal control system. These developments have increased the importance of ERM. This chapter outlines the effects of accounting fraud on ERM.

3.1 Frequent Accounting Fraud

3.1.1 Enron

Enron Corporation was established in 1985 when Kenneth Lay merged his company, Houston Natural Gas, Houston, with InterNorth, located in Nebraska, to create the new energy company. In the 1980s, when Ronald Reagan was president, the United States witnessed significant deregulation of the energy market, with instruments such as futures contracts used for energy, or forward contracts used for delivery of energy at a future date (forward **delivery)**. During this deregulation period, the late 1980s, Enron became a leading company in cash flow management, engaging in derivatives trading in addition to the traditional natural gas sales and transportation.

[1]Enron (energy sales, bankruptcy filing on 2 December 2001), K-mart (retail supermarket, bankruptcy filing on 22 January 2002), Global Crossing (optical communications, bankruptcy filing in January 2002), Tyco International (finance, 3 June 2002, executives alleged misappropriation of funds), ImClone Systems (drug development, 12 June 2002, alleged insider trading), WorldCom (long-distance communication, 25 June 2002, illegal accounting processing discovered), Xerox (office equipment, suspected increase in sales on 28 June 2002), Quest Communications (telecommunications, suspected increase in sales on 4 July 2002), Merck (pharmaceutical, July 2002, alleged increase in sales on 8 August).

H. Lee, *Risk Management*, Springer Texts in Business and Economics,
https://doi.org/10.1007/978-981-16-3468-0_3

In 1990, Enron hired Jeffrey Skilling, a consultant, who changed the company's business model from physical energy plant to financial investment firm, for example by splitting large contracts into derivatives to be sold. Jeffrey Skilling made a significant contribution, raising the company to the top in the gas and electricity sales industry; he became company chief executive officer (CEO) on 12 February 2001, with an annual compensation of USD 132 million.

Enron lobbied with the Securities and Exchange Commission (SEC) to become the first non-financial company allowed to calculate profits for the fiscal year using the market-to-market method. The company used this method to forecast its profits at future market values, rather than the historical or present value of transactions.

The company was alleged to have used market value accounting to spoof its sales and profits since the early 1990s. In the late 1990s, by exploiting the derivative transactions, the company generated transactions of buying and selling the same amount of power, to ultimately show zero generation but excessively high sales (circular transactions).

Also, Andrew Fastow, the chief financial officer (CFO), transferred the transaction losses to a non-consolidated subsidiary (special purpose entity: SPE) to prevent discovery of the fraud. This transfer resulted in an off-book loss, but the auditing firm (Arthur **Andersen** & Co) did not divulge these facts to investors.

The company was also a pioneer in weather derivatives, a hedging method using financial analysis, to hedge the risk of fluctuations in earnings due to weather. In the 1990s, price liberalization intensified price competition in the United States, placing utilities at the risk of earnings volatility. For example, in a particularly cool summer, the use of air conditioners falls, potentially leading to reduced gas consumption. Similarly, a particularly warm winter would reduce the need for electric heaters, with reduced electricity consumption. Insurance is sold to cover this risk, but a problem with insurance is that it involves a complicated investigation procedure before paying claims, making it difficult to interpret the range of collaterals in insurance contracts upon payout.

Enron successfully signed an agreement including these derivatives with Koch Energy Trading Inc. in 1997. If the temperature were below average, Enron would pay Cork USD 10,000 each time, and if it were above the average, Cork would pay Enron USD 10,000 each time.[2] Thus, Enron's aggressive trading of these derivatives accounted for more than 80% of its profits in 1998.

Enron was the seventh largest company in the United States in 2000, with annual sales of USD 110 billion, to become a leading company with nearly 20,000 employees in 2001. Fortune magazine selected Enron as America's most innovative company from 1996 to 2001.

Enron's stock price was over USD 90 per share in August 2000 and held in high regard. The company's management told investors that its stock prices would rise from USD 130 to USD 140 per share. However, Enron's management had inside

[2]*Houston Business Journal* (21 November 1999) (www.bizjournals.com/houston/stories/1999/11/22/story7.html).

information about the loss concealment and disposed of their shares in large quantities. Furthermore, the company's alleged accounting fraud was reported in the *Wall Street Journal* on 17 October 2001, at which point its stock price plummeted, leading to a search by the SEC. Meanwhile, many analysts suggested the purchase of company shares when their prices fell below USD 20 per share in October 2001. However, the rating agencies had reduced their ratings due to worsening earnings, and the company's stock price at the end of November 2001 was less than USD 1 per share. Thus, investors who had purchased the company's shares suffered huge losses.

Eventually, on 2 December 2001 the company filed for bankruptcy, when its share price was 26 cents per share. At this point, the company's total assets were USD 63.4 billion, whereas its total debt was USD 31 billion; this increased to over USD 40 billion when off-book debts were included. Thus, Enron was the largest bankrupt company in the United States before WorldCom's collapse in July 2002.

Former CEO Jeffrey Skilling was fined about USD 45 million by a federal district court in Texas on 23 October 2006, for fraud and collusion. He was also sentenced to 24 years and 4 months in prison. Former CEO founder Kenneth Rey was also found guilty, but he died of heart attack at age 64 on 5 July 2006. The District Court of Houston sentenced former CFO Andrew Fastow to 6 years in prison and 2 years of community service on 26 September 2006. Enron's audit firm, **Arthur Andersen** & Co,[3] was found guilty by the district court and, although this was overturned in the Supreme Court, the firm lost credit and had to close down because they lost most customers as well.

3.1.2 WorldCom

With a turnover of USD 35.2 billion and 85,000 employees, WorldCom was once the second largest long-distance telephone company in the United States after AT&T.[4] In 1998, the company bought Microwave Communications Inc. (MCI), then the fourth largest long-distance communications company in the United States, for USD 37 billion, at that point the largest ever price in US history. WorldCom's growth was largely due to its mergers in the 1990s. In the words of their then CEO Bernard Ebbers, the company's policy was: "We don't need cash. As long as we maintain a high stock price, we can acquire companies larger than ourselves." The company acquired 75 companies through stock swaps.

[3]Arthur Andersen & Co, founded in 1913, became one of the world's largest five accounting firms, especially relevant in the United States. During the Enron case, Enron instructed Arthur Andersen to destroy their internal material, and so the court found Arthur Andersen guilty of obstructing public affairs in criminal investigations; however, this was overturned on appeal.

[4]Long Distance Discount Service (LDDS), the predecessor of WorldCom, was founded in 1983, and Bernard Ebbers became CEO in 1985. It then changed its name to LDDS WorldCom in 1995. Again, after acquired MCI, a major telecommunications company, in 1998, it changed its name to MCI WorldCom; however, in April 2000, the company changed its name back to WorldCom.

However, WorldCom's stock prices continued to fall when the long-distance telephone company MCI, which it had acquired in 1998, suffered a revenue slump after the collapse of the IT bubble. Then, by the end of April 2002, Bernard Ebbers resigned, to be replaced by John Sidgmore as CEO.

In June 2002, WorldCom's internal audit department, led by Cynthia Cooper, found an accounting falsification of USD 3.8 billion during a regular audit, to then become an independent investigation organization within the company. Cynthia Cooper was named one of Time 2002's "persons of the year" for her courage and integrity in confronting fraud.

Then, on 25 June 2002, CEO John Sidgemore fired Scott Sullivan, the treasurer, pointing out that "in 15 months of window dressing, there were USD 3.8 billion of profit over-reporting". The company's stock price began to plummet, falling from USD 64.5 per share in June 1999 to six cents on 1 July 2002. Meanwhile, the SEC began its investigation of the company on 26 June 2002, to find a total assets inflation of about USD 11 billion in 2003.

The company's main window dressing method was to record the costs incurred for interconnection with other telecommunication companies (line costs) as an investment, although they should have been recorded as expenses. For example, if a service is provided to a building in which another operator has already laid an optical fiber, the line must be leased from the previous operator. These line costs would have to be recorded as expenses, but WorldCom wrote them off as investments.

Thus, the company applied for consideration under Chap. 11 of the Federal Bankruptcy Code (equivalent to the Japanese Corporate Reform Act) to the Bankruptcy Court of New York on 21 July 2002. The company's total assets amounted to USD 103.8 billion, nearly twice the size of Enron's assets of USD 63.4 billion, and with the company's total debt of USD 41 billion, this became the largest bankruptcy in US history. However, this record lasted only until the collapse of Lehman Brothers in September 2008, with total liabilities of USD 6130 billion. The company's former CEO Bernard Ebbers was found guilty of fraud and conspiracy and of submitting false documents to regulators, and on 15 March 2005 was sentenced to 25 years in prison. The then CFO Scott Sullivan was sentenced to 5 years in prison on 11 August 2005.

3.1.3 Cockroach Theory

This cockroach theory states that the finding of a single piece of bad news relating to a company reveals the existence of more bad news still hidden. The term "cockroach theory" comes from the notion that seeing a single cockroach is usually evidence of many more cockroaches hiding in the house. Under this theory, if you see one cockroach, you could expect 30 more cockroaches in the house. So, the finding of one problem pertaining to a company perhaps suggests the presence of 30 times more problems still hidden in the company.

For example, the Enron accounting fraud clearly showed that WorldCom had committed an accounting fraud. Furthermore, New Century Financial, a sub-prime lender, incurred losses in February 2007 when its borrowers failed to fulfill their payment obligations, leading to a liquidity crisis. WorldCom was the first of many companies to face liquidity problems due to sub-prime issues. In other words, the exposure of one sub-prime lender (one cockroach) to financial problems indicated the presence of similar problems in many other companies in the same industry.

From this theory, once a bad event relating to a company surfaces, investors would expect the same event to occur in other companies; they would stop investing in that industry as a whole, and this could cause stock prices to fall. For example, if an accounting fraud occurred in one company, the supervisory authority would check all the other companies to prevent the occurrence of further fraud, and investors, fearing the probability of further fraud, might sell their shares and withdraw from the financial markets, leading to further stock price crashes. Thus, investors who know about an accounting fraud that caused stock prices to plummet would tend to hold back from stock investment until the market stabilizes. In fact, in about 7 months, that is from 2 December 2001 when Enron filed for bankruptcy to July 2002 when WorldCom filed for bankruptcy the Dow index fell by 22.3%.[5]

3.2 SOX Act

The SOX Act is a US federal law enacted in July 2002 to prevent investors from losses due to accounting fraud. The law is also known as the Sarbanes-Oxley Act, from the names of Senator Paul Sarbanes and Representative Michael G. Oxley who filed the bill. The law is officially known as the Public Company Accounting Reform and Investor Protection Act of 2002; it is sometimes called the Corporate Reform Act in Japan.

The SOX Act represents one of the major changes in financial business law under the Federal Securities Act of 1933 and the Federal Securities and Exchange Act of 1934. The law applies to companies listed on the US securities markets and their consolidated companies as well as foreign companies listed on any US securities market. The most important points of this Act are as follows.

First, the listed companies' CEOs and CFOs have to personally guarantee the authenticity of accounting reports. Article 302 of the law requires CEOs and CFOs to sign the annual and quarterly reports confirming that (1) the officer signing the reports has read the report, (2) no important facts are misrepresented or omitted to cause any misunderstanding in the financial reports, (3) the information in the financial statements correctly represents the financial condition and operating results of the company, (4) the CEO and CFO are responsible for establishing and maintaining internal controls, with an internal control mechanism to ensure that

[5]It was USD 10,021.57 at the end of December 2001, but went down to USD 7784.58 by 21 July 2002, when WorldCom filed for bankruptcy.

the validity of the consolidated financial statement is in place and has been evaluated on its efficacy not more than 90 days before the closing date, (5) the serious deficiencies in the design and operation of internal controls if any have been disclosed to the auditor and audit committee, and (6) any misconduct of the management or employees having an important role in internal control has been disclosed to the auditors and audit committee.

Second, companies are required to submit an internal control report. Section 404 that deals with "management assessment of internal controls" states that in addition to the annual SEC financial report, companies are required to submit an "internal control report". The management has to establish and maintain an appropriate internal control mechanism for financial reporting and include the management's assessment of the control mechanism in the report. In addition, audit firms conducting audit of the company must note the internal control mechanisms of the company in their report (direct reporting).

Third, the CEOs and CFOs of companies would be liable to criminal penalties for willful violation of the law. Section 802(a) that deals with the criminal penalties for altering documents provides for "penalties of up to 20 years imprisonment for altering, destroying, mutilating, concealing, falsifying records, documents or tangible objects with intent to obstruct, impede, or influence a legal investigation". Section 906(c) that deals with corporate responsibility for financial reports provides for penalties for false reporting of financial statements. If any false statement is found in the SEC filing documents, the CEO[6] and CFO[7] would be held personally responsible, and could be fined up to USD one million and/or imprisonment for up to 10 years if they know that the disclosure is inappropriate, and USD five million and up to 20 years of imprisonment if the misstatement is intentional.

3.3 Companies Act

The Japanese commercial law, limited company law, and law for special exceptions to commercial law were congregated into a new single law in 2005, to form the Companies Act. This Act was applied to all companies for the establishment of an internal control system. Although the main purpose of the Companies Act is to

[6]In American-style companies, "ownership" and "management" of the company are considered separate, and the board of directors (shareholders) appoints and supervises the executive officers who execute business. At the head of these executive officers is the CEO. In the United States in the 1990s, outside directors representing the interests of institutional investors and others occupied the majority of the board of directors, and it became natural for the chairman of the board to concurrently serve as CEO. Thus, the risk of authority concentrating with the CEO made it difficult for the chairman of the board of directors, who oversees the management, to fully perform their functions.

[7]The CFO is a top management officer responsible for planning and executing corporate finance strategies. For listed companies in the United States, the CFO is the second-most important post after the CEO.

promote compliance, it requires the establishment of "a system to ensure that the directors execute their duties according to laws and regulations and the Articles of Incorporation". The details of this "system to ensure compliance to laws and regulations" are listed in Articles 98 and 100 of the Enforcement Regulations of the Companies Act, as follows:

1. a system for the storage and management of information related to directors' duties;
2. rules and other systems for managing the risk of loss;
3. a system to ensure that the directors execute their duties efficiently;
4. a system to ensure that the employees execute their duties according to laws and regulations;
5. a system to ensure the appropriateness of operations in the corporate group, which includes the interested company and its parent company and subsidiaries.

3.4 Financial Instruments and Exchange Act

The Financial Instruments and Exchange Act is commonly referred to as the "Japanese version of the SOX Act", and is a revision of the conventional Financial Instruments and Exchange Act. The SOX Act in the United States[8] influenced Japan to enact the Financial Instruments and Exchange Act in June 2006 and apply it since April 2008. The Japanese version of the SOX Act stipulates a stronger management system to prevent in-house fraud and requires that an internal control report based on inspection and evaluation of the management system be submitted to the prime minister along with a securities report (Article 24-4-4).

The Act requires the listed companies to prepare an "internal control report" and be audited by a certified public accountant or audit firm (Article 192-2-2); the internal control report is then submitted along with the external audit report. This system is called the "internal control reporting system". Furthermore, when submitting its securities report, the company should attach a "confirmation of adequacy by the representative",[9] similar to the one prescribed under Article 302 of the US SOX Act. If the internal control report includes false statements, the management will incur civil liability under the Act (Articles 24-4-6 and 22).

In addition, for non-submission or misrepresentation, the Act prescribes punishments of prison sentences of up to five years or fines of up to five million yen for individuals, and up to 700 million yen for corporations (Article 197-2 No 5, No 6, Article 207(1)).

[8]The United States, United Kingdom, France, South Korea, etc., introduced their own versions before Japan.

[9]Cabinet Office Ordinance No 28 (a Cabinet Office ordinance that partially revised the Cabinet Office ordinances on disclosure of corporate content, etc., in April 2003).

Since the internal control audit and financial audit are performed by the same auditor, the report of one audit can be used for the other. In addition, the internal control audit report should in principle form part of the financial statement audit report.

3.5 Companies Act and the Financial Instruments and Exchange Act

The Companies Act applies to all companies, but the Financial Instruments and Exchange Act (the Japanese version of the SOX Act) is applicable only to listed companies. In addition, the Companies Act mainly promotes compliance, whereas the Financial Instruments and Exchange Act focuses on the appropriate disclosure of financial reports.

Both the Companies Act and the Financial Instruments and Exchange Act require internal control, but each with a different purpose and content. Internal control in the Companies Act is for the board of directors, who the shareholders entrust to properly manage the company. On the other hand, internal control under the Financial Instruments and Exchange Act is to ensure the reliability of the financial reports and protect investors. The main differences between the two are shown in Table 3.1.

Table 3.1 Comparison of internal control between the Companies Act and the Financial Instruments and Exchange Act

Classification	Companies Act	Financial Instruments and Exchange Act
Interested companies	Large companies and companies with committees	Listed companies and consolidated subsidiaries
Purpose	To ensure proper operations	To ensure the reliability of financial reports
Interested party	Board of directors	Manager (the company)
Disclosure	Business report	Internal control report
Audit	Auditors and audit committee	External auditor (audit firm/certified public accountant)
Report	Audit report	Internal control report
Penalties	None in particular	If the internal control report is not submitted, or if false statements are made with regard to important matters in the internal control report, imprisonment for up to 5 years or a fine of not more than five million yen, with a fine of not more than 700 million yen for corporations

Source: Created by the author

Discussion Questions

1. Compare and explain the SOX law and the Financial Instruments and Exchange Act, the Japanese version of the SOX law. Also, explain the law that acts like the SOX Act in your country.
2. Discuss the impact of accounting fraud on risk management.

COSO ERM Framework

4

The COSO ERM and ISO RM are two framework types. This chapter outlines the COSO ERM framework.

4.1 COSO Organization

The 1980s saw corporate bankruptcy rampant in the United States due to accounting fraud. In response to this, the National Commission on Fraudulent Financial Reporting was formed in June 1985, with James C. Treadway, Jr., as the first chairman, giving it the name Treadway Committee. The Treadway Committee included five institutions that have now become part of the Institute of Management Accountants (IMA): the American Accounting Association (AAA), the American Institute of Certified Public Accountants (AICPA), Financial Executives International (FEI), the Institute of Internal Auditors (IIA), and the National Association of Accountants.

In the same year, the Treadway Commission COSO was formed. This COSO is a committee supported by the five accounting organizations mentioned above. The purpose of this COSO is to provide a pioneering mindset on three points: ERM, internal control, and fraud deterrence.[1]

4.2 Internal Control Framework

Internal control is a mechanism set up inside a company to ensure the appropriateness of corporate operations, and is maintained and operated by the management to supervise employees. This was originally understood as an activity to ensure the

[1]Based on the COSO website (https://www.coso.org/Pages/aboutus.aspx).

H. Lee, *Risk Management*, Springer Texts in Business and Economics,
https://doi.org/10.1007/978-981-16-3468-0_4

appropriateness of financial reporting in financial accounting. In the 1990s, the definition of internal control was broadened to encompass the control of compliance, particularly related to business policies and rules, the effectiveness and efficiency of business and their improvement, RM, and more. It also became a tool for corporate governance.

However, corporate governance is a mechanism for stakeholders, such as shareholders, banks, creditors, directors, and employees, to monitor the company's business and ensure that it is healthy and efficient from an external perspective. Therefore, corporate governance is a mechanism between stakeholders and management, while internal control is a mechanism between management and employees.

The de facto international standard for internal control is the Internal Control Integrated Framework (1992, revised in 2013)[2] (hereinafter: the COSO report), published by the Treadway Commission COSO.

The COSO report was compiled in response to the Treadway Commission's 1987 report, the *Report of the National Commission on Fraudulent Financial Reporting*, and its recommendations. This report consists of four volumes: Executive Summary, Framework, Reporting to External Parties, and Evaluation Tools.

In the COSO report, internal control is an ordinary process for normal business activities. It is performed by the board of directors, management, and all the other members of the company to ensure the achievement of three objectives: effectiveness and efficiency of business, reliability of financial reporting, and compliance. The five elements needed to achieve the objectives of internal control are a control environment, the evaluation of risk, control activities, information and communication, and monitoring activities.

Furthermore, in the COSO's Internal Control Framework (2013), the objective of reliability of financial reporting was changed to reporting, to include internal reporting, which includes non-financial items that have become important in recent years. Also, 17 principles are proposed as indices to achieve effective internal control.

The internal control framework of the COSO report (2013) is presented in Fig. 4.1.

[2]Coopers & Lybrand (now PricewaterhouseCoopers) was commissioned by COSO to produce the COSO report.

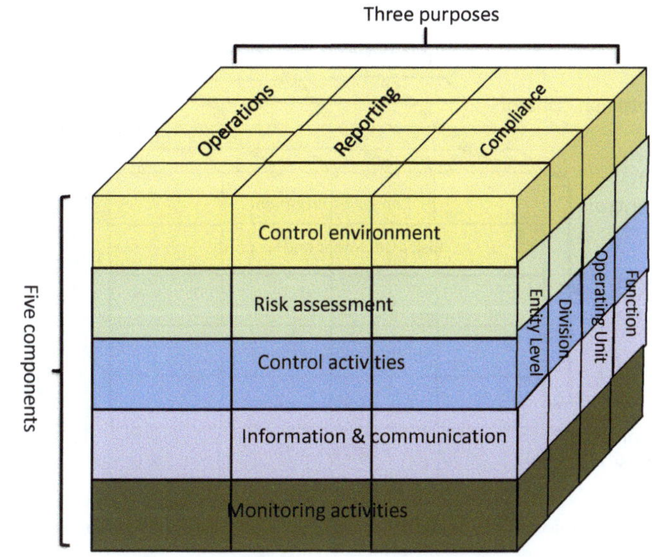

Fig. 4.1 The COSO Internal Control Framework (2013) (*Source:* COSO)

However, the internal control framework in Japan has four objectives and six components, one more for each category compared to the COSO framework.[3] The additional objective is preservation of assets, to ensure that the assets are properly acquired, stored, and liquidated, with the additional component of "response to technology", reflecting the importance of technology in today's enterprises.

Fig. 4.2 shows the Japanese version of the internal control framework.

[3]Internal Accounting Subcommittee, Corporate Accounting Council, "On Standards for Evaluation and Audit of Internal Control over Financial Reporting" (8 December 2005), pp. 3–4.

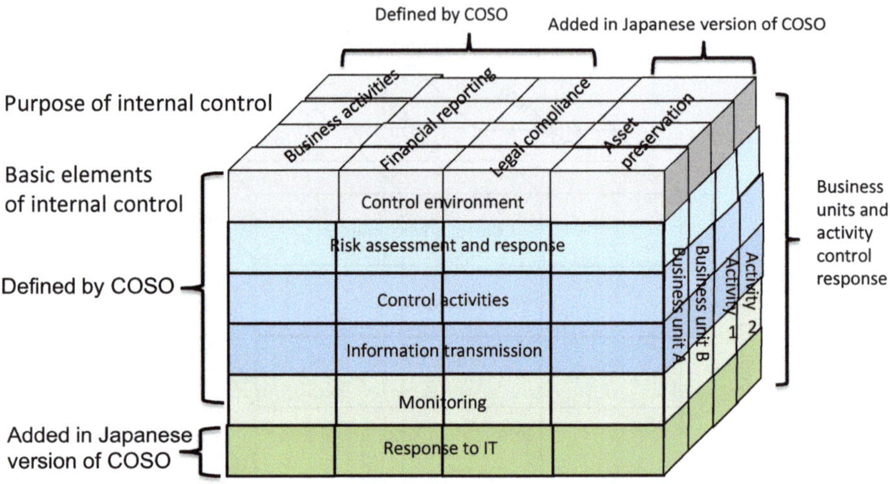

Fig. 4.2 Japanese version of the internal control framework (*Source:* Financial Services Agency)

Thus, the four objectives of the internal control framework in Japan are to ensure the effectiveness and efficiency of operations, reliability of financial reporting, compliance with the laws and regulations related to business activities, and preservation of assets. Internal control in Japan is a process in which everyone in the company achieves the four objectives.[4] The six components are the control environment, risk assessment and response, control activities, information and communication, monitoring, and technology response.

The objectives of the Japanese version of the internal control framework are as follows.

1. *Effectiveness and efficiency of business*. This ensures that the company's day-to-day operations are carried out in an efficient and effective manner to achieve the business objectives.
2. *Reliability of financial reports*. This ensures the reliability of financial statements and information significantly affecting the financial statements. The mechanism provides reliable financial reports to the company's stakeholders.
3. *Compliance with laws and regulations related to business activities*. This promotes compliance with the laws and regulations relating to business activities and other norms, such as company guidelines.
4. *Preservation of assets*. This ensures that the acquisition, use, and disposal of assets take place under due process and approval.

[4]The Business Accounting Council's "Standards for the Evaluation and Audit of Internal Control over Financial Reporting" (15 February 2007), refer to the internal control designed to achieve these four objectives. It is a process involving everyone in the company.

The basic components of the Japanese version of the internal control framework are as follows.

1. *Control environment*. Establish the ethos of the organization, to lead to the awareness of control of all persons in the organization. This forms the basis for all other components, such as the company's integrity and ethical values, management policies and strategies, and organizational structure and practices.
2. *Risk assessment and response*. The process of recognizing, analyzing, and evaluating the risks affecting the organization's goals, and responding appropriately to those risks.
3. *Control activities*. Policies and procedures to ensure implementation of the management's orders and instructions.
4. *Information and communication*. This ensures that necessary information is identified, understood, processed, and properly communicated to all interested parties inside and outside the organization.
5. *Monitoring activities*. This is to ensure continuous monitoring and evaluation of the effectiveness of internal controls.
6. *Response to information technology*. For the internal controls to function effectively and efficiently, the company needs to determine the appropriate policies and procedures related to information technologies incorporated in the business and respond appropriately to any information technology-related issue that may arise in the course of business.

4.3 The COSO ERM (2004) Framework

4.3.1 ERM Framework Establishment

In 2001, COSO commissioned Pricewaterhouse Coopers[5] to develop a framework for continuously and comprehensively assessing and improving the risks and opportunities of a corporation. The results were compiled into a report entitled the Enterprise Risk Management Integrated Framework (COSO ERM), and published in September 2004.

The COSO's internal control framework was published in 1992, and COSO ERM (2004) was published 12 years later, in September 2004. Fig. 4.3 shows the COSO internal control and ERM frameworks.

[5]PricewaterhouseCoopers is the world's largest professional services firm, headquartered in London, with 163,000 staff in 151 countries. Along with Deloitte Touche Tohmatsu (DTT), KPMG, and Ernst & Young, it is one of the "big four" accounting firms. Arthur Andersen & Co., one of the five major accounting firms, was closed in the aftermath of the aforementioned Enron incident.

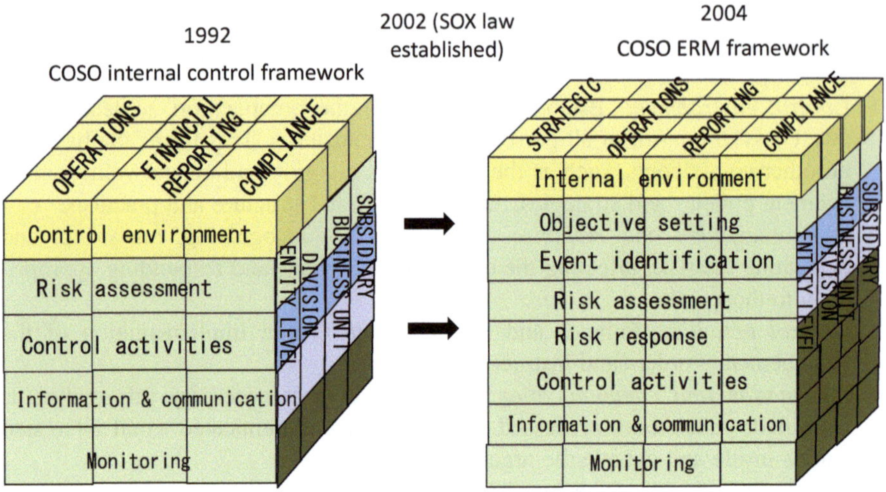

Fig. 4.3 The COSO internal control and COSO ERM (2004) frameworks (*Source:* COSO)

As can be seen in Fig. 4.3, COSO changed the internal control framework of 1992 to the ERM framework of 2004 after enactment of the SOX Act of 2002. That is, the question was raised as to whether the internal control reports required under the 2002 SOX Act should be prepared and audited according to the 2004 ERM framework. In response to this question, according to a "FAQ" on its website[6] COSO explains that the two are independent, and that the internal control reports created in accordance with the 2002 SOX Act are sufficient. In other words, the COSO ERM (2004) framework does not substitute the internal control framework, but includes it and expands on its scope.

4.3.2 Definition of ERM

Within the COSO ERM (2004) framework, ERM is defined as follows[7]: "ERM is a process effected by an entity's board of directors, management, and other personnel, applied in strategy setting and across the enterprise, and designed to identify the potential events that may affect the entity, manage the risk within its risk appetite, and provide reasonable assurance regarding the achievement of entity objectives." This definition of ERM exemplifies the following concepts of ERM.

- an ongoing and flowing process through an entity,
- effected by people at all levels of an organization,

[6]See FAQ No 8 of the COSO Enterprise Risk Management—Integrated Framework Update Project, and FAQ No 8 of the COSO Internal Control-Integrated Framework (May 2013).

[7]COSO, *Enterprise Risk Management—Integrated Framework* (September 2004).

- applied in a strategy setting,
- applied across the enterprise, at every level and unit, and that takes an entity-level portfolio view of risk,
- designed to identify the potential events that, if they occur, would affect the entity, and to manage risk within its risk appetite,
- that provides reasonable assurance to an entity's management and board of directors,
- geared to achieve objectives in one or more separate but overlapping categories.

4.3.3 Features of COSO ERM (2004)

The COSO internal control framework has three objectives and five basic components, while the COSO ERM (2004) framework has four objectives and eight basic components. The COSO ERM (2004) framework differs from the internal control framework in that the objectives are "strategic" and the components have an "objective setting". In other words, the three objectives of the COSO internal control are effectiveness and efficiency of business, reliability of (financial) reports, and compliance with laws and regulations related to business activities. COSO ERM (2004) adds a strategic objective. The five components of COSO internal control are control environment, risk assessment and response, control activities, information and communication, and monitoring. The eight components of COSO ERM (2004) are internal environment, objective setting, event identification, risk evaluation, risk response, control activities, information and communication, and monitoring.

The relationship between the COSO ERM (2004) objectives and basic components is shown in Fig. 4.4.

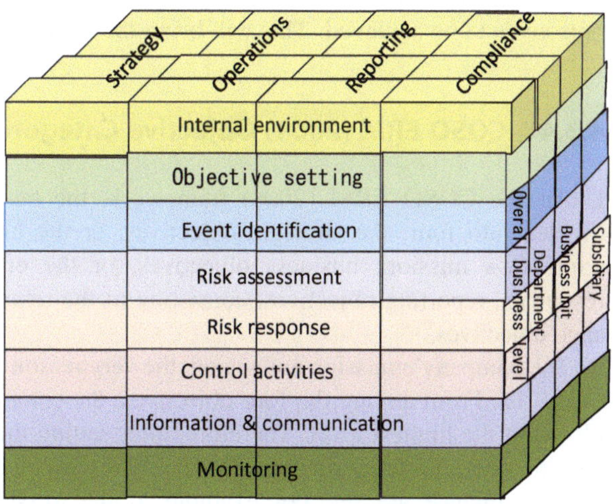

Fig. 4.4 Relationship between the COSO ERM (2004) objectives and components (*Source:* COSO)

In the COSO ERM (2004) framework, the relationship between the ERM objectives and the components necessary to achieve them is represented in a three-dimensional cube. The four objectives categories—strategic, operations, reporting, and compliance—are represented by the vertical columns, the eight components by horizontal rows, and an entity's units by the third dimension.

COSO internal control is mainly based on financial reporting, whereas the COSO ERM (2004) is based on management. COSO internal control is a process that can provide "reasonable assurance" of achieving the business objectives, while COSO ERM (2004) further includes RM. Although COSO internal control has no "risk appetite", COSO ERM (2004) introduces this concept.

COSO internal control considers only the risk of loss, whereas COSO ERM (2004) considers both the risk of loss, a negative aspect, and the opportunity to earn revenue, a positive aspect. In the COSO ERM (2004) framework, risk is limited to "the possibility of occurrence of an event having a negative effect on achievement of the organizational goals", with the positive effects classified as opportunities. The main objective of COSO internal control is "reliability of financial reporting", but for COSO ERM (2004) "strategy" is the main objective, making it important to eliminate uncertainties while executing the said strategy. COSO ERM (2004) covers all the businesses, including the subsidiaries and overseas bases, that is the entire corporate group. Furthermore, COSO ERM (2004) is a process that manages risk and provides reasonable assurance of achieving the entity's objectives.

The most important features of COSO ERM (2004) are the following. (1) It is applied across an organization, with the board of directors, management, and employees all participating. (2) It is inseparable from management and can be used to formulate business strategies for achieving the business objectives of the company (increase in corporate value). (3) Events affecting the organization can be specifically known. (4) Risk is managed within the risk appetite.

The COSO ERM (2004) framework has eight components in each of the four objectives and, if they function properly, we can reasonably expect the four ERM objectives to be achieved. This will bring the entity's risk within its risk appetite.

4.3.4 COSO ERM (2004) Objective Categories

Under the COSO ERM (2004) framework, the business entity's objectives are divided into four: the strategic objectives, or the high-level goals based on the company's mission; business objectives, or the effective and efficient use of resources; reporting objectives, consisting of the reliability of reports; and compliance objectives.

The company's mission and vision, the very reason for its existence, are at the top of the list. From among the four objectives, the company's strategic objectives are placed at the highest level. Therefore, after setting the strategic objectives and the specific strategies for realizing them, the objectives related to the business, reporting, and compliance are set. For example, if the mission is to become the largest manufacturer of high-end consumer electronics, the strategic objective is to fulfill this mission by "reaching 25% of market share". The strategy for this is to increase the number of retail stores, with the related objectives set for implementing this strategy. While the reporting and compliance objectives can be controlled by the entity, the strategic and operational objectives may depend on external events.

4.3.5 The COSO ERM (2004) Basic Components

COSO ERM (2004) is not a strictly continuous process in which one component affects only the next. ERM is a multifaceted and iterative process where almost every component potentially affects all other ones.

The eight basic components of COSO ERM (2004) are as follows.

1. *Internal environment*. The internal environment shows how members of an entity should perceive and deal with risks, such as the concept of RM, risk appetite, integrity, ethics, and the working environment of members.
2. *Objective setting*. The objective setting clarifies the management, business, strategic, and other COSO ERM (2004) objectives to be achieved. ERM ensures that the objectives chosen are aligned with the mission of the entity and are consistent with the entity's risk appetite.
3. *Event identification*. The events that affect the attainment of objectives must be identified for risks and business opportunities. Opportunities are fed back to the management's strategy and objective-setting process.
4. *Risk assessment*. This analyzes the likelihood and impact of risks. Risks are assessed on both intrinsic and residual basis.
5. *Risk response*. This selects the risk countermeasures, such as avoiding/accepting, reducing, and sharing risks, while ensuring that those choices match the risk tolerance and risk appetite of the business entity.
6. *Control activities*. Policies and procedures established and implemented to ensure that risk is handled effectively.
7. *Information and communication*. Relevant information is recognized, captured, and communicated using methods and timings that allow all members to fulfill their responsibilities. Effective communications, in a broad sense, flow in all directions: from top to bottom, horizontally, and bottom to top.
8. *Monitoring*. The entire ERM is monitored and modified as needed. Monitoring is performed through ongoing management activities, independent evaluation, or both.

4.3.6 Effectiveness and Limitations of COSO ERM (2004)

Determining the effectiveness of COSO ERM (2004) is based on the presence and functioning of the eight basic components. Thus, having the component is an important criterion in the first step of determining a valid ERM. If the components are present and function properly, the risk is expected to fall within the entity's risk appetite. The eight components may not function in the same way in all entities, but as long as each component is present and functioning properly, even a small entity can properly perform ERM.

However, the COSO ERM (2004) has limitations due to the following factors: (1) the board and management cannot guarantee achieving the entity's objectives; (2) when choosing to respond to risk, the costs and benefits must be considered; (3) the possibility of human error in decision making; (4) two or more people could collude and evade the control procedures; (5) management can ignore the ERM decisions.

4.4 COSO ERM (2017)

4.4.1 Outline of COSO ERM (2017)

COSO released a revised version of its 2004 ERM framework on 6 September 2017.[8] The revision was in response to the progress of technology and globalization of business, the diversification and complexity of risks, and the emergence of new risks. Furthermore, the COSO ERM (2004) framework was not yet adopted as a global standard for RM. This was due to various misunderstandings regarding ERM. More specifically: (1) ERM is a function or department; (2) it is intended to list risks; (3) it is to target internal control; (4) it is a checklist; and (5) it cannot be applied to small and medium-sized organizations. These and other misunderstandings are said to have led to several management groups shunning ERM.

COSO ERM (2017) defines ERM as "the culture, capabilities, and practices, integrated with strategy-setting and performance that organizations rely on to manage risk in creating, preserving, and realizing value". However, COSO ERM (2004) defined ERM as a process. In other words, in COSO ERM (2017), the concept of ERM was greatly expanded from a "process" to a "culture, ability, and practice".

Furthermore, COSO ERM (2017) draws on the ERM framework from the flow of management strategy formulation, and, in order to clarify the relationship between risk, strategy and performance, employs something similar to the basics shown in Fig. 4.5.

[8]Following the revision of the internal control framework in 2013, for the first time in 20 years, the ERM framework was revised. The PwC project team that led the revision was commissioned by the COSO; they published the exposure draft in June 2016, and then, after considering the public comments, released the revised version in September 2017.

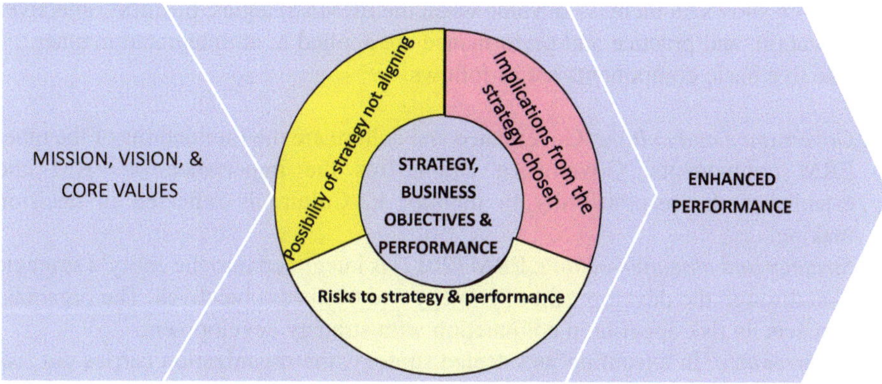

Fig. 4.5 Positioning of strategy (COSO ERM, 2017) (*Source:* COSO, *Enterprise Risk Management—Integrating with Strategy and Performance* (June 2017))

COSO ERM (2017) examined the strategies from three perspectives. First, the strategies and business goals may not align with the company's mission, vision, and core values. The missions are the core objectives of an entity and clarify what the entity wants to achieve and the significance of the entity. A vision is a goal that an entity seeks to achieve in the long run. A core value is an entity's belief or philosophy about what is right and what is wrong, or what is acceptable and what is not, affecting the entity's behavior. The second is the impact (implications) of the chosen strategy. This is because each of the selected risks has a unique risk profile. The third is the risk of executing the strategy. The flow of these management strategies is defined as the "basis of ERM", with the ERM framework built on top of it.

The COSO ERM (2017) framework includes five components and 20 principles. Fig. 4.6 shows the components and their relationship with the mission, vision, and core value of the entity. The three ribbons of strategy and goal setting, performance, and review and correction represent the common processes. The two ribbons governance and culture, and information, communication, and reporting, support ERM.

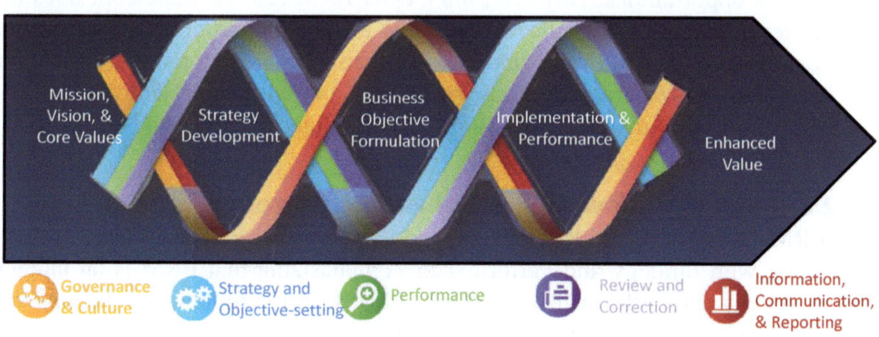

Fig. 4.6 COSO ERM (2017) (*Source:* COSO, *Enterprise Risk Management—Integrating with Strategy and Performance* (June 2017))

Fig. 4.6 shows an increase in value when the ERM strategies, business objectives organization, and practice and performance are applied in an integrated manner.

The five basic components are as follows.

1. *Governance and culture*. Governance and culture are the foundations of the other ERM components. Governance emphasizes the importance of ERM and establishes the responsibility to monitor it. Culture is reflected in decision making.
2. *Strategy and objective-setting*. ERM (2017) is integrated into the entity's strategic plan through the development of strategy and business objectives. The organization sets its risk appetite in conjunction with strategy development.
3. *Performance*. In executing its selected strategy, the organization carries out risk identification, risk analysis, risk evaluation, and risk response, the core RM processes affecting objective achievement.
4. *Review and revision*. The organization reviews whether the RM activities are carried out properly, whether they perform as expected, and whether the planning strategies, objectives, and risk assessment have changed the situation.
5. *Information, communication, and reporting*. Information is gathered and shared throughout the business.

The above five basic components include the 20 principles shown in Fig. 4.7.

These principles explain the basic concepts associated with each component and describe the practical implementation of ERM.

4.4.2 Main COSO ERM (2017) Revisions

4.4.2.1 Definition of Risk

The COSO ERM (2004) framework defines risk as the "events that negatively impact the organization's pursuit of its objectives". The events with a negative impact on this were classified as risks, and those with a positive impact were classified as opportunities. However, the COSO ERM (2017) framework does not use the term "event", but collectively refers to the "opportunities" that have a positive impact and the "risks" that have a negative impact as risks. It states that risk is an "uncertainty affecting business strategy and business objectives". COSO ERM (2017) appears to agree with ISO 31000, the international standard for RM.

4.4.2.2 Integrate Risk with Strategy and Performance

The ERM framework's title was changed to "Enterprise Risk Management—Integrating with Strategy and Performance", emphasizing that ERM is an integral part of strategy and performance. The COSO ERM (2017) framework explains that the concept of risk in strategy planning and daily activities can be useful, making it helpful to know how much risk is existed and how much is accepted in pursuit of a certain performance level.

Fig. 4.7 RM Principles within each of the five components (COSO ERM, 2017) (*Source:* COSO, *Enterprise Risk Management—Integrating with Strategy and Performance* (June 2017))

Since the implementation of COSO internal controls is required by law, the COSO ERM (2017) assumes that they are in place, and emphasizes the need to maintain and increase the organization's value.

4.4.2.3 Five Components and 20 Principles

In the COSO ERM (2004) framework, ERM consisted of eight interrelated components: (1) internal environment, (2) setting objectives, (3) event identification, (4) risk assessment, (5) response to risks, (6) control activities, (7) information and communication, and (8) monitoring. These can be visually represented through the COSO ERM cube (Fig. 4.4), based on the COSO cube.

However, the COSO ERM (2017) framework changed the interconnected components to: (1) governance and culture, (2) strategy and goal setting, (3) performance, (4) review and correction, and (5) information, communication, and reporting, as represented in the COSO ERM cube.

Table 4.1 compares the COSO ERM (2004) and COSO ERM (2017) basic components.

Table 4.1 Comparison of the COSO ERM (2004) and COSO ERM (2017) components

The eight elements of COSO ERM (2004)	The five elements of COSO ERM (2017)
Internal environment	Governance and culture
Objective setting	Strategy and objective setting
Event identification	Performance
Risk assessment	
Risk response	
Control activities	Omitted because COSO internal control is assumed to be in place
Information and communication	Information, communication, and reporting
Monitoring	Review and revision

Source: Created by the author

The integration of ERM and business practices improves the information, decision making, and performance, with the focus on creating, maintaining, and realizing value.

COSO ERM (2017) significantly changed the way the framework is presented. In COSO ERM (2004), the framework components were represented in a three-dimensional cube with six faces. In other words, the overall purpose of the ERM was expressed in one dimension, the eight concrete elements were expressed in two dimensions, and the organizational unit that implements them was expressed in three dimensions. However, in COSO ERM (2017), the framework cube was changed to "basic (positioning of strategy) + 5 elements + 20 principles", as described above.

4.4.2.4 Risk Capacity

Risk capacity (or limit) is a new term for the total risk that the organization can take.

Risk profiles (or reference information) indicate how much risk to take and the relationship between performance and the risk generated in aiming for a target performance. Risk appetite is a target set by an organization based on the risk profiles and risk capacity, and indicates how much risk the organization wants to take. Risk appetite literally means "the amount of risk the organization wants to take". In other words, it shows whether the organization chooses a "high-risk, high-return" or "low-risk, low-return" strategy.

The relationship between risk profiles, risk appetite, and risk capacity is shown in Fig. 4.8.

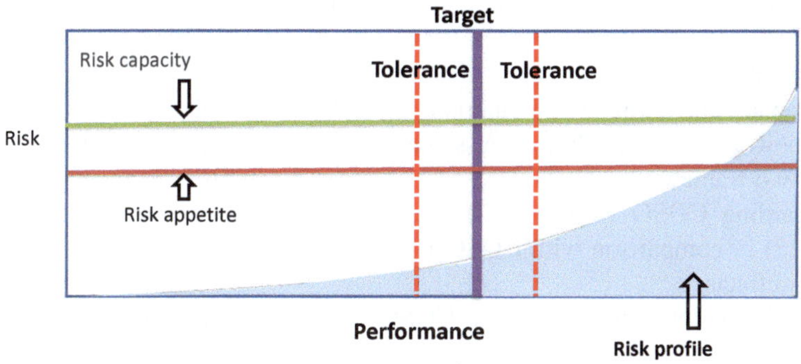

Fig. 4.8 Relationship between risk profile, risk appetite, and risk capacity (*Source:* COSO, *Enterprise Risk Management—Integrating with Strategy and Performance* (June 2017))

COSO ERM (2017) actively manages risk and performance, enabling the achievement of strategies, with focus on how risk and performance can be integrated. It considers the tolerance for performance variability, but in terms of achieving strategies and business objectives, and not as individual risks.

4.4.3 Relationship Between COSO Internal Control and COSO ERM (2017)

The COSO ERM (2017) is a framework for internal control and a complementary mechanism. Although both use the structure of elements and principles, COSO ERM (2017) does not specify any characteristic common to both. The main difference between COSO ERM (2017) and COSO internal control lies in its purpose. The purpose of COSO internal control is mainly to "comply with laws and regulations", whereas that of COSO ERM (2017) is to "create, maintain, and increase the value of the organization." For example, COS-ERM (2017) considers "establishing risk appetite" and "establishing strategies and setting goals", unlike COSO internal control, which mainly focuses on regulatory compliance, taking these activities for granted, but moving outside their scope.

Conversely, when some items are found in both guidelines, they are given priority in COSO internal control, and omitted from COSO ERM (2017), to avoid confusion. Specifically, this applies to the "control activities" in COSO internal control. Here, the "control activities" are the activities introducing and fixing the already established control methods by creating policies and procedures and executing the operations based on them, for example. The items common in both guidelines are emphasized and explained in more detail in COSO internal control than in COSO ERM (2017). Specifically, the above-mentioned "governance and culture", "review and correction", and "information, communication, and reporting" in COSO ERM (2017) and COSO internal control cannot be covered by a single set of guidelines, and users have to switch between them as needed.

Discussion Questions

1. Compare and explain the internal control framework and the COSO ERM framework. In particular, discuss the areas of application and effectiveness of the two frameworks.
2. Regarding COSO ERM (2017), please explain the revision of COSO ERM (2017) in comparison with COSO ERM (2004). Discuss the changed parts and their effects.
3. Explain the relationship between COSO ERM (2017) and internal control.

ISO RM Framework

5

ISO announced their RM framework as an international RM standard. This chapter outlines the ISO 31000 RM framework.

5.1 ISO Organizations and RM Standards

The ISO was established in 1947 as an international private non-governmental organization headquartered in Geneva, Switzerland, and has since established international standards in all fields, except the electrical field. Only one organization from each country can participate in this, but in 1952 the Japan Industrial Standards Committee (JISC),[1] the organization that investigates and deliberates on the Japanese Industrial Standards (JIS),[2] joined the ISO.

The ISO standards include a quality management system standard, the ISO9000 series, and an environmental management system standard, the ISO14000 series. The ISO9000 series certifies the quality management systems, from product design/manufacturing to inspection, while the ISO14001 series requires the creation of an environmental management system (EMS) as described in the ISO14000 series.

Furthermore, as an RM standard, on 15 November 2009 the ISO published the ISO 31000 series, the 2009 Risk Management Principles and Guidelines, and ISO Guide 73, a collection of definitions of RM terms. ISO 31000 was created on the basis of the RM standards used in Japan, Australia, New Zealand, and the United Kingdom. Following the issuance of ISO 31000, the RM system standard JIS Q 31000 "Risk Management Principles and Guidelines" was enacted on 21 September

[1]The JISC is a council established by the Ministry of Economy, Trade and Industry in accordance with Article 3, paragraph 1 of the Industrial Standardization Law (Act No 185 of 1 June 1949).

[2]The JIS is a national standard established based on the Industrial Standardization Law (1949) aimed at promoting industrial standardization.

H. Lee, *Risk Management*, Springer Texts in Business and Economics,
https://doi.org/10.1007/978-981-16-3468-0_5

2010.[3] Furthermore, the second edition of ISO 31000, "ISO 31000: Risk Management Guidelines (ISO 31000)", was issued in February 2018. Although ISO 31000: 2018 is not largely different from ISO 31000: 2009 in general terms, it makes the terms easier to understand and strengthens governance by clarifying the responsibilities of the supervisors and top management.

ISO 31000: 2018 offers RM guidelines for all risks and for all organizations. These guidelines can be used as a reference, and are not mandatory, unlike other practices or specifications.

5.2 Risk and RM Definitions

ISO 31000: 2018 defines risk as "the effect of uncertainty of objectives". Thus, RM includes negative risks as well as the risks that potentially offer positive effects.[4] It therefore includes speculative as well as pure risk.

The definition of risk in ISO 31000 includes both unfavorable and favorable effects, making ISO 31000 applicable to all business operations with speculative risk. If the definition of risk is limited to undesired effects, RM would be limited to prevention and safety activities related to disasters, etc. In addition, "effect of uncertainty on objectives" indicates that risk is a factor influencing the achievement of organizational objectives, thereby positioning RM as supporting the organization's objectives.

However, since risk is regarded as "the effect of uncertainty on various objectives", the scope of RM according to ISO 31000 is limited to the proactive activities dealing with risks, but only after the risks have materialized. CM (emergency response) and BCM are outside the scope of ISO 31000:2018.

ISO 31000:2018 also focuses on decision making under uncertainty and the responsibilities of management; the focus is on efficient decision making with limited knowledge. It states that management leadership has the responsibility to enforce governance and ensure that RM is incorporated into all organizational activities.

However, ISO 31000 defines RM in the usual manner of "coordinated activities to direct and control an organization with regard to risk". While RM is applied to activities individually, ISO 31000 is a standard to be applied to the activities of an organization.

[3] In March 2001, the Risk Management Standards Committee, the successor of the Crisis Management System Standards Review Committee, which was established in response to the Great Hanshin-Awaji earthquake in January 1995, released the "JIS Q 2001 Guidelines for Establishing a Risk Management System", which expand from simple CM to a wider, more comprehensive concept of risk management. With the enforcement of JIS Q 31000, JIS Q 2001 was abolished.

[4] ISO/IEC Guide 73:2002 defines risk as a "combination of the probability of an event and its consequence", that is, unfavorable results.

ISO 31000 does not define ERM, but shows that RM can be applied at all stages. Therefore, an ERM system can be built by applying this standard to every organization and risk in a company.

While COSO ERM manages risk from the perspective of a whole entity, ISO 31000 provides an RM framework that can be applied to any organization at any level. ISO 31000 is a guideline for RM, and not intended for certification, stating that its principles and methods should be applied flexibly according to the situation of each organization.

5.3 ISO 31000 System

ISO 31000 provides a general concept and is not intended to be applied to a particular field or enforced as a standard, such as for certification. It presents a "framework" and a series of general purpose "processes" for implementation.

The principles, framework, and processes of ISO 31000 are shown in Fig. 5.1.

A principle represents a policy outlining that must be observed when performing RM in an organization. ISO 31000:2018, as shown in Fig. 5.1, presents eight principles.

A framework is an operational system designed to manage processes according to certain principles and is a comprehensive RM framework for the whole organization meant for implementation, evaluation, and improvement. The framework is designed to help organizations integrate RM into their important activities and functions. The effectiveness of RM depends on the overall governance of the organization, including decision making.

A process is an iterative, ongoing activity of an organization under a framework, and can be applied to decision making related to the company's activities. These processes can be applied at each level of the enterprise, and when they are applied to the entire enterprise as a group, they become an ERM.

A framework refers to the activities designed, implemented, and reviewed so that the processes are consistent with the organization's management philosophy, mission, or objectives, such as its mid- to long-term goals. The processes relate to the implementation of RM, including the "scope, context, and criteria" of risk assessment (risk identification, risk analysis, risk evaluation), risk treatment, monitoring/review, communication and consultation, record creation, and reporting.

Depending on the organization, there could be one or more processes. Some organizations have a single process and do not differentiate between risk types, while others may have different processes for each type of risk, such as quality, environmental, business continuity, and financial risk.

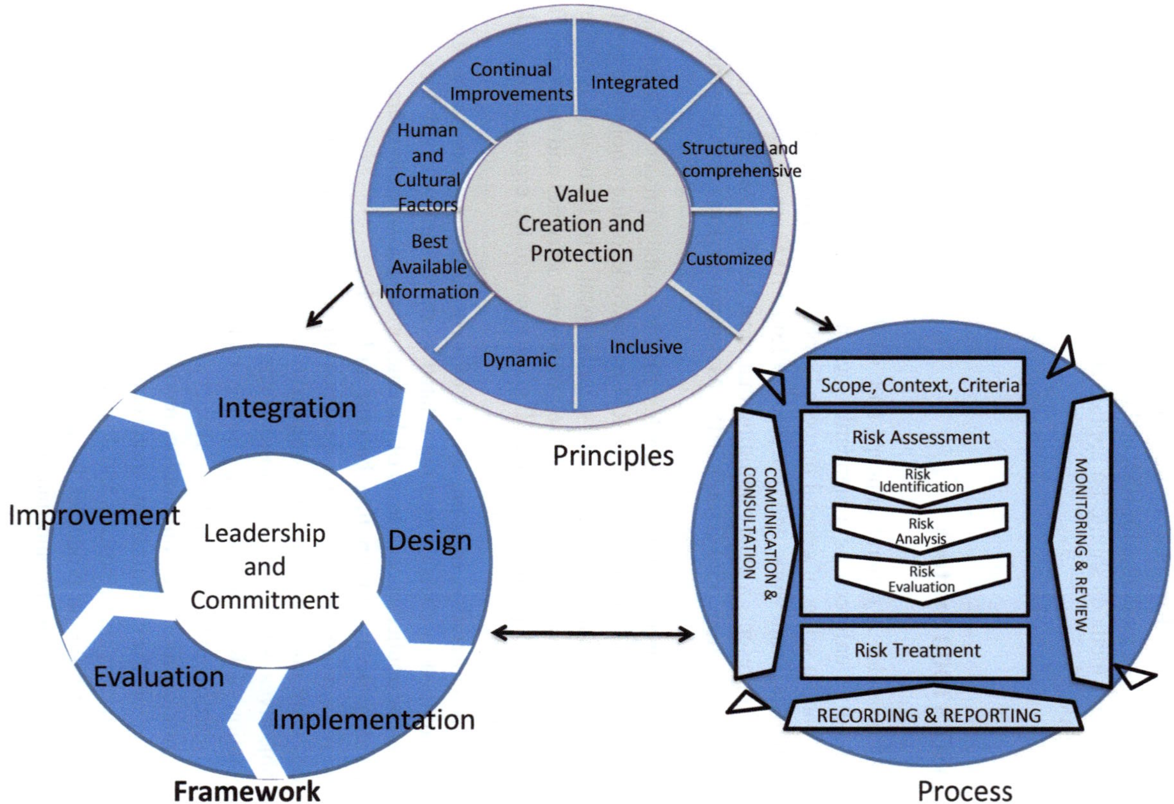

Fig. 5.1 Principles, frameworks, and process (ISO 31000:2018) (*Source:* ISO 31000:2018)

5.4 Principles (ISO 31000:2018)

The principles of ISO 31000:2018 describe eight issues that an organization must consider to make the RM effective. The purpose of RM is to create and protect value, improve performance, encourage innovation, and help achieve goals. The principles set out in these guidelines provide guidance on the effective and efficient RM and its value transfer, and an explanation of its intent and purpose. Principles are the basis of RM and need to be referenced when establishing an organization's RM framework and processes. They ensure that the organization can address the uncertainty related to its objectives.

The principles of RM (ISO 31000:2018) are shown in Fig. 5.2.

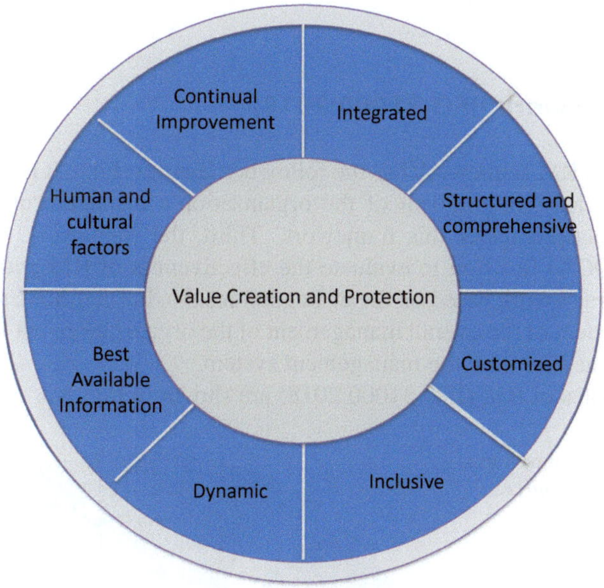

Fig. 5.2 Principles of RM (ISO 31000:2018 (*Source:* ISO 31000:2018)

An effective RM requires the following elements in terms of principles:

1. *Integrated.* Risk management is an integral part of all organizational activities.
2. *Structured and comprehensive.* A structured and comprehensive approach to risk management contributes to consistent and comparable results.
3. *Customized.* The risk management framework and process are customized and proportionate to the organization's external and internal context related to its objectives.
4. *Inclusive.* Appropriate and timely involvement of stakeholders enables their knowledge, views, and perceptions to be considered. This results in improved awareness and informed risk management.

5. *Dynamic*. Risks can emerge, change, or disappear as an organization's external and internal context changes. Risk management anticipates, detects, acknowledges and responds to those changes and events in an appropriate and timely manner.
6. *Best available information*. The inputs to risk management are based on historical and current information, as well as on future expectations. Risk management explicitly takes into account any limitations and uncertainties associated with such information and expectations. Information should be timely, clear, and available to relevant stakeholders.
7. *Human and cultural factors*. Human behaviour and culture significantly influence all aspects of risk management at each level and stage.
8. *Continual improvement*. Risk management is continually improved through learning and experience.

5.5 Framework (ISO 31000:2018)

The ISO 31000 RM framework has the following features. First, it is designed under the leadership and commitment of the organization's management. Second, processes are practiced under this framework. Third, the framework has a plan-do-check-act (PDCA) function to evaluate the effectiveness of RM and continuously improve the framework based on the evaluation results. Furthermore, the framework is not independent of the overall management of the organization, but is rather meant to help integrate RM with the management system.

The principles of RM (ISO 31000:2018) are shown in Fig. 5.3.

Fig. 5.3 The RM framework (ISO 31000:2018) (*Source:* ISO 31000:2018)

Leadership and commitment describe the responsibilities of directors and top management (for example, the CEO). In the previous edition of the ISO (ISO

31000:2009), the subject was top management only, but in the second edition the word "oversight bodies" has been added. Here, the directors and top management are responsible for the RM initiatives, roles, authorities, and accountability. Top management and the oversight bodies in leadership and commitment need to know that RM is integrated into all organizational activities, and implement them. The top management is responsible for RM, while the oversight bodies are responsible for overseeing RM.

Integration involves an organization's RM activities and governance, strategy development, strategy execution, culture, and more. The RM design needs to appropriately consider the overall RM policy, systems, roles and responsibilities, communication and consultation rules, and the RM processes.

Implementation requires that the organization actually implements and operates the RM processes determined in the design. In evaluation and improvement, the organization evaluates whether the various framework activities have contributed to achieving its objectives, such as the management philosophy, mission, and mid- to long-term goals and plans (effectiveness), and improving on them.

The framework introduces the concept of continuous improvement, known in management as PDCA (Fig. 5.4).

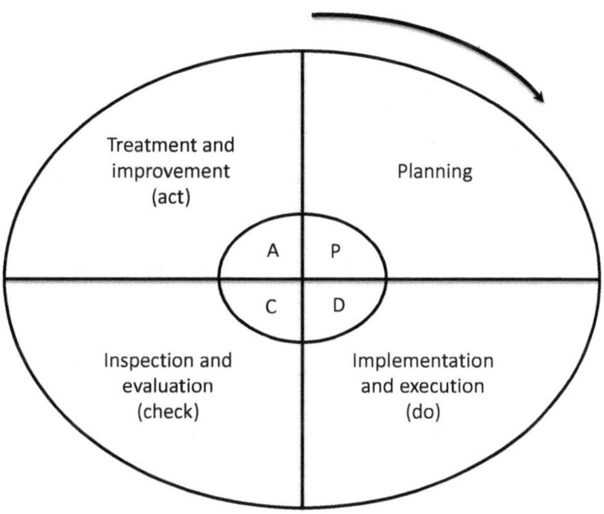

Fig. 5.4 The PDCA cycle (*Source:* Various materials)

The PDCA cycle was proposed by Walter A. Shewart and W. Edwards Deming, who formulated the concept of quality control management after World War II. It consists of the following:

Plan: Create a business plan based on past performance and future forecasts.

Do: Work according to a plan.

Check: Check whether the operation is in line with the plan.

Act: Investigate the areas where implementation is not in line with the plan and take remedial action.

This spiral structure is called spiral up.

5.6 Process (ISO 31000:2018)

In order to apply the RM processes at different levels (for example, strategies, operations, programs, projects, and other activities), they need to be aligned with the relevant objectives and the organization's general objectives. The purpose of establishing the "scope, context, and criteria" is to customize the process, allowing for effective risk assessment and appropriate RM. The scope defined relates to the RM activities. The context gives the internal and external environments of an organization trying to achieve its goals, including its external circumstances (such as laws and regulations; external stakeholder requirements; and social, cultural, and economic external environments). This includes contextual matters such as the internal status of the organization (organizational structure, roles, and responsibilities; available management resources, standards, and rules to be adopted or followed, and so on).

The risk criteria include an array of indicators set in advance so that there will be no significant difference in risk assessment, which is the next step, depending on the person performing it. Organizations need to specify the amount and type of risk they can take in terms of their goals, assess the significance of the risk, and set criteria to support the decision-making process. The criteria should be consistent with the RM framework and customized for the purpose and scope of the activity under consideration.

Risk assessment includes risk identification, risk analysis, and risk evaluation. Risk identification is the discovery, recognition, and description of the risks that may help achieve or hinder the organization's objectives. Risk analysis involves understanding the nature and characteristics of risks, such as their magnitude. In addition, risk evaluation compares the risk analysis results with the risk criteria and provides the basic data required to deal with the risks and determine viable options.

Fig. 5.5 shows the RM processes (ISO 31000:2018).

The risk response follows a risk assessment. In addition, responsible and interested individuals continuously monitor and review the scope, context, criteria, risk assessment, and risk response to ensure that they have been sufficiently effective.

However, communication and consultation promote the awareness and understanding of risk and provide feedback to reinforce decision making, and should be designed into each RM process. This underpins all the RM processes. In communication, information is transmitted, exchanged, and shared with stakeholders, whereas in consultation, the organization receives advice from all sources that could help solve its problems, including external experts. Communication and consultation are conducted at all stages as necessary.

Additionally, monitoring and reviewing the RM process as well as the results related to them improve the effectiveness of the process. For recording and reporting, the RM process results should be recorded so that they can be shared with the stakeholders and RM can be improved in the future.

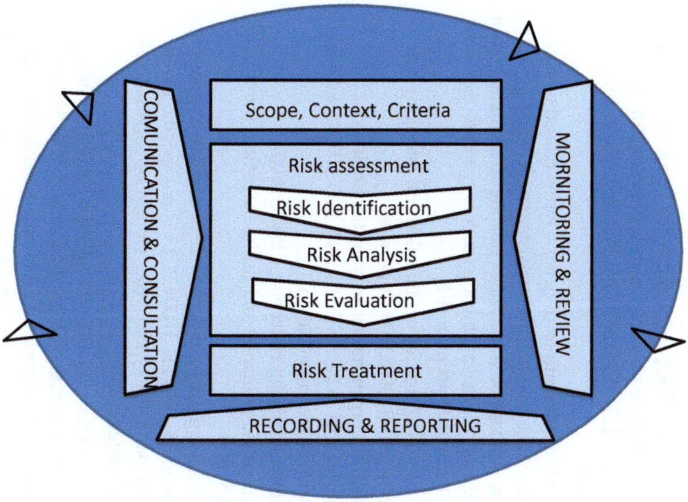

Fig. 5.5 RM process (ISO 31000:2018) (*Source:* ISO 31000:2018)

5.7 Features of ISO 31000

The most important features of ISO 31000 are as follows.

1. ISO 31000 is designed for all risks and organizations, to provide general use RM processes for all of them, and a framework, and to efficiently operate the said processes.
2. The framework shows the elements required for RM operation as an organization and the organic relationships between the elements.
3. It provides a system to continually improve the framework as well as processes using the PDCA model: plan, implement (do), monitor/evaluate (check), and correct/improve (act).
4. It focuses on day-to-day RM, and does not cover CM in emergency situations.
5. ISO 31000 is a guideline for RM, and not meant for certification.
6. ISO 31000 has the following complementary standards (see Table 5.1).

Discussion Questions

1. Explain the features of ISO31000 in comparison with COSO ERM (2017).
2. Explain the ISO31000 process in comparison with COSO ERM (2017).
3. Discuss whether there is a difference in the fields of application and effects of ISO31000 and COSO ERM (2017).

Table 5.1 Complementary standard of ISO 31000

Classification	Contents
IEC 31010:2009 Risk management—risk assessment techniques	IEC 31010:2009 is a dual logo IEC/ISO, single prefix IEC, supporting standard for ISO 31000 and provides guidance on selection and application of systematic techniques for risk assessment. This standard is not intended for certification, regulatory or contractual use
ISO GUIDE 73:2009 Risk management—vocabulary	ISO Guide 73:2009 provides the definitions of generic terms related to risk management. It aims to encourage a mutual and consistent understanding of, and a coherent approach to, the description of activities relating to the management of risk, and the use of uniform risk management terminology in processes and frameworks dealing with the management of risk
ISO/TR 31004:2013 Risk management—guidance for the implementation of ISO 31000	ISO/TR 31004:2013 provides guidance for organizations on managing risk effectively by implementing ISO 31000:2009. It provides: 1. a structured approach for organizations to transition their risk management arrangements in order to be consistent with ISO 31000, in a manner tailored to the characteristics of the organization 2. an explanation of the underlying concepts of ISO 31000 3. guidance on aspects of the principles and risk management framework that are described in ISO 31000 ISO/TR 31004:2013 can be used by any public, private or community enterprise, association, group, or individual. ISO/TR 31004:2013 is not specific to any industry or sector, or to any particular type of risk, and can be applied to all activities and to all parts of organizations
ISO 31022:2020 Risk management—guidelines for the management of legal risk	This document gives guidelines for managing the specific challenges of legal risk faced by organizations, as a complementary document to ISO 31000. The application of these guidelines can be customized to any organization and its context. This document provides a common approach to the management of legal risk and is not industry or sector specific

Source: Various materials

Risk Assessment

6

Risk assessment can be said to be the core of risk management (RM). This chapter outlines the concept of risk assessment.

6.1 Risk Assessment: An Overview

Risk assessment is the core of RM, and includes risk identification, risk analysis, and risk evaluation (ISO 31000).

The RM process and risk assessment (ISO 31000: 2018) are depicted in Fig. 6.1.

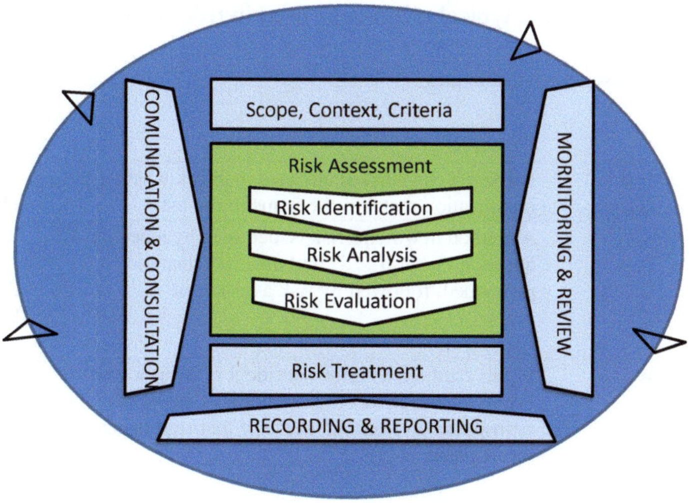

Fig. 6.1 RM process and risk assessment (ISO 31000: 2018) Source: ISO 31000:2018

H. Lee, *Risk Management*, Springer Texts in Business and Economics,
https://doi.org/10.1007/978-981-16-3468-0_6

The preliminary stage of risk assessment is to establish its "scope, context, and criteria". The objective of this is to customize RM. The next step after risk assessment is risk treatment, which is the process of adjusting the risk.

IEC/ISO 31010:2009 (Risk Management—Risk Assessment Techniques) was published in November 2009 as an international standard for the techniques in risk assessment. It was turned into a set of JIS guidelines in 2012 (JIS Q 31010:2012) and complements ISO 31000:2009 (Risk Management Principles and Guidelines) from a more technical perspective.

Risk identification is the process of finding and describing risks. Risk analysis is the process of understanding the nature of risks and determining their magnitude. Risk evaluation is the process of comparing the results of risk analysis with the risk criteria and determining the priorities in risk treatment.

The purpose of risk assessment is to provide evidence-based information and analyze the possible choices in responding to a particular risk. In other words, it helps make informed decisions on how to respond to a particular risk and select the most appropriate option. Specifically, risk assessment is the process of understanding risks and their causes, consequences, and probabilities. Risk assessment provides the basis for choosing the most appropriate approach to risk treatment.

6.2 Risk Assessment Technique

Risk assessment techniques may be used alone or in combination. In addition to the techniques shown in Table 6.1, companies develop their own techniques based on individual characteristics.

Table 6.1 presents the typical techniques used in risk assessment.

Table 6.1 Risk assessment techniques

Technique	Overview	Application field
Checklist method	Prepare a checklist in advance to check whether the organization matches the items in the list	Risk identification
What if	A method in which a risk is identified by repeating the question "what if . . .", and then risk analysis is performed, followed by risk assessment	Risk identification Risk analysis Risk evaluation
Fault tree analysis (FTA)	In this method, a serious accident is set as a start event, the progress of the accident is analyzed retrospectively, and the cause of that start event is investigated	Risk identification Risk analysis Risk evaluation
Event tree analysis (ETA)	This method analyzes the development of an initial event into an accident. By analyzing the scenario in which an event develops and determining the probability of occurrence for each branch point, the probability of the occurrence of a serious accident can be calculated	Risk identification Risk analysis

(continued)

Table 6.1 (continued)

Technique	Overview	Application field
Failure mode and effects analysis (FMEA)	This method evaluates the impact of a single fault condition, such as a component, on the entire product or system	Risk identification Risk analysis Risk evaluation

Source: Various materials

6.3 Risk Identification

Risk identification is the process of finding and describing risk. It identifies the possible risks, that is the effects of uncertainties on objectives, and creates a comprehensive risk list. This risk identification should be comprehensive because the risks that are not identified will be excluded from all subsequent RM processes, such as risk analysis, risk assessment, and risk treatment.

Since the number of risks are unlimited, risk identification based on risk criteria tries to determine the risks that should be considered for RM. While some risks can be adequately dealt with when they surface, there are others that may jeopardize the survival of the organization itself once they surface. In particular, organizations have recently become more complex, large, and sophisticated, and, in an increasing number of cases, the probability of organizations surviving a crisis depends on their response to risks. In addition to actual human, financial, and physical effects, decline in social credibility is now recognized as a risk.

In ISO 31000:2018, the risks are the same as that for COSO ERM (2017), but include not only the risks of negative impact, but also those of positive impacts, including the risk from not pursuing such opportunities. This requires the identification of risks that are beyond one's jurisdiction.

Here, one must identify the risk sources and events, and their causes and possible consequences. A risk source is an element with the potential to generate risk by itself or in combination with other elements. ISO 31000 uses the term "risk" instead of "hazard", because hazard is associated with unfavorable effects, but risks can also include favorable effects. The possible consequences are the potential outcomes of events that influence the objectives both negatively, such as through disasters, and positively, such as through profits. Furthermore, in some cases, an event may lead to a plurality of consequences, where the first consequence leads to a chain of further reactions. Consequences can be certain or uncertain, and expressed both qualitatively and quantitatively.

6.4 Risk Analysis

6.4.1 An Overview

The purpose of risk analysis is to understand the nature of risk and its characteristics, including its level. Risk analysis includes a detailed discussion of uncertainties, the risk factors, consequences, likelihoods, events, scenarios, controls, and their effectiveness. Risks have multiple causes and consequences, and can affect multiple objectives. Risk analysis provides the input for risk assessment, to determine whether risk treatment is necessary, and the optimal response strategies and methods.

Risk analysis also includes identifying the possible results (consequences) and likelihood of risk occurrence (probability). The level of risk is determined by combining its consequence and occurrence probability. Risk analysis should identify the factors affecting the outcomes and probability of risk occurrence.

Risk can be analyzed using quantitative, semi-quantitative, and qualitative methods.

In Table 6.2, the quantitative and qualitative analysis of risk are summarized.

Table 6.2 Overview of quantitative and qualitative risk analysis

Classification		Quantitative analysis	Qualitative analysis
Conditions		Uses past data or statistics (accidents, breakdowns, and s on)	Uses no past data, or data are too scattered to be useful
Calculation method		Engineering calculations based on data and statistics	Intuitive estimation Consideration of past experiences Referring to expert opinions
Example	Occurrence probability	0.1×10 cases per year 0.1×10 cases per time	Large probability Medium probability Small probability
	Loss magnitude	**** yen **** people	Large scale Medium scale Small scale

Source: Various materials

Risk analysis methods include quantitative analysis, semi-quantitative analysis, and qualitative analysis. Quantitative analysis is a method of calculating the result and its occurrence probability as a practical value, and calculating the value of the risk level in a specific unit defined at the time of risk criteria. However, complete quantitative analysis may not always be possible, or may not be desirable, such as when information or data is lacking. In such cases, semi-quantitative or qualitative analysis is more effective than quantitative analysis. Qualitative risk analysis is effective when past data does not exist or when the data variability is too large to be used. This qualitative analysis refers to performing risk analysis by intuitively estimating or taking into account past experience.

In a qualitative risk analysis, the outcome and probability of occurrence of each risk is indicated by risk level or rank, such as high, normal, or low (large, medium, small). In addition, the result and the probability of occurrence may be combined to determine the risk level against qualitative criteria. For qualitative analysis, it is advisable to record a clear explanation of the terms used and the basis for all criteria.

Semi-quantitative analysis is a method of deriving a risk level by using a numerical rating scale for results and probability of occurrence and combining the two.

6.4.2 Consequence Analysis

Consequence analysis assumes that a particular event has occurred and analyzes its effects. An event can have several effects and affect different objectives and stakeholders. Consequence analysis may include a simple outcome description, a detailed quantification model, or a vulnerability analysis.

As for effects, some have a high probability of occurrence but minor consequences, some have a low probability of occurrence but significant consequences, and some have intermediate consequences. Risks with the probability of extremely significant consequences tend to be emphasized. Furthermore, chronic events occurring frequently but with little effect as individual events may have large cumulative or long-term results.

6.4.3 Scenario Analysis

Scenario analysis is carried out to find the final impact of a risk. It analyzes the effects of risk under several different conditions. For example, it can analyze the effects of both a worst-case and best-case scenario that have a 30% chance of occurring.

A typical scenario analysis includes event tree analysis (ETA) and fault tree analysis (FTA). Both methods analyze the relationship between the causes and effects of an event. ETA first determines the initial event considered to be the cause, and then follows its development to the final event, for example an explosion. FTA first determines the start event, such as an explosion, and then traces back the cause of the event to the initial cause through its development process.

6.4.3.1 Event Tree Analysis

ETA starts from the initiating event, traces forward the possible events according to the passage of time, and analyzes how this develops into the final event. This is an inductive analysis method. In other words, it identifies the initiating event, carries out an accident progress analysis, and estimates the results and probability of occurrence after the risk has surfaced.

A visualization of ETA is shown in Fig. 6.2.

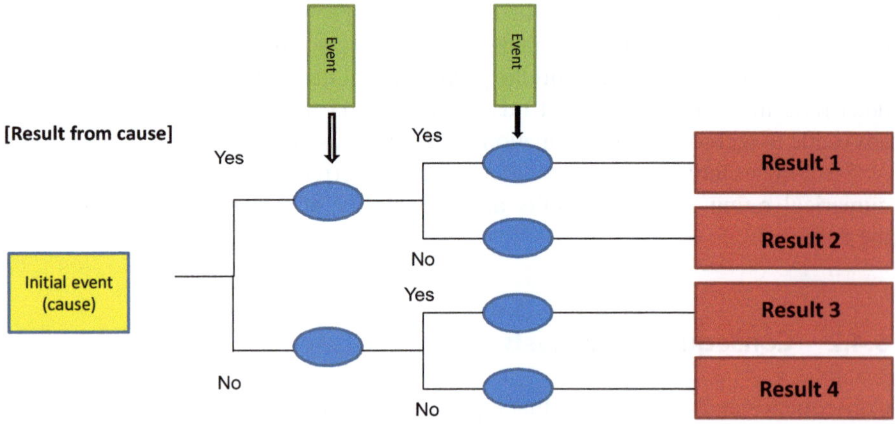

Fig. 6.2 Visualization of ETA (Source: Various materials)

This ETA lists the events or measures to stop the problem from developing, as well as the progress from the initial event (cause), and shows the event effects in a tree shape, branching into both success and failure scenarios. The key goal of ETA is to identify the events that may prevent unwanted results. It analyzes the relationship between the event expansion and events (such as disaster prevention equipment or activity) that prevent it.

The advantage of ETA is that it shows the progress of an event clearly like the branching of a tree, and sets a countermeasure (event) for each stage of the progress. Its most prominent limitations are as follows. First, events such as partial successes and failures cannot be expressed because the countermeasures' effectiveness is expressed in one of two ways—success or failure. Second, since it analyzes the progress of the accident, it does not show the risks of the entire analysis target.

6.4.3.2 Fault Tree Analysis

FTA follows a deductive method in which a start event, such as an explosion, is determined first, and the cause of the event is traced back to the initial cause through its development process. Its analysis of the relationship between the risk event and its cause makes it possible to find a method to reduce the risk and perform both quantitative and qualitative analyses. FTA evaluates the occurrence probability of each event extracted using the ETA.

Fig. 6.3 depicts a visualization of FTA.

FTA is an analytical method introduced by H.A. Watson of the BELL Research Institute in the United States and completed by Boeing in 1965. This analysis method refers to the start event, such as a fire, as the "top event", and all the factors that caused it as events. The individual factors leading to the top event are then analyzed. This is a top-down deductive analysis method that analyzes all the causes behind the occurrence of the top event. Since the diagram of this analysis resembles a tree, it is called a "fault tree" (FT) (Table 6.3).

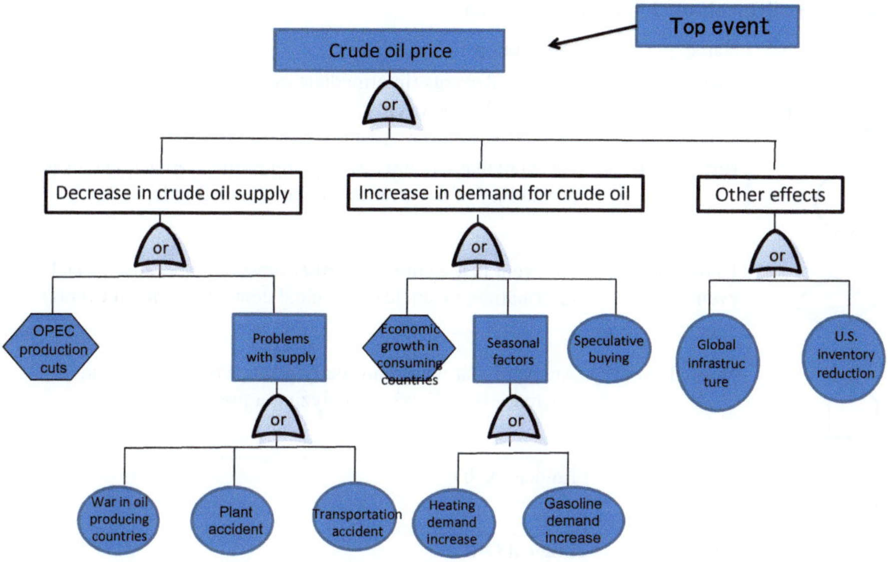

Fig. 6.3 FTA visualization (Source: Various materials)

The main advantages of FT are as follows. (1) If the occurrence probability of an event (lower-order event) can be calculated, the occurrence probability of the top event can be calculated as well. (2) Since the FT is represented by a simple theoretical structure using mainly the AND and OR gates, one can visually interpret the routes and factors leading to the top events, accidents, and disasters.

The main limitations of FT are as follows. (1) Since the conditions and factors for generating an event are expressed as a tree, a simple FT can easily be understood, but a complex one may become too large for easy understanding. (2) It is difficult to represent each event on an FT over time.

6.4.3.3 Weakness Analysis

Weakness analysis examines the weaknesses found when risks occur. For example, through scenario analysis, it extracts the hazards that can be a common cause of multiple risks, and performs analysis unsure of whether a system exists that captures the events and signs that trigger an accident and the events that may delay its discovery.

6.4.4 Quantitative Risk Analysis Indicators

The three main indicators used for quantitative risk analysis are as follows.

Table 6.3 Symbols used in the FTA diagram

Symbols	Name	Description
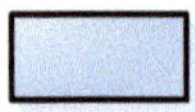	Event	Individual events (intermediate events) caused by a combination of top and basic events
	Basic event	An event that will not develop any further, or basic events whose probability of occurrence can be obtained independently
	Undeveloped event	An event that cannot be further developed because of lack of information, or unclear technical content (diamond events)
	Normal event	An event that would normally occur. For example, "the existence of air", when analyzing a fire, and so on
	AND gate	Logical AND
	OR gate	Logical OR
	Transfer gate	Shows the transition or link to related parts on the FT diagram
	Inhibit gate	Conditional probability output event; this occurs only when the conditions are satisfied

Source: Various materials

6.4.4.1 Value at Risk

Value at risk (VaR) is an index for evaluating the maximum loss amount at a certain occurrence probability, such as once every 200 years with a maximum loss of ten billion yen. Probable maximum loss, which will be described next, is similar to VaR. Both represent a risk at a certain point ("at"), and do not represent the entire risk.

6.4.4.2 Probable Maximum Loss

Probable maximum loss (PML) is the maximum expected loss under certain conditions. While "earthquake PML" refers to the "expected maximum loss" due to an earthquake—this was first used in the United States as fire insurance information, and more recently in real estate and construction industries—PML has been used in Japan as the basis for setting the total payment limit for household earthquake insurance since its establishment in 1966.

PML has limitations in that it does not include the probability of occurrence, represents a worst-case scenario, and therefore cannot be considered an overall risk representation.

6.4.4.3 Expected Loss

Expected loss (EL) is obtained by multiplying the "probability of loss" by the "loss amount".

$$\text{EL} = \text{probability of loss} \times \text{loss amount}$$

Since this index contains two factors, it expresses two indicators, the probability of occurrence and amount of loss.

6.4.5 Risk Curve

The risk curve is a graph showing the relationship between the amount of loss and the probability of exceeding it.

The risk and event curves are shown in Fig. 6.4.

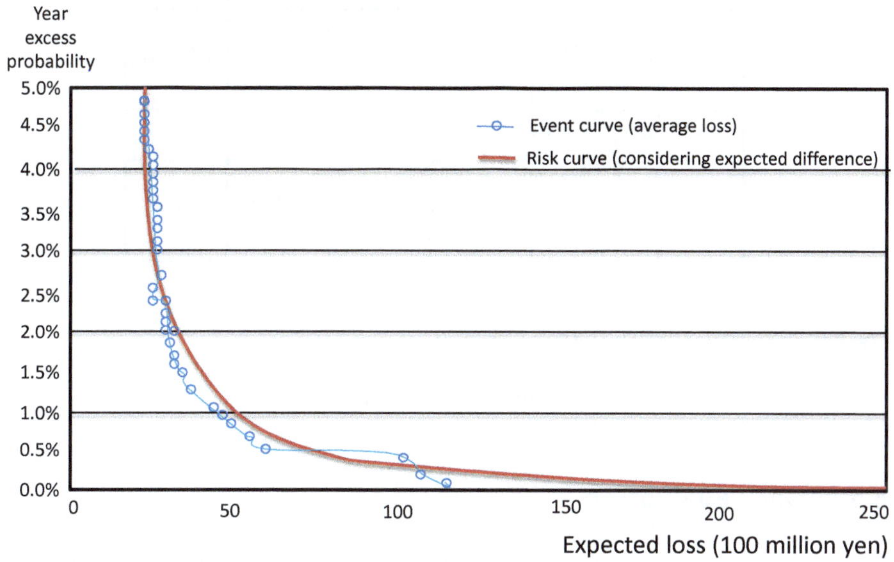

Fig. 6.4 Risk and event curves (Source: Various materials)

An event curve shows the EL on the horizontal axis and the probability of exceeding it on the vertical axis. It can be created by calculating the EL of a possible disaster (earthquake, typhoon, and so on), creating a list of the EL and its probability of occurrence, and calculating the probability of exceeding the said loss.

The risk curve and event curve have different meanings for annual excess probability on the vertical axis. For the event curve, it is the probability of the occurrence of an event that causes a further loss, whereas for the risk curve, it is the probability of further loss. Therefore, the event curve shows the relationship between the loss and probability of the event that causes it, whereas the risk curve shows the relationship between the loss and probability of excess loss.

6.4.6 Risk Matrix

A risk matrix is created by dividing risk into four or five steps, with the horizontal axis indicating its intensity (impact) and the vertical axis indicating its frequency (occurrence probability). By placing the analyzed risk into a matrix by degree of impact and the probability of occurrence, and color-coding them into high-risk (for example, red), medium-risk (for example, yellow), and low-risk (for example, green), the risk situation can be visualized and made easier to understand at a glance.

Fig. 6.5 shows a risk matrix.

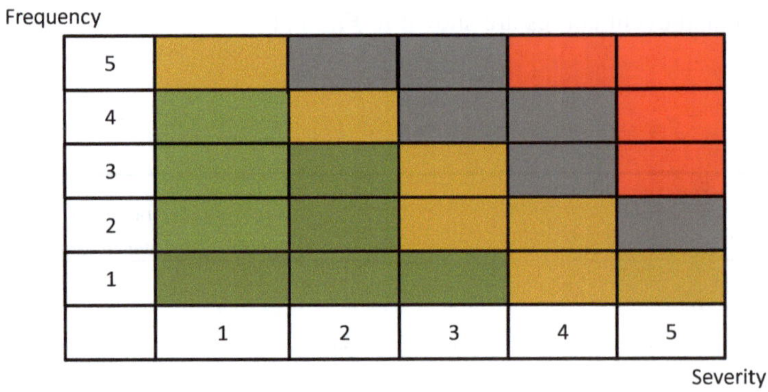

Fig. 6.5 Risk matrix (Source: Various materials)

The risk matrix is useful for qualitative risk analysis.

6.5 Risk Evaluation

Risk evaluation is carried out by comparing the risk analysis results with the risk criteria to determine whether the risk frequency or probability is acceptable. Its purpose is to compare the risk analysis results with the established risk criteria and provide the basic data required for decision making in risk treatment. This includes the following decisions: (1) Stop proceeding further. (2) Consider options for risk treatment. (3) Analyze further to better understand the risks. (4) Continue existing controls. (5) Rethink the objectives.

Risk criteria are judgment standards set in advance to prevent a large difference in evaluation results depending on who performs the risk evaluation. International standards (ISO 31000 Guide 73) define them as "conditions for assessing the significance of risk". In other words, they can be said to be the indexes for determining whether or not to respond to a risk, and the response priorities. For example, if a risk analysis calculates the magnitude of risk as 16, 12, and 9, respectively, this risk criteria result is a judgment standard that makes it unnecessary to deal with risks below a certain score.

However, a risk portfolio would manage all risks collectively. By setting the risk tolerance and risk appetite levels in the risk matrix, one can understand the range of risks within the portfolio. Thus, one would be able to perform RM while optimizing the entire organization's risk instead of individual risks.

The risk portfolio is shown in Fig. 6.6.

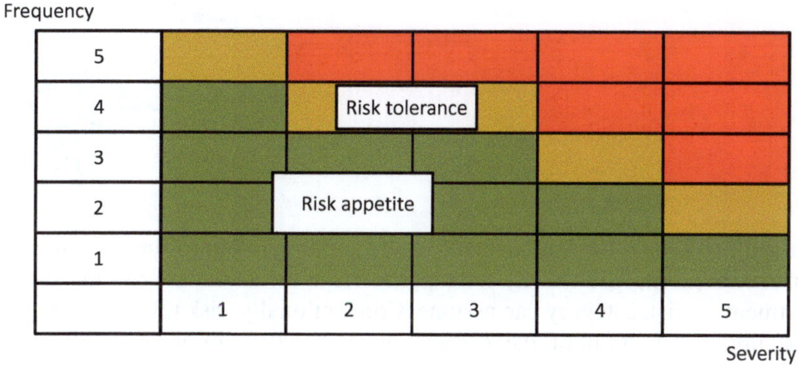

Fig. 6.6 Risk portfolio (Source: Various materials)

Risk appetite is the amount of risk an entity is willing to take in order to achieve its goals. It is the (monetized) amount of risk an organization is willing to accept as possibly occurring in the course of business. Risk appetite is defined as a combination of risk frequency and risk severity, and varies from company to company, with no absolute standards or criteria.

In contrast, risk tolerance is an allowable range, that is, a risk limit that can be accepted when the risk deviates from the level set by risk appetite. For example, if production has to be completed within a certain budget and time, a 5% surplus in budget and 10% surplus in deadline can be tolerated. Therefore, in the risk matrix, risks above the tolerance level are those that exceed the risk limits of a company, and these must somehow be reduced or avoided.

The risk tolerance depends on the circumstances of each company. For example, a company with a capital of 100 million yen may be able face a loss of ten million yen, but a company with a capital of ten million yen may not be able to do so. In recent years, frequent scandals, financial crises, terrorism, earthquakes, and so on, have shown that a single risk can compromise the existence of a whole company. The risk tolerance of an enterprise is based on the risk criteria.

The "risk appetite" of an organization is tied to its organizational strategy, whereas its risk tolerance is primarily tied to a specific activity. In other words, risk appetite is, across the company, a more common indicator than risk tolerance, which can be said to be an individual indicator mainly set for individual activities. For example, if the call center of an organization sets a standard such as, "at worst, let 10% of the total number of inquiries wait 10 min", this would define their risk tolerance.

The relationship between risk appetite and risk tolerance is shown in Fig. 6.7.

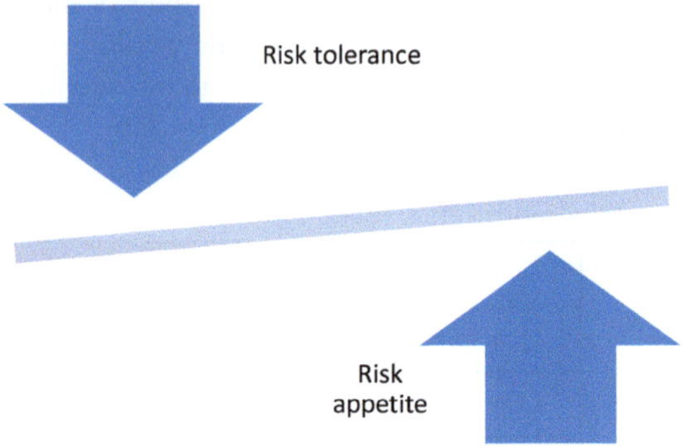

Fig. 6.7 Relationship between risk appetite and risk tolerance (Source: Various materials)

In sum, risk appetite is a business strategy that determines the risks that can be taken to earn profit, whereas risk tolerance refers to the amount of risk that each base, department, or risk category can assume. Conventionally, risk tolerance has been set as the upper risk limit of the organization regardless of its risk appetite on a company-wide basis or risk category. However, from an ERM viewpoint, the upper risk limit should be set on a company-wide basis since risk tolerance is based on the risk appetite.

6.6 Risk Communication

Risk communication enhances the effectiveness of the RM system by sharing risk information about specific risks among all stakeholders and communicating and enhancing mutual understanding. To do so, an organization needs to establish a risk communication channel for the internal (such as directors, employees, and labor unions) and external (such as investors, business partners, consumers, and supervisors) stakeholders.

The internal risk communication tools include meetings, committees, and e-mails. Establishing a whistleblower system based on Japan's Whistleblower Protection Act would also be effective. The whistleblower system informs the organization before reporting to the media or other external organization. The Whistleblower Protection Act (enforced on 1 April 2006) is a law to protect the employees of a company who report any serious law and regulation violation of their employer. According to the Act, if more than 20 days have passed since the violation has been reported but the company has not acted on the report, for example by not conducting an internal investigation or ordering the reporting employee not to leak this information externally, the Act will not apply.

External risk communication is becoming more complex. Until recently, shareholders and customers were the main target, but now this has been expanded to include non-profit organizations (NPOs), non-government organizations (NGOs), social networks, and so on. External risk communication is mainly used to share risk information with local residents and build cooperative relationships with them on environmental issues, such as nuclear facilities and garbage incineration facilities, and risks, such as natural disasters. For example, in the event of a natural disaster, accident, or terrorism, risk communication will consist of requesting the cooperation of residents in evacuation and rescue operations and confirming the safety of neighboring residents.

Since judgments on risk acceptance are strongly influenced by psychological factors, it would be necessary to provide appropriate knowledge and exchange information to reduce anxiety, and enable the stakeholders to make rational judgments. Risk communication can be considered a technique to provide accurate and sufficient information and alleviate anxiety through consensus building.

The factors that render risk communication effective can be summarized into four types: sender factors, recipient factors, message factors, and media factors.

The sender is often a government or company, but the citizens have low trust in the government or company. Therefore, experts such as university teachers, international organizations, or neutral third parties such as NGOs are often interposed.

Factors on the recipient side influence the effectiveness of risk communication more strongly than do those on the sender side. The receiver and sender of risk communication do not have the same knowledge, cognition, emotions, and so on. Often, citizens accept much smaller risks than experts do. For example, citizens tend to demand a situation where there would be no accident or side effects related to life or health. Experts make judgments considering both the probability of occurrence and risk based on magnitude of loss, whereas citizens tend to consider only the magnitude of loss. Thus, citizens usually do not accept the risk of large losses even if the probability of occurrence is low. This risk acceptance varies between individuals because of their differences in knowledge and information, information-processing ability, values, personality, gender, age, occupation, and so on. Therefore, the characteristics of the parties need to be understood before entering into risk communication.

The risk communication message entails the following factors. Since the recipient would find it difficult to understand risk through the probability of occurrence and scale of risk, it would be necessary to recognize the recipient's attributes and provide an easy-to-understand explanation. Moreover, the receiver's risk perception could be different depending on the method used to explain the risk. For example, data provided in terms of survival rate rather than mortality rate can make the message more acceptable. Besides, the recipient may distrust a professional and confusing explanation.

From among the various media available for risk communication, mass media are excellent for alerting and interpersonal media are better for consensus building. Electronic media, such as the Internet, are excellent for fast communication over a wide area.

Discussion Questions

1. Give an overview of risk assessment and its techniques.
2. Explain risk-specific concepts and techniques.
3. Explain the concept of risk analysis and its technique.
4. Explain, by comparing, quantitative analysis and qualitative analysis.
5. Explain the main indicators of risk quantitative analysis.
6. Explain the risk curve.
7. Are there any principles for the concept of risk assessment and the application of that technique? Discuss your thinking.

Value at Risk

7

Value at risk (VaR) is a typical technique for quantitative risk analysis. This chapter outlines VaR.

7.1 Probability

7.1.1 Concept of Probability

The history of probability theory is said to have originated in a series of letters exchanged in 1654 between French mathematicians Blaise Pascal (1623–1662) and Pierre de Fermat (1607–1665). Chevalier de Méré, a French nobleman known for his gambling expertise, is said to have asked Blaise Pascal in 1654 how to determine the best betting method that would be advantageous to him, which resulted in the aforementioned letters.

Probability is a fraction, where the number of times an event occurs is the numerator and the sum of the number of times the event occurs and number of times it does not is the denominator. A probability of 1 means that the event always occurs, and a probability of 0 means that the event never occurs. Probability values range from 0 to 1. If the probability of an event happening is 0.2, the probability of it not happening is $1 - 0.2 = 0.8$.

Before they happen, all events can be explained only through probabilities. For example, before rolling a dice, you do not know which number you would obtain, but you can explain your chance of rolling a "6" as 1/6.

However, according to the law of large numbers, if, for example, a coin is tossed a very large number of times, the number of both "head" and "tail" events approaches 1/2; if the number of trials is sufficiently large, the statistical appearance of an event will approach its calculated probability.

The probability of default is expressed as follows.

H. Lee, *Risk Management*, Springer Texts in Business and Economics,
https://doi.org/10.1007/978-981-16-3468-0_7

Assume an event A where a certain company α will go bankrupt within 1 year. The probability of this event occurring is expressed as P(A). Here, P stands for probability. Since P(A) is a probability, the condition $0 \leq P(A) \leq 1$ must be satisfied. The probability of event A not occurring is $1 - P(A)$.

If another company β goes bankrupt within 1 year in event B, "A∩B" means that events A and B occur simultaneously and both α and β go bankrupt within 1 year.

A∩B is read as "A and B" or "A cap B," and is the portion of overlapping events shown in Fig. 7.1.

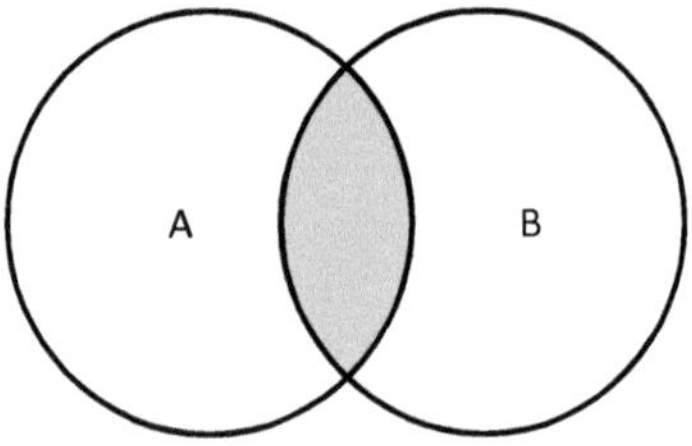

Fig. 7.1 A∩B (Source: Various materials)

"A∪B" means that either A or B will occur. This, therefore, indicates that either company α or company β will go bankrupt within 1 year.

A∪B is read as "A or B" or "A cup B," and is the whole set of events shown in Fig. 7.2.

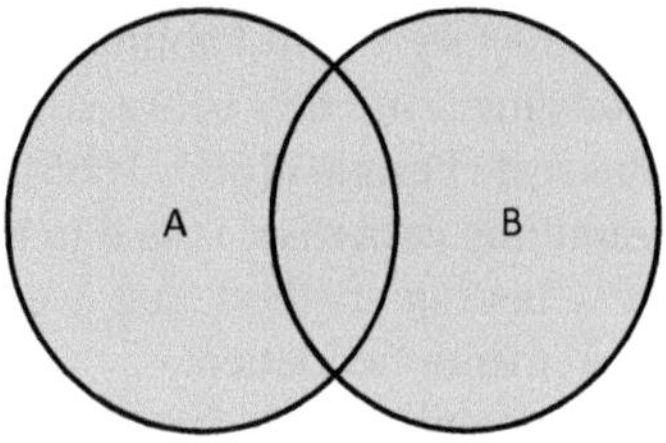

Fig. 7.2 A∪B (Source: Various materials)

7.1.2 Variance and Standard Deviation

7.1.2.1 Variance

A simple average is often used to calculate a mean value.

$$\overline{x} = \frac{1}{n}\sum_{i=1}^{n} x_i = \frac{x_1 + x_2 + \cdots + x_n}{n}$$

x_i (i = 1, 2, 3... n): all samples; n: number of samples.

This average is written as $\overline{x}$ (X bar) or μ (mu).

However, "variance" is an average value obtained by summing the squares of the difference (distance) between the value of each sample and the average value.

$$\sigma^2 = \frac{1}{n}\sum_{i=1}^{n}(x_i - \overline{x})^2$$

Variance is calculated as follows. First, the average value is calculated from the values of each sample, ($\overline{x}$), and then the distance to the average of each single sample (deviation) is calculated. Variance can be calculated by dividing the sum of the squares of these distances (deviations) by the number of samples.

Variance is a numerical value indicating the degree of dispersion of the samples, but this cannot be directly compared with the individual sample or average values because the distance between the value and the average value of each sample is squared. Taking the square root of this value leads to the standard deviation.

7.1.2.2 Standard Deviation

The standard deviation (SD) is a numerical value that indicates the degree of dispersion of a sample, similar to the variance. The SD is represented by σ or s (sigma) and is the square root of the sum of the squares of the deviations, which is the difference between the value of each sample and the mean value.

$$\sigma = \sqrt{\frac{1}{n}\sum\nolimits_{i=1}^{n}(x_i - \overline{x})^2}$$

For example, if a test is performed in a class of n persons, and their scores are x_1, x_2, ..., x_n, the arithmetic mean is expressed as follows.

$$\overline{x} = \frac{1}{n}\sum_{i=1}^{n} x_i$$

Variance is the average squares of the difference between the value of each sample and the mean.

$$\sigma^2 = \frac{1}{n}\sum_{i=1}^{n}(x_i - \overline{x})^2$$

The SD is the root mean square (RMS) of this variance.

$$\sigma = \sqrt{\sigma^2}$$

If the average and SD values are known, the degree of spread in the data can be measured as a distance from the average. SD σ is the average of the absolute values of the distances from the average value, and is a numerical value indicating the degree of data scatter. The smaller the σ, the lesser the distribution, and the larger the σ, the greater the distribution.

SD is depicted in Fig. 7.3.

It is determined that the risk is smaller for a distribution with a small σ, that is a sharp distribution, than with a distribution with a large σ, that is a flat distribution.

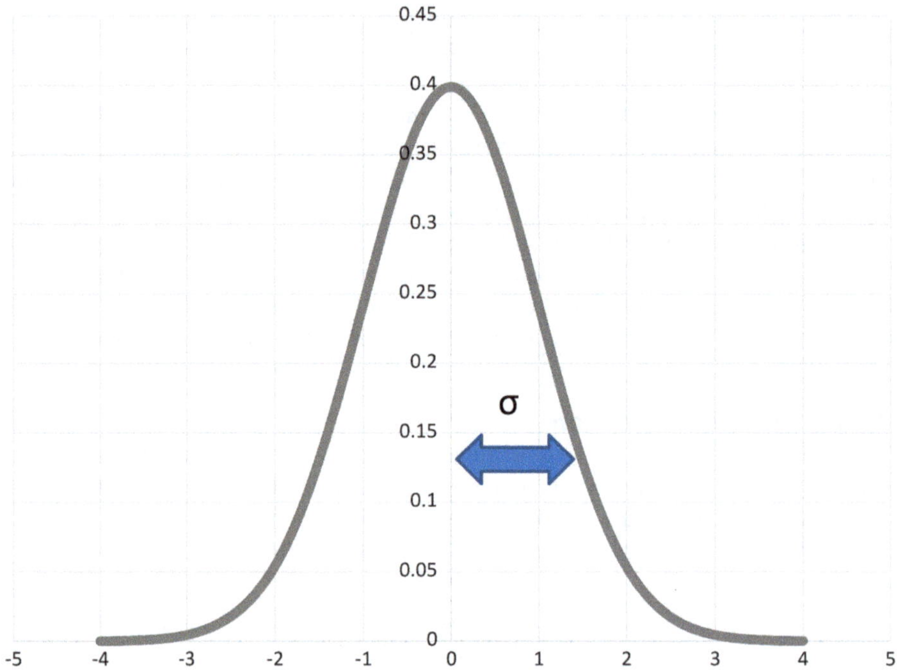

Fig. 7.3 Standard deviation (Source: Created by the author)

The relationship between SD and risk is shown in Fig. 7.4.

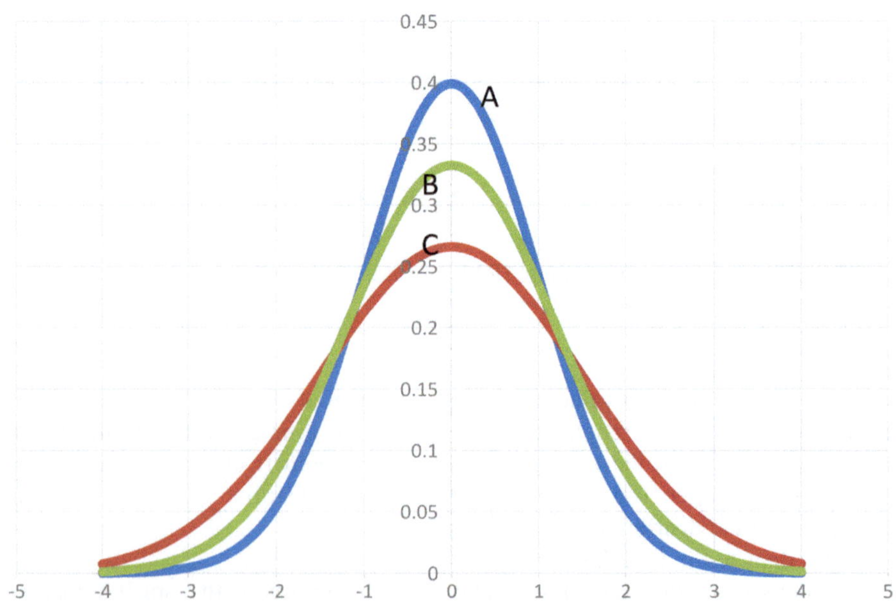

Fig. 7.4 Standard deviation and risk (Source: Created by the author)

In Fig. 7.4, B has a greater risk than A, and C has a greater risk than B.

However, a normal distribution is a bell-shaped distribution with the highest density at the average, and is symmetrically distributed around the average of μ.

This "normal distribution" establishes the following relationship between the mean value (μ), SD (σ), and frequency (Table 7.1).

Table 7.1 Relationship between mean (μ), standard deviation (σ), and frequency in normal distribution

Range	Frequency (data percentage)
$\mu \pm \sigma$	0.6827 (about two-thirds)
$\mu \pm 2\sigma$	0.95450
$\mu \pm 3\sigma$	0.9973

Source: Various materials

In the normal distribution, $\mu \pm \sigma$ means that 68.27% of all the data is distributed in the range of the average value (μ) ± SD (σ), and $\mu \pm 2\sigma$ means that 95.45% of all the data is distributed in the range of average value (μ) ± 2 × SD (σ) (Fig. 7.5).

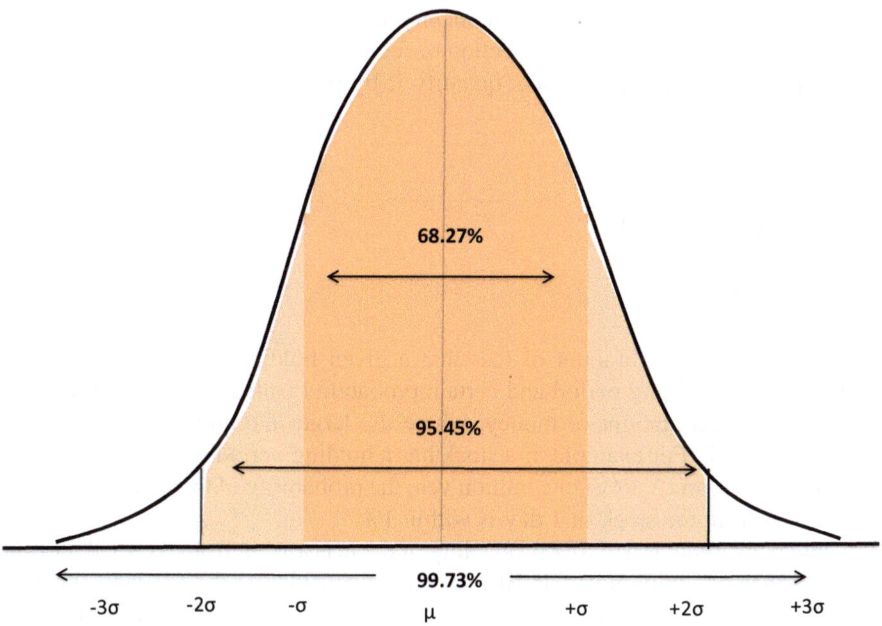

Fig. 7.5 Standard normal distribution table (Source: Various materials)

7.1.2.3 Volatility

Volatility is the average price fluctuation of an underlying asset expressed as an annual rate (%), and often uses the SD. If the volatility is large, the price fluctuation is also large, indicating a large risk. Therefore, an increase in volatility causes an increase in risk, and this increases the price of futures and options for dealing with that risk (see Table 7.2).

Table 7.2 Example of price volatility (HV) (σ = 5%). USD/JPY, Validation period 3 years

SD	Price volatility	Confidence level
1.00σ (sigma)	5.00%	68.27%
2.00σ	10.00%	95.45%
3.00σ	15.00%	99.73%

Source: Various materials

Historical volatility (HV) is the average price volatility of the underlying asset over a certain period in the past, and corresponds to the SD. This volatility predicts future volatility.

For example, when USD 1 = 100 yen and the price volatility (historical volatility) is 5.00%, the confidence level is assumed to be 68.26% in the SD. In this case, it means that 68.27% (250 × 68.27% = 170.67 days) will remain within the range of 100 yen ± 5.00% within 250 trading days during the year. This is the case of 1 SD (1σ), and the probability of 68.27% is called the confidence level. The 2 SD (2σ) are 1σ × 2, and the 3 SD (3σ) are 1σ × 3.

Implied volatility (IV) is a term mainly used in options, and is also called "expected volatility". This is a projection of future volatility from the current option payments, and market participants quantify it by predicting the future changes in option payments.

7.2 Value at Risk

7.2.1 Overview

VaR is the maximum amount of loss that a given holding can statistically incur within a certain holding period and certain probability called confidence level. It is represented by an amount of money, where the larger the amount of money, the greater is the risk. For example, if a stock has a holding period of 1 day, confidence level of 99.00%, and VaR of one million yen, the probability of losing more than one million yen from the stock in 1 day is within 1%.

Conversely, there is a 99.0% probability of the loss arising from the stock in 1 day to be less than one million yen. In RM, instead of considering the 1% cases that have losses of over one million yen, we recognize the loss that will occur with a 99% probability as the expected maximum loss and prepare for it accordingly. This confidence level can be changed, for example, to 99.5% or 95%, in accordance with the RM policy.

In Fig. 7.6, the shaded area accounts for 99% of the possible events. The possible events show the distribution of the data for each profit and loss statistic, but a 99%

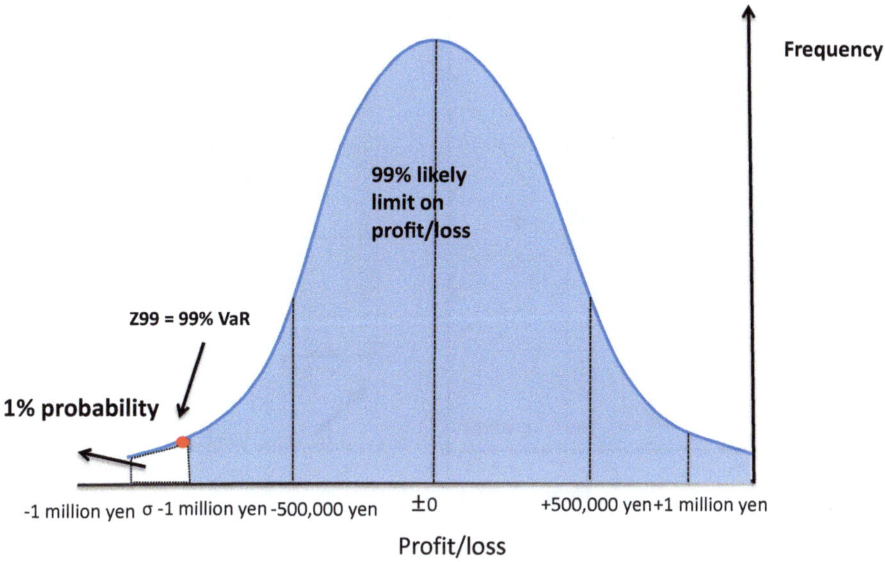

Fig. 7.6 Distribution of asset price fluctuations (Source: Various materials)

confidence level means that 99% of the total data is considered and the remaining 1% loss, ignored. In this case, the largest loss in the 99% confidence level is minus one million yen, on the leftmost point "Z99". In other words, the statistical maximum loss within the set confidence level of 99% is one million yen, and the statistical probability of the loss exceeding this maximum loss is 1%. The "99% VaR" of this asset, or simply "VaR," is a loss of one million yen at the point Z99.

7.2.2 Origin and Development

In 1989, JP Morgan CEO D. Weatherstone requested the creation of the "4.15 report", that is a report on the amount of risk incurred by the company's portfolio that was to be submitted by each department within the next 24 h and then every day at 4.15 p.m. To address this, JP Morgan's experts in econometric analysis found that past fluctuations such as in interest rates, stocks, and foreign exchange could be used to estimate the maximum loss that can occur within a certain probability, thus developing the "risk metrics" measurement model. This is the market risk VaR.

Market risk VaR is outlined in Fig. 7.7.

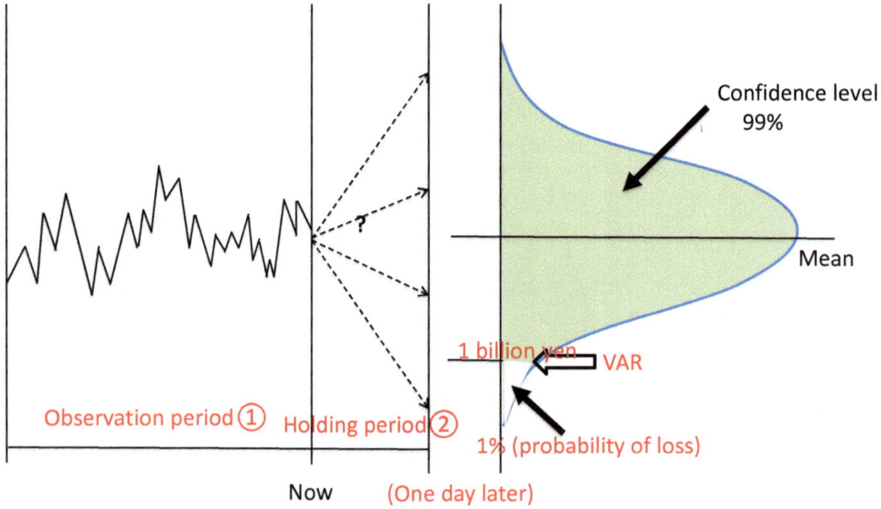

Fig. 7.7 Market risk VaR concept. VaR with 99% confidence level = 1 billion yen Source: "Understanding and Managing Market Risks," lecture material of the Bank of Japan (2013)

Market risk VaR can be calculated as follows. Using data for a certain period of past observations, predict the distribution of the observation period that will also occur in the future holding period, and calculate the maximum loss that the assets may cause within a certain probability, that is the confidence level.

Fig. 7.8 predicts price fluctuations 1 day later based on the statistical distribution of data during the observation period. This shows that the amount of the largest loss

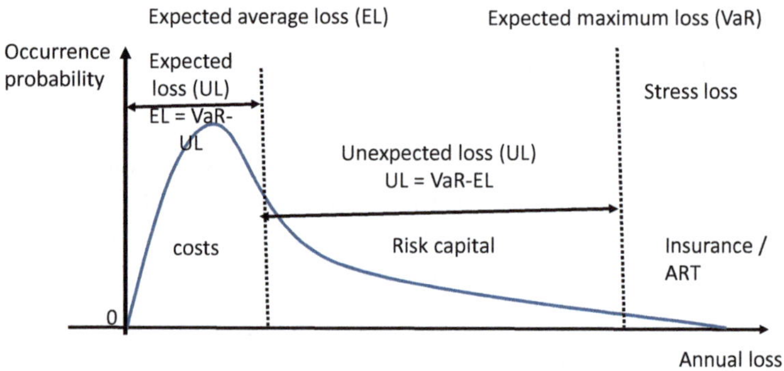

Fig. 7.8 Loss distribution and risk financing (Source: Various materials)

in the 99% number of specimens, that is the region of distribution, is one billion yen. In addition, the number of specimens of the remaining 1% shows that the amount of loss exceeds one billion yen. Here, the amount of this loss of one billion yen is defined as VaR.

This VaR is now used by banks and insurance companies as well as business companies. This is further to the second BIS regulation in 1993, recommending a market RM method for banks. Furthermore, in addition to market risk, an increasing number of financial institutions and companies using VaR calculate their credit risk and operational risk. Each of these risks is calculated using a common measure, VaR, and the risks are managed in an integrated manner.

7.2.3 Measurement Method

VaR measurement methods include a variance–covariance method, a historical simulation method, and a Monte Carlo simulation method. In many fields, such as military, economics, politics, and physics, the term "simulation" refers to the creation of an imaginary model for predicting changes, using computers, and so on. A model is an abstraction of actual items and systems that reduces the burden and risk of having to use actual systems for evaluation and analyses. For example, in marketing a product or advertisement that requires a large amount of money but fails to penetrate the market would lead to a considerable loss. However, using a computer model to simulate and predict the effects and results of executing the plan can avoid the possibility of launching a product or advertisement that could result in a significant loss.

In market risk measurement, the major banks of Japan and other countries are migrating from the variance–covariance method to the historical simulation method. For credit and operational risks, the method generally used is Monte Carlo simulation.

7.2.3.1 Variance–Covariance Method

The variance–covariance method is based on the assumption that market risk is normally distributed, and that the distribution falls within a certain magnification of the mean (μ) $\pm$ SD (σ). Covariance measures the relationship between the two types of data, and is the average of the product of the two variables' deviations from the average.

This method is appropriate to analyze the correlation between risk factors, and is based on the assumption of normal distribution, which is not always the case. Therefore, a market risk not following a normal distribution could be underestimated.

7.2.3.2 Historical Simulation Method

The historical simulation method does not assume a normal distribution, but assumes that price fluctuations similar to those that occurred in the past will continue to occur in the future, and VaR is obtained based on past values. Since this method calculates VaR using actual data, it can respond to price fluctuations that are not normally distributed. However, this method considers only the past price fluctuations data, and therefore, in case of vast differences in the distribution of data depending on the observation period, the resulting amount of risk too will change vastly depending on the period.

The variance–covariance method has often been used for measuring the VaR for market risk, but an increasing number of companies have shifted to the historical simulation method in recent years. This method uses past price fluctuation data from actual events that have occurred, without making any specific assumptions, and therefore has the advantage of being easily explained externally. In addition, the method has a problem in that the distribution of data may vary greatly depending on the observation period, but also has an advantage in that price fluctuations data, such as stock prices, can be acquired on a business day basis, making it easy to acquire observation data.

7.2.3.3 Monte Carlo Simulation Method

The Monte Carlo simulation method, named after one of the four districts of the Principality of Monaco famous for its casinos, is also called the random method. This method uses a random number to calculate the profit and loss of owned assets, assuming a change in risk factor, and then calculates the VaR. Specifically, this method stochastically observes the phenomenon by giving a large number of random numbers as input and observing the output values. A random value is numerical, has no regularity, and cannot be predicted.

The Monte Carlo simulation method is as follows. First, a random number is used to repeatedly generate an expected value of the risk factor. Second, the present value of the asset/liability corresponding to the fluctuation values of the risk factors is calculated. Third, VaR is calculated using values within the range of the confidence level by arranging the present values obtained through simulation in descending order.

The Monte Carlo simulation method can be used even when the probability distribution of risk factors is not normal. The disadvantages of this method are that it considers the distribution of risk factors (model risk) and takes time to calculate when large volumes of data are required.

7.2.4 Limitations

VaR is an "estimated value" of risk measured using a statistical method. Therefore, an abnormal event not caught in the observation VaR period will not be included in the statistical data, and hence will not be measured or prepared for. For example, if a stress event, such as a financial crisis that occurs once every 20–30 years, is not included in the observation VaR period, its occurrence risk cannot be measured. Therefore, the VaR may underestimate future losses for abnormal events.

In addition, as a confidence level of VaR, generally, neither 99% (3 SDs) nor 68% (1 SD) is used, in favor of 95% (2 SDs), ignoring any risk beyond this level. This is because it would not be reasonable to run a business that has to provide for the worst risks that are very unlikely to occur. For example, farmers take countermeasures against floods, heavy snowfall, and droughts that may occur by accident, but on this account do not prepare for meteorite falls or similar catastrophic events. As described above, even if their data are included in the observation period, events exceeding the set confidence level will be ignored, and hence the losses may be underestimated. In view of this VaR limitation, one would have to use a stress test, as described later.

7.3 Expected and Unexpected Loss

As described above, the maximum loss in VaR is not truly the "maximum" loss, but the "maximum loss expected to occur under a certain probability". Unexpected loss (UL) is the difference obtained from subtracting the average loss, that is expected loss (EL), from VaR.

$$\mathrm{UL} = \mathrm{VaR} - \mathrm{EL}$$

In traditional RM, EL (plural) mean relatively small or routine losses, and UL mean large or rare losses.

However, in RM in recent years, EL has come to mean specifically the average loss. Smaller losses are referred to as daily or minor losses, and are recognized as daily expenses.

If the VaR in this case is USD 500 and the EL is USD 300, the UL (singular) will be USD 200 (USD 500 − USD 300).

This UL is deemed to be appropriately handled by risk capital. Further, although ELs exceeding VaR occur only rarely, if they do occur, the loss amount becomes large, and insurance or alternative risk transfer (ART) would be appropriate.

7.4 VaR by Risk Type

Market risk is often described by assuming a normal distribution. In the long run, market risk is supposed to have an equal probability of generating loss and profit, and so the loss distribution of market risk is assumed to spread symmetrically with zero expectation.

Fig. 7.9 depicts the loss distribution by risk type.

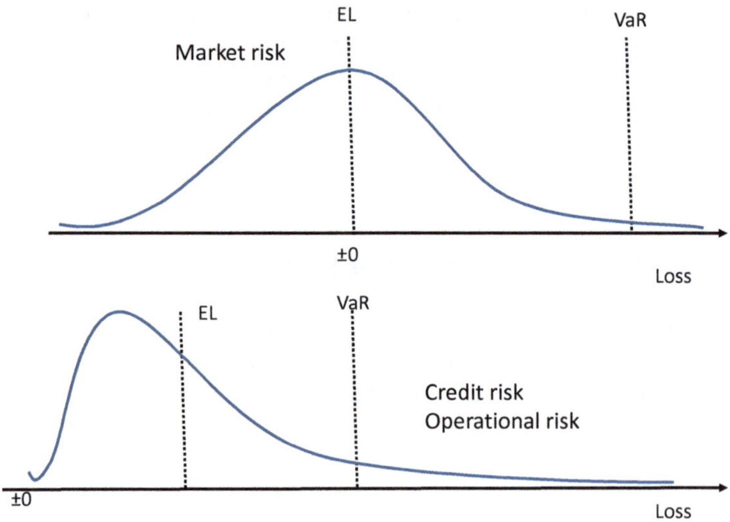

Fig. 7.9 Loss distribution by risk type (visualization) (Source: Various materials)

However, since credit and operational risks are pure risk, they do not consider the possibility of profit as a premise. As regards credit risk, business partners have their own unique default rate. Also, operational risks have different probabilities for each risk factor, meaning that the probability distribution of these risks cannot be a normal distribution. Therefore, they are shaped in what is known as a "fat-tailed distribution", with a long tail showing a large loss and the expected value is not zero.

Credit risk can be calculated from the default credit, default probability, and default loss rate.

$$\text{Credit risk} = \text{EAD} \times \text{PD} \times \text{LGD}$$

Exposure at default (EAD) is the credit amount at the time of default. Probability of default (PD) is the probability of a debtor defaulting within a certain future period. Loss given default (LGD) is the ratio of the EL at the time of default (LGD = 1 − recovery rate).

The credit risk varies depending on the recovery rate. Since real estate is a collateral security in lending and other transactions, no credit risk would exist if the credit amount can be fully recovered by disposing off the collateral.

7.5 Stress Test

Stress testing is a risk-management approach to assess the loss severity (expected) when it exceeds the level normally predicted for a stressful event, such as a market crash or large-scale disaster. This test verifies whether the system can withstand the occurrence of an unexpected event or loss larger than that predicted. In the stress tests of financial institutions, assumptions (stresses) of abnormal events such as "exchange rate fluctuating by 15%" or "government bond price dropping by 20%" are set to evaluate whether the capital adequacy ratio can be maintained under these conditions.

The term "stress test" has been widely used since 2009, when the US Federal Reserve used it to check the asset health of 19 major financial institutions. The FRB's (Federal Reserve Board) stress test was used as a basis for determining whether there would be a capital shortfall in the next 2 years in the event of loss due to more rapid deterioration in the economy than expected.

In the past, there have been unpredicted large price fluctuations every 10–20 years due to events such as Black Monday, the Asian currency crisis, and the Lehman Brothers bankruptcy. In general, a stress test extracts the risk scenarios under abnormal circumstances from historical data, measures the amount of potential risk inherent in, for example, current assets, and aims to make RM sustainable even when such events do occur.

A stress test has the following characteristics. (1) Because the risk occurrence status can be set arbitrarily, there is no need to rely on real past data from VaR. (2) Because the stress test is not based on statistical data or its distribution, there is no concept of frequency/probability or holding period, and it cannot be compared with VaR or other stress tests results that have different preconditions.

The following factors need to be noted with regard to the stress test. (1) Because the concept of probability is pointedly absent, the chance of such an event really occurring is unknown. (2) The assumption of stress is subjective. In many cases, the selection of risk factors, the magnitude of risk (variation), and the observation period are subjective. (3) It is difficult to create a stress scenario that properly predicts future changes in situation. (4) It is important to match the perceptions of management.

Discussion Questions

1. Explain the variance and standard deviation.
2. Explain the origin and development of VaR.
3. Explain the VaR measurement method and limitations.
4. Explain VaR by type of risk.
5. Discuss each method of dealing with the risks of expected loss and non-expected loss.
6. Discuss, with examples, the relationship between VaR and stress testing.

Part II

Risk Financing

Risk Treatment and ART

8

Risk treatment is divided into risk control and risk financing, while insurance and alternative risk transfer (ART) are two important means of risk financing. This chapter outlines the relationship between risk treatment measures and ART.

8.1 Risk Treatment: An Overview

ISO 31000:2018 states that the purpose of risk treatment is to select and implement options that correct risks. Risk treatment involves the following iterative steps. (1) Formulate and select options for risk treatment. (2) Plan and implement risk treatment. (3) Evaluate the effectiveness of responses. (4) Judge whether the residual risk is acceptable. (5) If the remaining residual risk is not acceptable, continue risk treatment.

To choose the most appropriate risk treatment option, one needs to consider the potential benefits and costs associated with achieving the objectives. The risk treatment options are not mutually exclusive and may not be appropriate in all situations. The options for risk treatment (ISO 31000:2018) include one or more of the following seven steps:

Avoid risks by not starting or continuing risky activities.
Take or increase risks to pursue opportunities.
Eliminate the risk sources.
Change the possibility of a risk occurring.
Change the consequences of risk, that is the scale of loss.
Share risks with, for example, contractors or insurance purchasers.
Control risks by making decisions based on risk analysis.

The choice of the risk treatment option needs to be based on the organization's objectives, risk criteria, and available resources. When choosing a risk treatment, to

H. Lee, *Risk Management*, Springer Texts in Business and Economics,
https://doi.org/10.1007/978-981-16-3468-0_8

select the most appropriate mode to communicate and consult with stakeholders, one has to consider their values, mode of thinking, and potential involvement. Monitoring and review are an integral part of implementing risk treatment to ensure that the responses are effective and sustainable. Risk treatment can introduce new risks that need to be managed.

If no treatment options are available, or if the available ones do not sufficiently address the risk, the risk has to be recorded on an ongoing review basis. Decision makers and other stakeholders should be aware of the nature and extent of the residual risks after treatment. These risks should be documented, monitored, reviewed, and addressed as needed.

8.2 Risk Treatment Measures

8.2.1 An Overview

Risk treatment measures are classified into risk control and risk financing, as shown in Fig. 8.1.

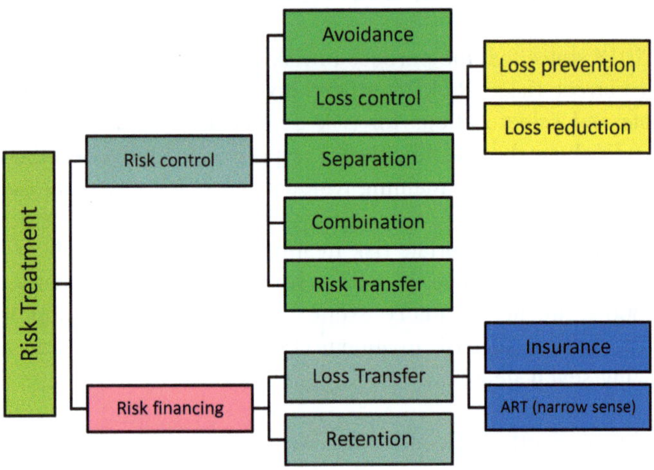

Fig. 8.1 Risk treatment measures classification (Source: Various materials)

Risk control is a prophylactic measure taken in advance to prevent or reduce the occurrence of loss. With risk control, it is difficult to completely prevent losses from occurring, and therefore risk financing is performed to financially manage the losses due to residual risk. Actual risk treatment is not limited to a single risk control or risk financing method, but often combines a plurality of methods. The choice of risk treatment options needs to be based on the organization's objectives and risk criteria.

However, there are four possible combinations of transfer, avoidance, possession, and reduction in risk treatment based on the risk matrix (see Fig. 8.2).

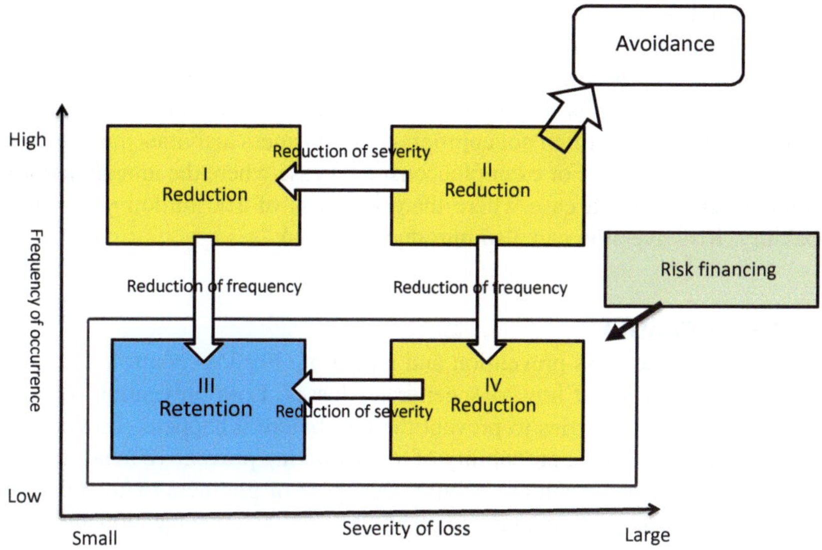

Fig. 8.2 Risk matrix and risk treatment (Source: Various materials)

As shown in Fig. 8.2, risk control, which will be described later, generally prevents losses from intensifying in magnitude and frequency (occurrence probability). As for residual risk, risk financing will be performed in areas III and IV. That is, retention will be performed in area III, and either insurance or ART, which will be explained later, will be performed in area IV. However, risk aversion will be performed in area II since it has a high occurrence frequency and loss intensity.

8.2.2 Risk Control

Risk control targets both pure risk and speculative risk and aims at reducing the frequency and severity of losses before they occur. Risk control does not prepare resources for restoration or compensation but focuses on the actual losses themselves. For example, in a traffic accident, a pedestrian might suffer injuries, and this would be a loss to the pedestrian. Now, the driver would be subject to liability for the damage caused to the pedestrian, and this would be a loss for the driver. Thus, loss prevention can be measured only subjectively. Similarly, sprinklers are effective against almost all fires, but when fires are caused by lubricating oils, and so on, they could worsen the situation. This shows that loss control is effective against specific risks.

8.2.2.1 Risk Avoidance

Avoidance is the cessation or abandonment of risky activities, that is blocking all expected risk. It includes "avoiding any contact with risky people, goods, businesses, and so on", and "eliminates the risk itself by severing all relations with it", such as stopping the production of foods that are likely to cause food poisoning.

However, some risks cannot be avoided, whereas others should be actively pursued. Risk aversion is a simple and passive measure, but since it involves abandoning returns, it is often not appropriate for business activities that seek returns commensurate with risk. For example, consider a case where the annual net profit is ten billion yen against a case where there is a loss of 100 billion yen with 10% probability. Risk aversion can also introduce new risk.

8.2.2.2 Loss Control

Loss control includes loss prevention and reduction. For loss control, one needs to understand the process of how risk generates losses. Loss prevention reduces the probability of a loss and tries to prevent the loss before it happens. In other words, loss prevention reduces the probability of loss by taking preventive measures, which include physical means, such as vacuum packaging of products to keep them from spoiling, and human resources-related means, such as safety education and periodic inspections.

However, loss reduction reduces the scale of loss, and prevents and mitigates its expansion to reduce the damage it causes. Examples of loss reduction methods are a recall system for defective products, and sprinklers and other safety devices to cope with accidents before and after they occur. Crisis management is a management method to systematically reduce losses after a crisis occurs.

EL = frequency of loss (probability) × scale of loss

8.2.2.3 Separation and Combination of Risk

Risk separation is a method to separate and diversify risks. For example, factories may be separated and spread in different locations to reduce economic damage in case of an earthquake. However, the combination and accumulation of risk reduce uncertainty and make it possible to predict losses. For example, following the law of large numbers, insurance companies increase the number of contracts with risks of the same nature to stabilize the probability of occurrence of loss. With this risk combination, the probability of stable loss occurrence can be calculated, and this makes it possible to hold risk through internal reserves, and so on.

8.2.2.4 Risk Transfer

Transferring risk in risk control, unlike that in risk financing, involves the passing on of the risk itself, such as the transfer of property or liability to others through contracts. Lease contracts and outsourcing of operations are examples of risk transfer.

8.2.3 Risk Financing

Risk financing involves the raising of funds that would be required after a risk has occurred. Unlike with business finance, the funds in risk financing cannot be expected to produce additional revenue because fund-raising is performed in a situation where a large disaster has caused losses.

Risk financing is classified into retention and transfer.

8.2.3.1 Retention

Retention is holding a risk after recognizing it. Holding risk without realizing it would not count as retention in risk financing. Examples include reserves, captives, loans, and self-insurance. Operating costs are financed through immediate funds, surpluses, and other general resources, and reserves are held to cover losses caused by a specific risk. Captives basically are risk-taking subsidiaries that take over the risk of their parent company. In some cases, they also take over the risks of other companies, and can even develop into insurance companies. Loans include borrowings from financial institutions and the issuance of corporate bonds. Self-insurance is a method of retaining expected or higher losses in an organization based on the probability of occurrence.

8.2.3.2 Loss (Risk) Transfer

Unlike in risk control, loss (risk) transfer in risk financing is the opposite of risk retention, and refers to the transfer of financial losses. Loss transfers include insurance and non-insurance transfers. Insurance is a traditional means of risk transfer viable only for pure risk. ART includes pure risk as well as market risk. In insurance, an organization pays an insurance premium to the insurance company, and this company bears the burden of loss in case it occurs. Thus, risk is transferred from the organization to the insurance company. The transfer of financial losses through insurance transforms irregular damages into a recurring risk (in the form of an insurance premium) and, in the event of an accident, the loss is covered by insurance.

However, while risk transfer through insurance functions as a response to risk from the standpoint of a company, for society as a whole the risk does not fundamentally reduce. For example, insurance can cover the loss on account of an explosion in a factory but cannot reduce the risk that an explosion poses to society.

Non-insurance transfers include insurance-like instruments, risk transfer contracts, risk offsets, and ART. Mutual aids, guarantees, and other insurance-like pool methods are mechanisms to reduce risk for mutual alliances or groups. Risk transfer contracts are a method to clarify the burden of the other party in a contract when a loss occurs. Risk cancellation is a method to reduce risks by combining the inversely correlated risks (such as price fluctuations), and ART is a risk hedging method that combines insurance and financial technologies.

8.3 Risk Financing and Corporate Finance

8.3.1 Relationship Between Risk Financing and Corporate Finance

As mentioned above, the means of dealing with risk in risk management are classified into risk control and risk financing. Risk control is a precautionary measure to reduce the probability of loss and severity. Since it is difficult to completely eliminate the probability of loss occurrence by risk control, risk financing is used as a financial measure against the loss caused by residual risk. Risk financing is the activity of raising the necessary funds after a risk occurs. There are insurance and ART for the transfer of loss (risk) in this risk financing. Insurance is a traditional and representative means of risk financing in risk management. This insurance will be outlined in my book Insurance Theory (Hakueisha, 2021), which will mainly explain ART.

This risk financing is different from corporate finance in a situation where there is a possibility of bankruptcy due to a disaster. This is because if a loss occurs due to a major disaster, additional business income cannot be expected from the financing. In other words, corporate finance generally means "procurement of funds necessary for corporate activities for profit" and "efficient management of the raised funds". Risk financing, on the other hand, is not aimed at profits, as seen in insurance, but is focused on monetary measures against potential losses. In addition, risk management limited to the operation of financial companies is called "financial risk management", but it is used in a different sense from risk financing.

8.3.2 Insurance and ART

ART has two elements, as its name implies, risk transfer and being "alternative". "Alternative" means that something is available as a different choice, or that it departs from traditional norms. In a narrow sense, ART can be used as a generic term for new non-insurance risk transfer instruments, but in a broad sense it has come to collectively refer to RM methods that replace traditional insurance. ART also includes innovative insurance approaches.

Table 8.1 shows the main risk-financing methods.

Table 8.1 Risk-financing methods

Category	Risk-financing method	Underwriter's risks and characteristics	Example
Retention	Internal funding	Provisions to be set up in the company	Internal funding
	Captive insurance company	An insurance company established, owned, and managed by a business company exclusively to undertake its own or its group companies' risks	Insurance contract

(continued)

Table 8.1 (continued)

Category	Risk-financing method	Underwriter's risks and characteristics	Example
	Contingent capital (debt)	A mechanism that enables borrowing of funds in an emergency based on predetermined loan limits and interest rate conditions	Contingent commitment line
	Finites	An insurance program involving a multi-year contract where insurance premiums are accumulated by a fixed amount for a certain period	Insurance contract
Transfer	Insurance	Insurance is paid in the event of a loss	Insurance Reinsurance
	Insurance-linked securities	Insurance is paid in the event of loss through the securitization of risk	CAT bond Sidecar ILW (see Chap. 13) Collateralized reinsurance
	Contingent capital (equity)	A mechanism where a company purchases an option to issue stock at a predetermined price in an emergency	Contingent equity put
	Insurance derivatives	Derivative transactions (such as option swap transactions) targeting changes in indicators linked to insurance-related risks	Weather derivatives

Source: Various materials

Risk financing and ART can be classified as shown in Fig. 8.3.

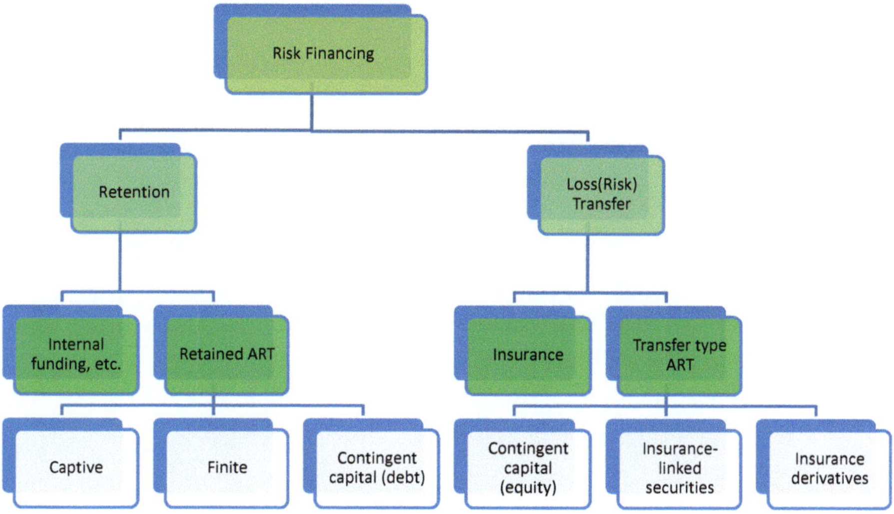

Fig. 8.3 Risk financing and ART classification (Source: Various materials)

The definition of ART varies. It is a new product, vehicle, or solution that transfers risk between the insurance and capital markets for RM. The ART market combines different innovative solutions from the insurance and capital markets for RM.[1] The new products, vehicles, or solutions that transfer risk can be categorized as follows. (1) The new products that transfer risk are the means or mechanisms used in RM and typically include insurance-linked securities, contingent capital, and insurance derivatives. (2) The new vehicles that transfer risk are typically captive and special purpose companies (SPCs) used in RM. (3) The new solutions that transfer risk are extensive programs of multiple products or vehicles used in RM, such as an ERM program.

With some characteristics of both insurance and financial instruments, ART employs mechanisms such as finites in the field of insurance to limit the risk timing and distribution to insurance as well as a scheme to raise funds from financial markets using innovative financial methods called derivatives and securitization, thus diversifying itself, and overlapping with both fields.

Fig. 8.4 presents a visualization of ART classification.

[1]Erik Banks, Alternative Risk Transfer (John Wiley & Sons Ltd., 2004), pp. 49–50.

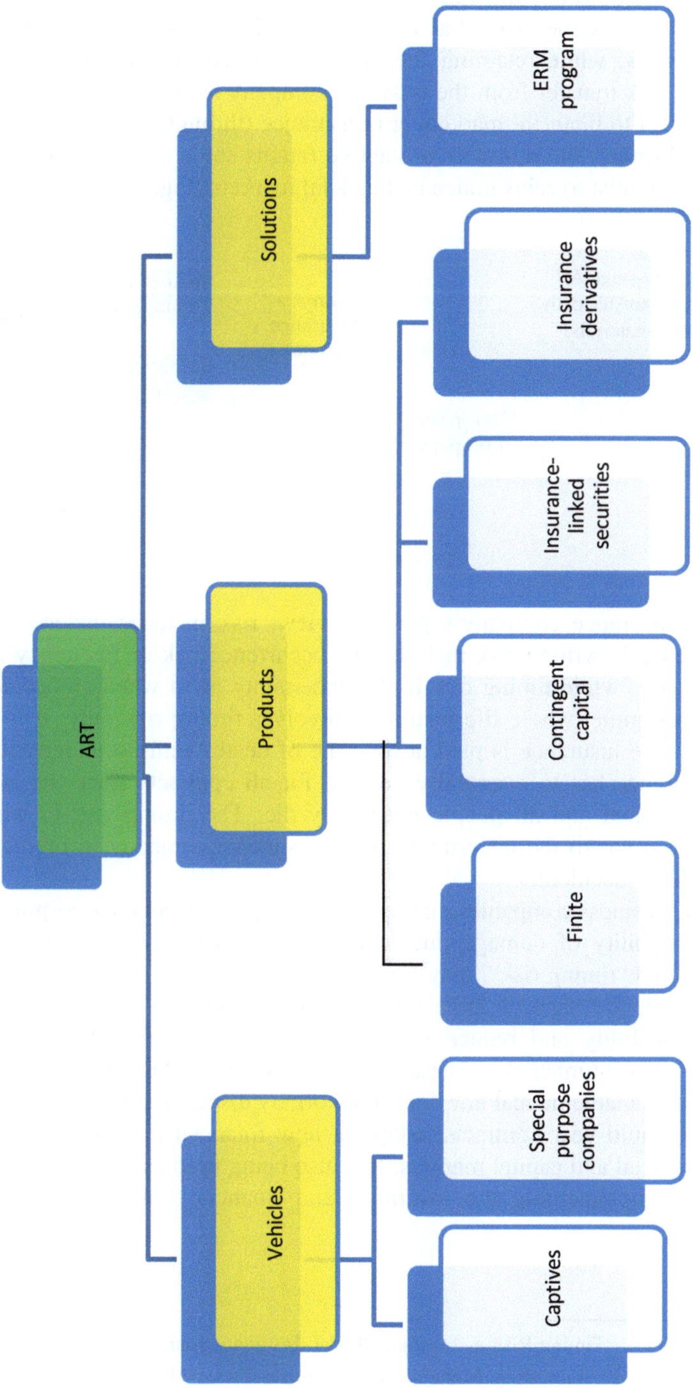

Fig. 8.4 ART classification in RM (Source: Various materials)

ART follows the following stages in an ideal risk transfer "path". The business company transfers some risks that it holds directly to insurance companies and financial markets, while retaining the others. Subsequently, the primary insurer receiving the risk transfer from the business company retains some of the risk and transfers the rest to financial markets or reinsurance (through reinsurance or captive companies). Further, the reinsurer or captive retains some of its underwriting risk and transfers the rest to reinsurance or financial markets (Fig. 8.5).

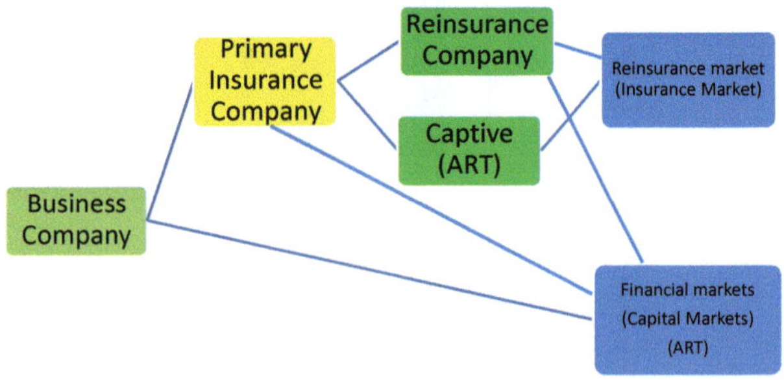

Fig. 8.5 Stage-by-stage ART treatment in risk transfer path (Source: Various materials)

From an insurance company's point of view, risk includes underwriting and timing risks. Underwriting risk includes the occurrence risk or frequency risk and the severity risk, while timing risk is the uncertainty as to when an accident will occur.[2] For example, whole life insurance involves timing risk only. It is a death insurance, where insurance is paid at the time of death, with no underwriting risk because insurance has to eventually be paid for all contracts since the insurance period is unlimited and all people eventually die. The timing risk in whole life insurance is similar to the uncertainty of an insurance company in predicting the occurrence of an accident.

However, business companies mainly use finance to protect their corporate value from the possibility of damage due to delays in financing, because this lag in financing, called "timing risk", may impair corporate value.[3]

In insurance, the "law of large numbers" means that an insurer can stabilize statistical probability and reduce fluctuations in risk occurrence probability by collecting a large number of contracts of the same type. ART mainly deals with the risk that this mathematical law does not work by dispersing the risk over time by entering into multi-year contracts, adopting new financial methods, and utilizing abundant financial and capital markets. It is also being used as a new risk-financing method by complementing the insurance and financial functions through their integration.

[2]Takuya Yoshizawa, "Timing Risk as Insurance Risk", Insurance Journal, 600 (March 2008).

[3]Ginsen Co Ltd., Risk Financing Methods in Enterprises-Types of Alternative Risk Transfer Methods (ART) and Their Use Cases (2014), pp. 3–4.

8.4 Financial Market

In a broad sense, the financial market can be considered to be a place where funds are borrowed or loaned, or a market where the supply and demand of funds are regulated. Interest rate is the price of a financial transaction in the financial market. Depending on the length of transactions, financial markets are classified into short-term money markets (money market) with a period of less than 1 year, and long-term financial markets (capital market) with a period of more than 1 year. The money market is further classified into an interbank market, where transactions are conducted between financial institutions, and an open market in which general companies and investors can participate. The capital market is classified into a stock market and bond market.

Fig. 8.6 shows the financial market classification.

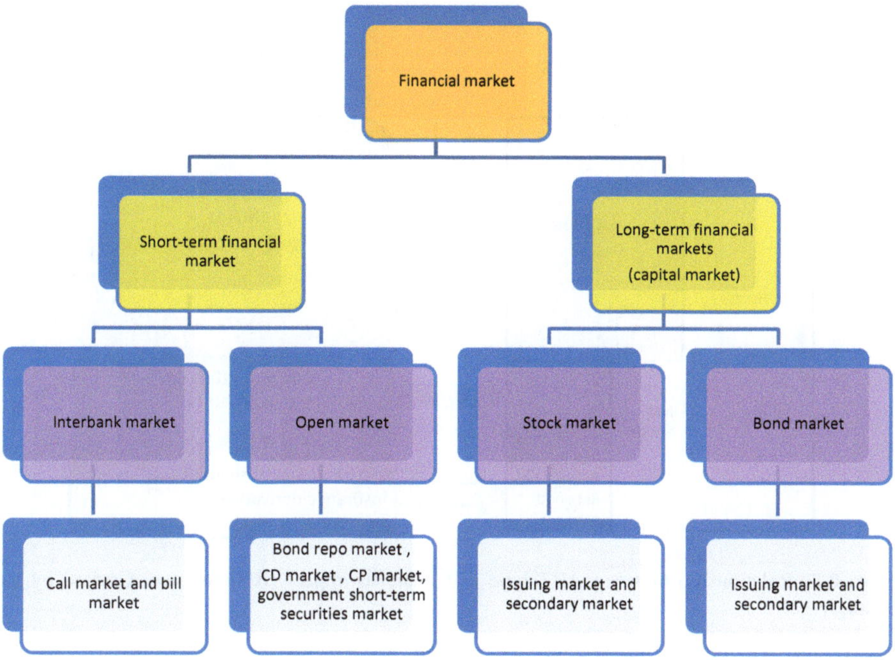

Fig. 8.6 Financial market classification (Source: Various materials)

Money markets include interbank markets and open markets. The call market and bill market are interbank markets where financial institutions can borrow short-term loans. In contrast, the repo market, certificate of deposit (CD) market, and government securities market are open markets where ordinary companies and investors can participate in transactions.

Long-term financial markets are also called capital markets or securities markets. Some definitions of financial market exclude capital (securities) markets.

8.5 Impact of ARTs on Finances

In general, risk has a negative effect on the income statement and balance sheet in terms of effect. That is, a decrease in profits, increase in costs, or occurrence of damage reduces profits in the income statement. Furthermore, if the balance falls into negative, the net assets, such as retained earnings, capital surplus, and capital in the balance sheet will decrease. However, risks affect the profit and net assets of a company as well as the balance of funds.

Fig. 8.7 depicts the relationship between the effects of ART types and finances on the balance sheet (B/S).

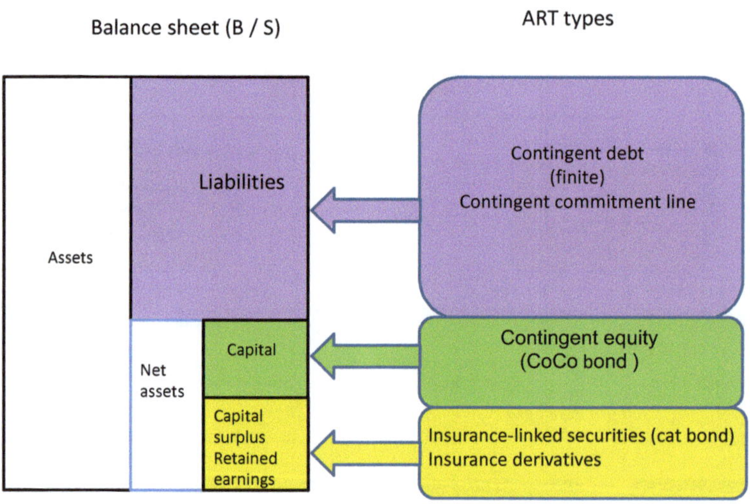

Fig. 8.7 Relationship between ART type and financial impact (B/S) (Source: Created by the author)

Insurance companies have a loss compensation function that reduces the negative impact of occurred losses on the profits, losses, and net assets in the balance sheet. However, it may not be suitable as emergency funding because a certain period of time is required for loss investigation and insurance payment. However, finance can prevent the risk of insolvency or late payment of funds, but cannot directly protect corporate profits and net assets. Therefore, when selecting a risk-financing method, one should analyze the extent to which a risk may affect the company's financial statements and select measures that have the appropriate effects.

Fig. 8.8 depicts the relationship between the effects of ART type and finances on the balance sheet (P/L).

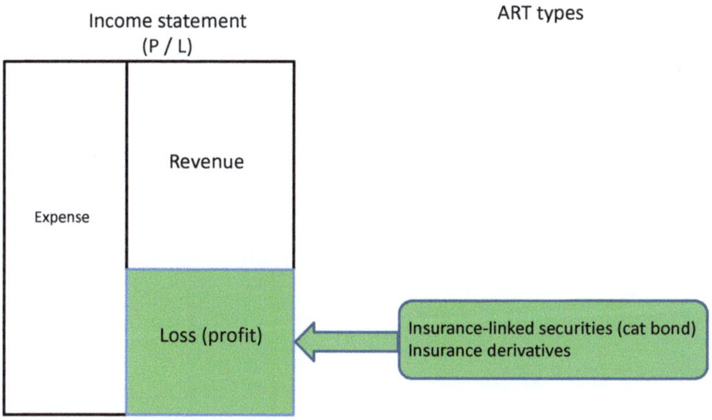

Fig. 8.8 Relationship between ART type and financial impact (P/L) (Source: Created by the author)

For insurance derivatives, for example, the difference between the settlement amount and the option fee is recognized as revenue, although the actual accounting treatment varies. Insurance money on non-life insurance is recognized as revenue. Insurance-linked securities (CATs) and insurance derivatives are recognized as extraordinary income because, as with insurance claims, there is no obligation to repay or otherwise compensate for the occurrence of risks. On the other hand, contingent equity is recognized as equity and contingent debt is recognized as borrowings, but these have no effect on the balance sheet, although they have an impact on the income statement. Thus, insurance and insurance derivatives are the most effective mechanisms to eliminate accounting losses, followed by, in this order, contingent equity and contingent debt. The price of these is proportional to their effect, with insurance being the most expensive and contingent debt being the cheapest.

Because contingent equity can be used as capital in the event of a risk—with no obligation to repay—it can help cover losses without deteriorating the organization's debt ratio. However, since new shares will be issued in a situation where the stock price is likely to fall, that is after a risk has occurred, it could be difficult to draw in investors who may believe that the price could fall even further.

Discussion Questions

1. Explain the outline and means of risk response.
2. Explain risk control.
3. Explain the difference between risk financing and corporate finance.
4. Explain the relationship between insurance and ART.
5. Explain the types of ART and their financial impact. Discuss its strengths and weaknesses in terms of its impact on the income statement and its impact on the balance sheet.

9 Limitations of Insurance as a Risk Financing Tool

Insurance is a traditional means of risk financing. However, this insurance has limitations as a means of risk financing derived from its mechanism. This chapter outlines the limitations of insurance as a means of risk financing.

9.1 Insurance and Risk Financing

As mentioned in Chap. 1, there are pure risks that can be covered by insurance and speculative risks that cannot be covered by insurance; there is no insurance for these speculative risks. The lack of insurance against speculative risk has been the main limitation of insurance as risk financing. This is because risk financing needs to be dealt with regardless of the risk category.

In addition, the concept of insurable interests was introduced in the eighteenth century in the insurance system to distinguish between insurance and gambling, as will be described later. As a result, gambling using insurance will not be possible, and there will be a principle of compensation for actual loss in order to adhere to the principle of prohibiting gain, and subrogation will be carried out. As a result, the insurance system has been evaluated as socially beneficial, and the insurance industry has achieved sustainable development.

However, with the introduction of the concept of insurable interest into the insurance system, it is no longer possible to obtain profits from insurance, and the insurance market is no longer attractive to investors seeking profits. In addition, in the event of an insurance accident, a damage investigation was required to comply with the principle of compensation for damages, and it took time to pay insurance claims.

Further, in the case of under-insurance in which the insurance amount is less than the insurance value, the insurance money is calculated by multiplying the damage amount by the ratio of the insurance amount to the insurance value. This is called the

H. Lee, *Risk Management*, Springer Texts in Business and Economics,
https://doi.org/10.1007/978-981-16-3468-0_9

principle of proportional compensation. As a result, in the case of under-insurance, only a part of the damage amount will be covered.

In addition, even for risks that can be covered by insurance, fluctuations in the insurance market have caused an insurance crisis in which premiums have skyrocketed and insurance companies refuse to underwrite insurance.

Such problems, which can be said to be the limits of insurance, have led to a lack of underwriting capacity in the insurance market and complicated insurance practices, and have resulted in the development of new risk financing means such as ART. In this chapter, we will consider the limits of insurance as a means of this risk financing.

9.2 Insurable Interest and Insurance

9.2.1 Insurable Interest and Prohibition of Gain

Insurance is a system in which the policyholder pays the insurance premium to the insurance company as consideration for the transfer of risk, and the insurance company pays the insurance money to the policyholder (insured person) in the event of damage caused by the risk undertaken. It has been used as a traditional means of risk financing.

Around the seventeenth century, this insurance was used as a speculative means for the deaths and property of aristocrats and celebrities by having a third party who has no interest in the person or property take out the insurance. Such insurance contracts for non-interested people and property were called gambling insurance policies.

To ban this gambling insurance, the concept of insurable interest was introduced into insurance contracts. Insurable interest is defined as the interest between a person and the things when there is a risk of damage to the person in the event of an accidental accident. An insurance contract without an insurable interest is an insurance contract for a person or property that is unlikely to suffer damage, so no damage can occur to the insured.

Since non-life insurance aims to pay insurance money for damages, it is necessary to have an insurable interest as a prerequisite for the contract. As a result, the subject of the insurance contract becomes the insurable interest, and the insured object or subject-matter insured changes from things such as ships and cargo to the insurable interest. As a result, gambling and insurance were distinguished.

The Marine Insurance Act 1745 in the United Kingdom prohibited the issuance of insurance policies without an insurable interest. In addition, the Marine Insurance (Gambling Policies) Act 1909 defined an insurance policy without insurable interest as gambling insurance, and the policy was invalidated. The Marine Insurance (Gambling Policies) Act 1909 stipulates that a person who concludes a gambling insurance contract will be sentenced to imprisonment with hard labor or a fine for up to 6 months.

Also, in the United Kingdom, there were no restrictions on the conclusion of insurance contracts for the lives of others, but in the eighteenth century the harmful effects increased, and the Life Assurance Act 1774 was enacted, by which insurance contracts without an insurable interest were banned.

Insured interests are stipulated in the Japanese Insurance Law as "relationships in which the insured should suffer financial damage due to the occurrence of an insurance accident on the subject-matter of insurance" (Articles 3 and 9). Therefore, non-life insurance contracts without an insurable interest will be invalid. If the owner, security interest holder, creditor, and so on have different insurable interests in different positions for one insurance object, each could conclude an independent insurance contract.

This insurable interest must be monetarily valuable. The "principle of compensation for damages" is a principle in which the amount of insurance claims paid is limited to the actual amount of damages and can be understood as a derivative of the concept of insured interests. In addition, the principle of prohibiting gain is the principle that, in the event of damage, insurance money cannot be received in excess of the actual amount of damage.

If the "principle of compensation for damages"is from the perspective of insurance payments by insurance companies, the principle of prohibiting gains can be said to be from the perspective of receiving insurance claims from the insured. According to the principle of compensation for damages and the principle of prohibiting gains, policyholders and others receive insurance money up to the amount of damages and cannot gain from insurance, preventing moral risk. Moral risk refers to the psychological phenomenon of a policyholder or insured who seeks to gain by using the insurance system after taking out insurance.

On the other hand, in life insurance contracts in Japan, the presence or absence of insurable profits does not matter regarding the conclusion of the contract and its validity. Life insurance has its own business area of risk related to human life and death, and the parties can freely decide the insured, the beneficiary, and the amount of insurance. In non-life insurance contracts, the insurable value is the evaluation of the insurable interest. However, since life insurance does not require the insurable interest as a contract requirement, its valuation does not exist. Therefore, in life insurance contracts, there is no concept of compensation for damages and prohibition of gains.

Life insurance in Japan, unlike those in the United Kingdom and the United States, does not require the existence of an insurable interest. However, a consent principle is adopted that requires the consent of another person (insured person) only for the insurance contract of the life (death) of another person. Insurable interests are said to be effective in preventing gambling insurance, and the consent principle is said to be effective in preventing moral risk. In non-life insurance, the insured refers to a person who may receive insurance money, but in life insurance it is a person who is covered by an insurance contract (insured life). In a life insurance policy, a person who may receive insurance money is called a beneficiary.

In this way, insurance and gambling were separated by the introduction of the concept of insurable interest as a prerequisite for the validity of insurance contracts.

This increased the reputation of the insurance industry and recognized the insurance system as beneficial to society.

9.2.2 Relationship Between Insurable Value and Insurance Amount

The amount at which the insurable interest is evaluated is called the insurable value, which is the maximum amount that can be insured. In addition, the amount contractually contracted by the parties as the maximum amount that the insurance company should cover is called the insurance amount (insurance to value).

It is practically difficult to evaluate the insurance value of all contracts when concluding an insurance contract, and policyholders do not always want insurance for the entire insurance value in order to save premiums. Therefore, the insurance amount is freely decided between the contracting parties.

In addition, when an insurance accident occurs, the money that the insurance company pays to the insured is called insurance money, insurance payout, or insurance proceeds. The maximum amount of insurance money in non-life insurance is the lowest of the insurance value, insurance amount, and damage amount (however, there are exceptions such as new value insurance). As a result, the principle of prohibiting gain is maintained.

On the other hand, if the insurance amount is less than the insurance amount, it is called under-insurance. In this case, in the event of damage, the principle of average will be applied in principle, unless otherwise specified.[1]

Insurance claims based on proportional compensation are calculated as follows.

$$\text{Insurance Money} = \text{Damage Amount} \times \frac{\text{Insurance Amount}}{\text{Insurable Amount}}$$

For example, if an insurance contract with an insurance amount of three million yen is concluded for a car with a vehicle price (insurance value) of five million yen, the insurance money paid is the ratio of the insurance amount to the insurable amount for the damage amount. In this case, if this car suffers damage of three million yen, the insurance money will not be paid in the sum of three million yen and, unless a value agreement endorsement is attached, the principle of proportional compensation will be applied and the amount of damage will be applied. As a result, 1.8 million yen (three million yen × 60%), which is 60% of the total amount, will be paid as insurance money.

[1]The predominant reason for allowing proportional compensation is the lack of insurance premiums. In other words, since many small damages occur, a large amount of cost is incurred in the processing. However, all insurance premiums are calculated on the premise of full insurance, and the rate for small damages with a high probability of occurrence is not calculated. In order to make up for that, the premium rate for under-insurance should be raised, but it is difficult in practice, so it is adjusted at the time of payment.

An insurance contract in which the insurance amount is larger than the insurance value is called over-insurance. The portion exceeding this insurance value will not be paid due to the principle of prohibiting gain. The insurance money in this over-insurance is paid up to the lowest amount of the insurance value, insurance amount, and damage amount. This is because the amount of damage cannot exceed the insurance value.

In addition, double insurance is a special form of over-insurance. This is a case where there are multiple non-life insurance contracts with the same insurable interest and covered risk and overlapping insurance periods for the same insurance object, and the total of those insurance amounts exceeds the insurable value.

In other words, double insurance is when multiple insurance contracts exist for the same insurable interest, resulting in over-insurance, and even if some of the multiple contracts overlap, the overlapping part is over-insurance. Over-insurance refers to the case where all three elements of insured interest, covered risk, and insurance period are partially overlapped. In this over-insurance, each insurance company pays the amount of insurance money that it would have paid if there were no other insurance contracts, and the total amount of independent liability of the calculated amount was adopted. However, the insured cannot receive insurance money in excess of the amount of damage. After that, it is settled between insurance companies.

On the other hand, coinsurance refers to the fact that multiple insurance companies share the insurance amount, that is the risk, for the same insurable interest. In contrast to double insurance or over-insurance, coinsurance is a mechanism in which multiple insurance companies share the risk with one insurance contract, and the secretary company is decided and the paperwork is carried out through the secretary company.

In this way, the principle of proportional compensation is applied to some insurances, and institutionalized to prevent overpayment of insurance money in excess of the insurance value for over-insurance or double insurance.

On the other hand, unlike non-life insurance, life insurance in Japan does not require an insurable interest as a contract requirement, so it is a "fixed amount insurance" in which the insurance amount decided at the time of contract is paid as insurance money without considering actual damage. Since this life insurance does not require an insurable interest, there is no concept of under-insurance, full insurance, over-insurance, and double insurance, which is the relationship between the insurable interest and insurance amount.

9.2.3 Subrogation

Subrogation that is only allowed in non-life insurance includes subrogation regarding lost or destroyed property and subrogation regarding claim. Subrogation regarding lost or destroyed property means that the insurance company acquires the right to the insured's insurance object when the entire insurance amount is paid as a total loss.

In the case of partial insurance, the insurance company acquires the rights according to the ratio of the insurance amount to the insurance value and shares the remnants with the insured. This is because if the insured acquires both the insurance money and the right to the remnants, in the event of damage, the insured may actually get a gain (gain prevention theory). The total loss here means that the object of insurance cannot be used in the conventional usage (it may be used in other uses). In addition, although it can be physically repaired, it may be considered as a total loss because the estimated repair cost exceeds the insurance value (economical repair is impossible).

With this remnants subrogation, if the insurance company pays the insurance money as a total loss, the right to the remnants for the object-matter of insurance is legally acquired. Moreover, the acquisition of rights by subrogation of remnants does not require a manifestation of intention regarding the transfer of rights of the insured and naturally occurs at the same time that the insurance company meets the prescribed requirements. This remnants subrogation allows the insurance company to recover a portion of the insurance payments. However, by acquiring the right to this remnant, it is possible that the owner will be obliged to remove the remnant and will be forced to bear a huge cost.

In response to this, the insurance company avoids the burden on the insurance company due to the transfer of rights regarding the remnants by stipulating the following in the contract. First, when the insurance company expresses its intention not to acquire the rights of the remnants and pays the insurance money, it is stipulated that the rights held by the insured will not be transferred to the insurance company (private automobile comprehensive insurance, and so on). Secondly, it stipulates that the ownership will not be transferred to the insurance company unless the intention to acquire the ownership of the remnants is indicated (comprehensive housing insurance, and so on). Third, it waives the acquisition of rights by subrogation of remnants.

In addition, subrogation of claims means that if damage is caused by an insurance accident due to the actions of a third party and the insurance company pays the insured, the insurance company will get the right to claim damages that the insured has against a third party within the limit of the amount paid. It acquires the right (to claim damages) that a person has against a third party.

Fig. 9.1 illustrates the claim subrogation.

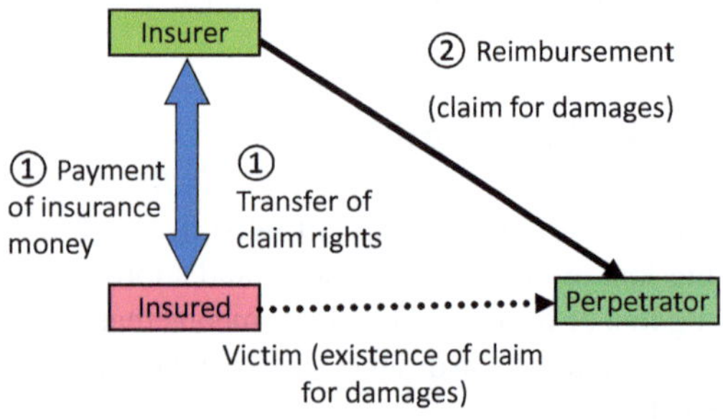

Fig. 9.1 Claim subrogation (*Source:* Various materials)

The requirements for subrogation of claims are that the insured has acquired the right to a third party due to the occurrence of an insurance accident (even in the case of partial loss), and that the insurance company has paid the insurance money to the insured. As a result, the insured's right to a third party is transferred to the insurance company within the limit of the amount paid by the insurance company to the insured.

Subrogation naturally occurs according to the provisions of the law, and it is not necessary for the parties to express their intentions and to have perfection requirements. The policyholder and the insured are obliged to protect their rights (terms and conditions). This subrogation also adheres to the principle of prohibiting gains in the insurance system.

9.3 Insurance Crisis in the United States

The characteristic of insurance from the standpoint of a company (insured person) is that by paying a certain premium, the possibility of causing a large amount of damage is transferred to the insurance company. However, due to the insurance crisis, insurance premiums have skyrocketed and insurance companies have refused to underwrite insurance contracts. This situation has made it difficult for companies to manage their risks in a stable manner.

9.3.1 The Start of the Insurance Crisis in the United States

The insurance crisis (commercial insurance crisis) has led to the following two problems. The first is the unavailability of insurance, "the insurance company does not sell the insurance, so the business company cannot obtain the insurance". The second problem is unaffordability, "the insurance premium is too high for the business company to buy insurance".

9.3.1.1 The First Insurance Crisis

From the end of the 1960s to the 1970s, PL (product liability) litigation, such as asbestos litigation, increased dramatically. As a result, the profits of insurance companies deteriorated, and insurance premiums increased five to seven times over the previous year. As a result, a number of companies that could not buy PL insurance were forced out of business or went bankrupt. It became a social problem during the first insurance crisis (commercial insurance crisis) around 1974–1976.

9.3.1.2 The Second Insurance Crisis

From 1985 to 1987, a second "insurance crisis" occurred on a scale far larger than the PL crisis, the first insurance crisis. For example, as a result of the liability insurance premiums soaring more than five times in half a year, 12% of obstetrics and gynecology departments refused to deliver and about half of the ice rinks in US were closed.

At this time, Lloyd's of London recorded the largest business loss in its 300-year history. Peter Miller, Chairman of Lloyds, issued the following warning as a condition of underwriting liability insurance or its reinsurance. First, American insurers should raise their premium rates on liability risk significantly. Second, the underwriting of insurance would be on a claims made basis, and the legal costs would be on an in-frame payment condition. Third, the legal system of the United States should be improved.

The claims-made base pays insurance claims only to insurance policies that meet the following two conditions. The first is when the disability or property damage that is the cause of the claim for damages occurs after the retroactive date. The second is when the insurance money is claimed within the insurance period.

There are various theories as to the causes of these insurance crises, but the underwriting cycle, cash flow underwriting, punitive damages, and the court system are highlighted.

9.3.2 Underwriting Cycle

The underwriting cycle is a cycle in which the soft market and the hard market alternate, that is the cycle in which the rise and fall of insurance premiums fluctuate periodically. The phenomenon in which insurance premiums soar and insurance companies limit their underwriting of insurance is called the hardening of the insurance market or the hard market. On the other hand, the phenomenon in which insurance premiums fall and insurance companies relax their underwriting conditions is called the softening of the insurance market or the soft market. It is argued that the insurance crisis is a hard market problem in the underwriting cycle, where the soft and hard markets repeat every few years.

In the United States, between 1989 and 1993, earthquake risk premiums have jumped about 2.5 times. Such hardening of the insurance market, once started, will continue for at least several years, causing a significant rise in rates and depleting the underwriting capacity of insurance companies. In addition, the earthquake-related insurance premium rate continued to decline for 6 years from 1993 to 1999. In such a soft market, not only the insurance premium rate is lowered, but also the underwriting conditions such as the insurance amount and the coverage range of insurance are relaxed.

9.3.3 Cash Flow Underwriting

The concept of cash flow underwriting is insurance underwriting that sets the insurance premium rate, taking into consideration the expected investment income up to the time of payment of the insurance premiums received. In the United States, cash flow underwriting was used to make up for the decline in profits and losses on insurance business due to competition to reduce insurance premiums with investment income.

Cash flow underwriting was popular during the high interest rate era around 1980. Products liability insurance and professional liability insurance for professionals are suitable for this purpose. The reason is that there is a long tail that takes a long time from the income of the insurance fee to the payment of the insurance money. With these liability insurances, the actual amount of damages is determined by trials, and so on, so there are many cases where a long tail appears, which takes a long time before the insurance money is paid and, during that time, the asset management of the reserve fund can be carried out.

An illustration of the long tail is as shown in Fig. 9.2.

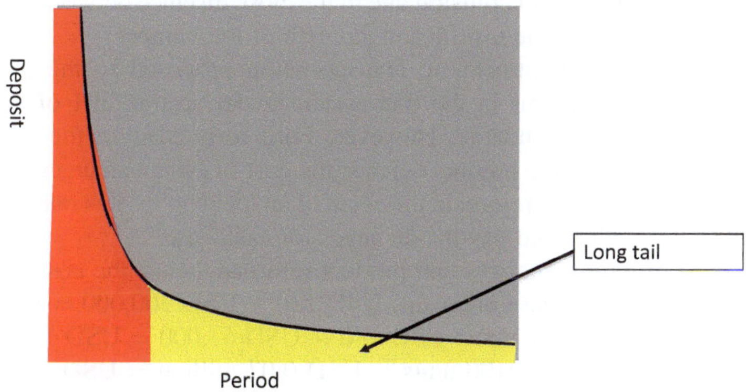

Fig. 9.2 Long tail (*Source:* Various materials)

However, this cash flow underwriting made it impossible to generate the expected investment profit in the low interest rate phase due to changes in the financial markets and, as a result, the insurer suffered a large loss. Insurers have responded by significantly raising premiums and severely restricting underwriting conditions.

As an example of cash flow underwriting, assume that insurance company A concludes an automobile insurance contract with an insurance amount of USD 100,000, an insurance period of 10 years, and an annual insurance premium of USD 250 (total insurance premium of USD 2500). However, the policyholder has a record of driving under influence, and the insurer knows that more than USD 2500 is expected to be paid. This is the case when an insurance contract is concluded on the premise of insurance underwriting loss. This cash flow underwriting is used as a short-term sales tactic at a low price. Then, the insurance company is betting that the premium income will be managed in a way that is expected to gain a high yield, and the investment return will be higher than the discount amount of the premium.

9.3.4 Punitive Damages

Punitive damages are, at the discretion of the court or jury, in addition to compensatory damages if the perpetrator is found to be malicious under the damages system. It is a damage compensation system adopted mainly in Anglo-American law countries and does not exist in Japan. In the United States, punitive damages cases appeared immediately after the founding of the country, which inherited British law.[2]

The Ford Pinto case, which is famous as a case of punitive damages, has the following content. Ford launched the Ford Pinto, an automobile model for the North American market, on 11 September 1970. In 1972, a Ford Pinto stalled while driving on the interstate highway, and was hit by a vehicle following at about 50 km/h and caught alight. The accident killed the driver and severely burned his passengers.

When developing the Pinto, Ford reduced the development period, which normally requires about 43–25 months by sharing parts with the existing Mercury model. During this development stage, a defect was discovered that could cause a fire in the event of a rear-end collision due to the close distance between the gasoline tank and the bumper and the insufficient strength of the bumper.

In 1973, the US Department of Transportation proposed to the Ford Motor Company to solve problems in the fuel system under section 301 of the Federal Motor Vehicle Safety Standards. However, Ford responded to the proposal by saying: "Although there are product defects, the cost of design changes and product refurbishments is high. Therefore, in the event of an incident . . . it is rational to judge the defect of the vehicle and pay the damages for each case."

In the case of design changes and product refurbishments, the cost reduction is USD 49.53 million (decrease in deaths: USD 180 × USD 200,000 = USD 36 million, reduction in serious injuries: USD 180 × USD 67,000 = USD 12.06 million, vehicle accident reduction: 2100 units × USD 0.07 million = USD 1.47 million), and it is estimated that the increase in manufacturing costs due to product refurbishment will be USD 137.5 million (12.5 million units × USD 11). Based on this estimate, Ford compared the costs of design changes and product modifications with and without it, and determined that the cost of not doing so would be low. And no safety measures were taken.

Ford's former employees testified that the company was aware of the existence of the flaw and proceeded with the development without taking safety measures. In addition, as a result of comparative calculation of costs, it was discovered that the company decided to launch a defective car without taking safety measures.

In the Ford Pinto case, a jury verdict for damages in excess of USD 100 million was issued and became famous (compensation for damages: USD 2.8 million, punitive damages: USD 125 million). This case was also the subject of the movie *Proceedings* (original title *Class Action*) produced by twentieth Century Fox in 1991.

9.3.5 Products Liability Lawsuit

Product liability (PL) was established in the United States in the 1960s for the purpose of relieving victims of product defects. In Japan, the Product Liability

[2]For example, the1784 *Genay v Norris* case.

Law was enacted on 22 June 1994, and it has been in force since 1 July 1995. In the Product Liability Law, which is also called the PL Law, when a defect in a product causes damage to life, body, or property, victims are able to claim damages from manufacturers without proving their negligence.

There are the following cases of PL proceedings in the United States. When a teenage woman sprinkled cologne on a candle in an attempt to scent the room, the vaporized alcohol ignited and her friend in the same room was burned. The cologne maker was held liable for the accident.

A dog also died of burns as a result of the wet dog being put in the oven to dry. In this case, the manufacturer, who did not warn about the dangers of drying pets, was held liable for damages. In addition, a robber who fell from the roof and was injured claimed damages from the landlord, and liability was recognized in the trial.

There is also the case of asbestos. Asbestos is a mineral fiber with a diameter of 0.02–0.2 microns, and has excellent heat insulation and hygroscopicity and is easy to process, so it has been widely used in building materials, electrical products, automobile parts, and the like. In the United States, inhaling asbestos fiber in the 1960s was found to pierce the lungs and cause lung cancer. A study conducted by the US Environmental Protection Agency (EPA) found that 15 million children were learning and 1.4 million workers were working in asbestos-based buildings across the United States. After that, the EPA ordered a partial ban on asbestos in 1986 and decided to ban it entirely 10 years later.

Schools and businesses have filed suits against asbestos makers for damages, with the cost of removing asbestos as damages (some of which include punitive damages). Especially since the manufacturer was granted PL in 1973, the number of PL proceedings against asbestos manufacturers has increased sharply. The plaintiffs' winning rate in asbestos proceedings for damages was close to 80%, and the average amount of damages in the winning judgment was USD 702,000.

9.3.6 Court System

Problems with the American system regarding attorneys are highlighted. The remuneration of corporate lawyers in the United States is said to be about USD 150–500 per hour. On the other hand, the remuneration of lawyers in individual damages proceedings is a success fee system. They do not take compensation from the client, but receive 30–50% of the damages that would be received from the other party if the case is won.

In the United States, after graduating from college, if you graduate from a 3-year law school and pass the bar exam, you can qualify as a lawyer. The bar examination is an absolute evaluation, so if it meets certain criteria, it will pass regardless of the number of people. The passing rate of the exam is about 80%, excluding New York and California (about 60%), which are considered difficult.[3]

While in the United Kingdom the jury system in civil lawsuits was abolished, in the United States, the jury system in civil lawsuits is maintained and the amount of punitive damages is also recognized by the jury. This jury system is mainly operated in countries of Anglo-American law.

In this jury system, a jury, which is usually a jury consisting of 12 jurors, finds facts and applies the law in criminal and civil proceedings as a committee without the participation of a judge. In principle, a jury in a civil proceeding is different from a criminal proceeding in which the defendant is judged to be guilty or innocent, and in addition to whether or not the defendant is liable for damages, the amount of damages is also determined. The jury receives a jury instruction from the judge regarding the doctrine and calculation criteria for damages, but this relates purely to general criteria.

The jury attends the court from the beginning to the end of the trial, confirms the evidence, and listens to witness statements and lawyers and prosecutors' arguments. Then, all the members of the jury consult in a separate room and, in principle, unanimously reach a "verdict" independently of the judge.

In the United States, the requirements for becoming a juror are that you must be an American citizen over the age of 18, have lived in the area for at least a year, be able to read and write, be mentally and physically healthy, and that you have no criminal records or pending cases of punishment for more than a year. The court will randomly select those who appear to meet these requirements from the electoral list, tax book, telephone directory, and so on and send a subpoena. You are obliged to respond to this summons, and you may be fined if you do not respond without good reason. The jury will be dismissed after the verdict, but contact between the jury and lawyers is prohibited during the trial.

Any juror who responds to this summon will not be able to work in a regular job until the end of the trial. Therefore, housewives, the elderly, and the unemployed who have time to spare often become jurors. Jurors often have little or no legal background and are easily influenced; so in cases of severe illness or death, there is a tendency to give a verdict in favor of the victim.

In contrast is Japan's Saiban-in system, which was implemented from 21 May 2009. This, unlike the American jury system, is limited to serious crimes in criminal cases and does not apply to civil cases. In addition, this Saiban-in system is a criminal trial for certain serious crimes, in which six Saiban-in selected for the case participate in the hearing together with the judge. The subjects of this Saiban-in system are criminal trials of the district court relating to murder, injury and death, robbery, arson, and kidnapping for ransom.

[3]It is said that there are about 1.33 million lawyers in the United States as of 2016. On the other hand, the number of lawyers registered with the Japan Federation of Bar Associations is 38,980 based on 2017.

Discussion Questions

1. Explain the relationship between insured interests and insurance.
2. Describe the principle of prohibiting gains and the principle of compensation for damages in insurance.
3. Describe the relationship between the insurance value and the insurance amount.
4. Explain the causes of the insurance crisis in the United States.
5. Discuss the impact of the underwriting cycle on risk management for companies in your country.
6. Discuss the limits of insurance for risk management.

Captive Insurers and Finite Insurance

10

Business companies are responding to the hardening of the insurance market by establishing a captive insurance company, an insurance subsidiary to flexibly take on the risks of their own or their group. On the other hand, with finite insurance, insurance companies and business companies share risks to deal with huge risks that are difficult to take out with ordinary insurance.

This chapter outlines captive and finite insurance, which are a type of held-type ART. Contingent debt, a type of possessive ART, will be outlined in Chap. 11.

10.1 Captive Insurance Companies

10.1.1 Definition of a Captive Insurance Company

A captive insurance company, or captive, is an insurance company established by a non-insurance business company or a group of business companies thereof as a subsidiary whose purpose is to assume only the risks of the company or its group. By using this insurance subsidiary, business companies can stably secure insurance even for risks that insurance companies generally do not undertake.

Here, captive means "prisoner of war", "under control", and is used in insurance to mean "only for the parent company". Many captive insurance companies are set up in a captive domicile, which means countries/regions that are willing to attract them. There, operation management companies, lawyers, accountants, actuarial scientists, financial institutions, and so on support the operation of captive insurance companies.

The captive insurance company was incorporated in Bermuda in 1950 under the Exempted Companies Act. Bermuda, a British overseas territory in the North Atlantic, is also known as a tax haven, backed by the financial and tourism industries.

From the latter half of the 1960s, major American business companies established a number of captive insurance companies in search of favorable location conditions

H. Lee, *Risk Management*, Springer Texts in Business and Economics,
https://doi.org/10.1007/978-981-16-3468-0_10

and regulatory and tax environments. The initial establishment of captive insurance companies in the 1960s was to respond to the outbreak of the first insurance crisis (see Chap. 9). In other words, commercial insurance transactions were aimed at transferring risks that could not be secured or had very high premiums. In the mid-1980s, the number of lawsuits for damages increased sharply in the United States, and the amount of damages judgments soared, causing a second insurance crisis (see Chap. 9). This made it difficult for even large multinational corporations to obtain corporate liability insurance, executive liability insurance, and other liability insurance.

Therefore, 34 American Fortune 500 business companies such as GM, GE, Dupont, Dow Chemical, and IBM combined to establish an insurance company in the Cayman Islands (later transferred to Bermuda) to take on only their own risks. There is also a case of developing as a multinational insurance group (Chubb non-life insurance).

In addition, the damage caused by Hurricane Andrew, which struck Florida in the United States in 1992, made it difficult to obtain insurance for natural disaster risk, and reinsurance premiums soared. In response to this, brokers, investors, and reinsurance companies, mainly in the United States, have established captive insurance companies specializing in underwriting abnormal disaster reinsurance. Since insurance companies alone cannot secure sufficient underwriting capacity, new know-how for securitizing insurance risks was also found, and the fusion of insurance and finance began in earnest.

10.1.2 Captive Insurance Companies Types

10.1.2.1 The Essence of a Captive Insurance Company

A captive insurance company is a type of self-insurance in which a business entity uses an insurance subsidiary to hold risks. Self-insurance means that a business entity maintains in-house a reserve commensurate with the probability of risk occurrence and the amount of damage. In simple self-insurance, a risk fund is formed with retained earnings or voluntary provisions. Self-insurance using a captive insurance company is the same as self-insurance in that it holds risks, except that it uses a mechanism called captive.

In risk financing, self-insurance is desirable for small predictable risks, and transfer of risk to a third party, including insurance, is suitable for large risks with a low probability of occurrence. However, the huge risk of not being able to purchase insurance from an insurance company is forced to own, that is, self-insurance. The background to the development of captive insurance companies is the difficulty in obtaining insurance in the traditional insurance market, the reduction of insurance costs, and the internal reserve of insurance profits.

10.1.2.2 Classification by Insurance Underwriting Form

Captive insurance companies can be classified as primary captive insurance or reinsurance captive insurance companies according to the type of insurance underwriting. The direct captive insurance company undertakes insurance contracts directly from the parent company without going through the insurance company. In addition, a reinsurance captive insurance company underwrites part or all of its contract as reinsurance through a non-life insurance company that has assumed the risk from the parent company. Both captive insurance companies will arrange the reinsurance and retrocession necessary for their own risk management as an insurance company. A captive insurance company will generate insurance underwriting profit if the number of accidents in the insurance contract undertaken is small, and will incur an insurance underwriting loss if the number of accidents in the insurance contract is high.

A direct captive insurance company is obliged to issue an insurance policy as an insurance company (in Japan, Article 649, paragraph 1 and Article 683, paragraph 1 of the Insurance Business Law), and damage investigation work, and so on. Therefore, there are few cases where a captive insurance company is established as a direct captive insurance company with a heavy work burden, and most of them are established as a reinsurance captive insurance company. This reinsurance captive company is a captive that underwrites part or all of the insurance contract that the non-life insurance company (fronting company) underwrites the risk from the parent company such as the business company as primary insurance. The operation is often outsourced to a specialized business company in the country where the captive insurance company was established.

The structure of a reinsurance captive company is shown in Fig. 10.1.

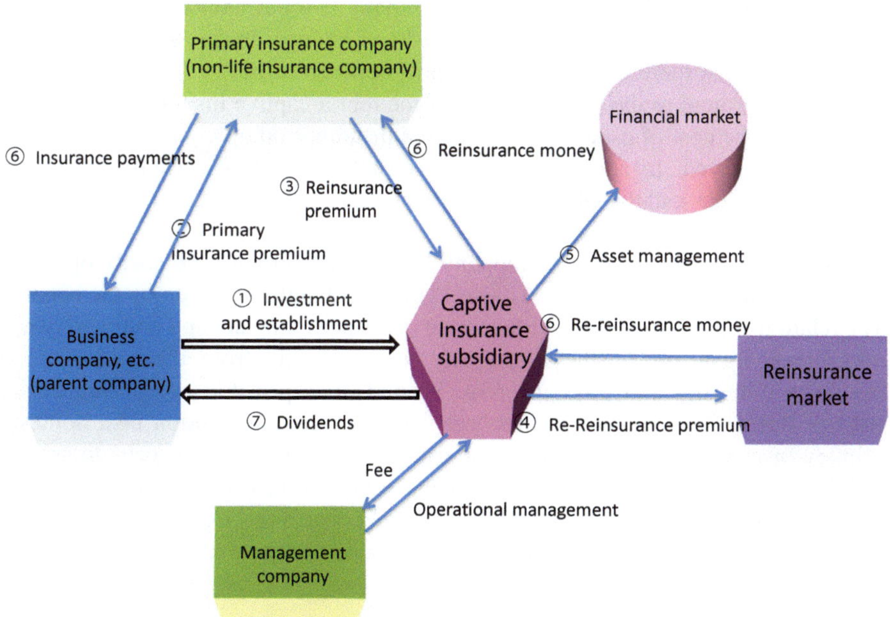

Fig. 10.1 Re-insurance captive insurance company (*Source:* Created with reference to materials from the Ministry of Economy, Trade and Industry)

10.1.2.3 Classification by Ownership

Captive insurance companies can be classified into the following three types according to their ownership form: the pure captive insurance company, which is owned by a single business company or group of business companies; the association captive insurance company, which is jointly owned by multiple non-capitalized business companies or groups of business companies; the rent-a-captive insurance company, which rents only the functions of the captive. In many cases, rental captive insurance companies can be established only with a deposit and do not require investment for their establishment, but there is a problem that the degree of freedom of operation is restricted.

The rent-a-captive insurance company provides the convenience of a captive insurance company and receives its management and rental fees. This rent-a-captive insurance company does not hold any risk, and the profit from underwriting the risk is returned to the user. The business company can acquire the preferred shares of the rental captive insurance company and receive dividends if the cell has an underwriting profit. The rental captive insurance company has an insurance company license and is able to access the reinsurance market through this rental captive insurance company.

One form of rental captive insurance company is called protected cell captive insurance company. This allows you to "rent" a cell (room) that is part of an overseas rental captive insurance company with an insurance company license. The primary insurance company, which has assumed the risk from the parent company, conducts reinsurance transactions with a part called a cell.

This protected cell captive insurance company is a mechanism that allows one captive insurance company to take on the risks of multiple business companies, and is blocked so that there is no financial impact between cells.

The background to the establishment of the rent-a-captive insurance company is as follows. The cost of establishing a captive insurance company is usually at least 20–30 million yen. In addition, the labor cost for operating a captive insurance company overseas and the labor and cost for annual operation such as office rent will be considerable.

The rent-a-captive insurance company leaves the laborious and costly operation of a captive insurance company to its specialists so that they only enjoy the benefits. The relationship between the rent-a-captive insurance company and policyholders is as follows. First, the business company rents a "cell" from the rent-a-captive insurance company and pays the rent. Second, it is possible to reinsurance the risks of business companies in this "cell" through the intervention of a domestic primary insurance company. Third, you can retrocession from the "cell" to another reinsurer. Fourth, if the "cell" has an underwriting profit, it will be returned to the business company that has acquired the preferred shares through a stock dividend.

The structure of a protected cell captive insurance company is shown in Fig. 10.2.

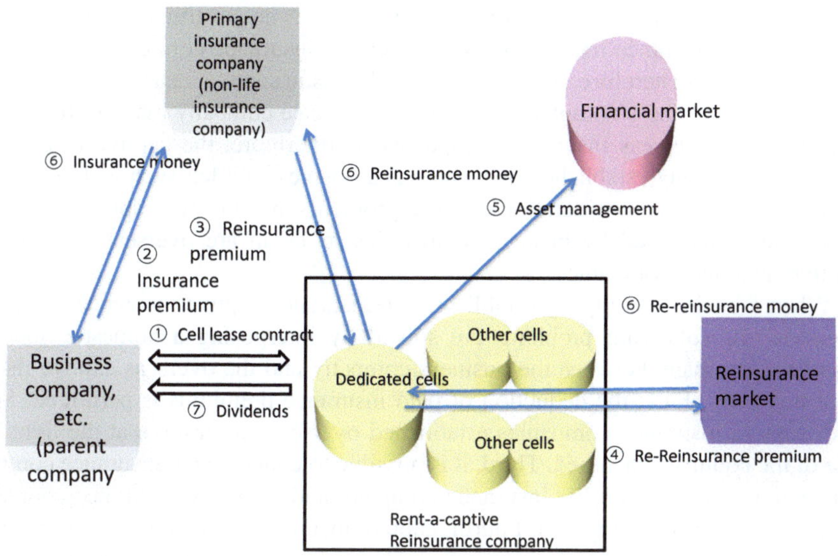

Fig. 10.2 Protected cell captive insurance company (*Source:* Created with reference to materials from the Ministry of Economy, Trade and Industry)

10.1.3 Japanese Business Companies and Captive Insurance Companies

Japanese business companies generally do not establish captive insurance companies in Japan, but as reinsurance captive insurance companies overseas. When considering the establishment of a captive insurance company in Japan, the following must be considered. First, it is possible to establish a direct captive insurance company in Japan. However, if the captive insurance company takes only the risk of the parent company, it is unlikely that an insurance company license can be obtained, so the captive is positioned as a business company rather than an insurance company. Therefore, the premium paid by the parent company in a captive manner will not be recognized as an insurance premium and will not be deductible under the tax law. In addition, when establishing a reinsurance captive insurance company in Japan, it seems that the insurance company license cannot be obtained only by the risk of the parent company. Therefore, when a primary non-life insurance company makes a reinsurance transaction with the captive insurance company, the deduction of policy reserves for the ceded portion of the primary non-life insurance company is not permitted. In addition, the reserve of the captive insurance company will be taxed.

Furthermore, in Japan, domestic policyholders such as business companies are not allowed to insure directly to overseas insurance companies. In principle, the Insurance Business Law prohibits domestic policyholders from directly insuring overseas insurance companies, except for maritime insurance and aviation insurance, in order to protect domestic policyholders through effective supervision (Insurance

Business Law Article 186). However, there are no restrictions on insurers conducting reinsurance transactions with overseas insurance companies or reinsurance companies. Therefore, if the established domestic captive insurance company is regarded as a business company, the captive insurance company may not be able to reinsure with overseas insurance companies. Furthermore, the captive as a direct insurance company established in Japan has a business burden such as issuance of insurance policy. In consideration of these problems, most of the captive insurance companies established by business companies in Japan are overseas reinsurance captive insurance companies.

When a business company establishes a reinsurance captive insurance company overseas, the following problems are solved by interposing a domestic non-life insurance company between the business company and the overseas captive insurance company. First, the deduction of paid insurance premiums is permitted. Second, captive insurance companies established overseas can reserve at the light tax rate of the country concerned. Third, it is possible to conclude a reinsurance contract between a domestic non-life insurance company and a captive insurance company (overseas insurance company). Fourth, captive insurance companies have obtained insurance company licenses overseas, and domestic insurance companies have reduced or deducted policy reserves for reinsurance contracts with the captive insurance companies.

For a domestic insurance company to take on the risk of a business company and reinsure it to an overseas captive insurance company, it is necessary that the solvency, which is the insurance payment ability of the captive insurance company, be sufficient. This condition is required for all insurers in which domestic insurers carry out reinsurance transactions, including captive insurers. Since primary insurance and reinsurance are independent contracts, in the event of an insurance accident the primary insurance company will pay insurance money to the business company even if the reinsurance money cannot be collected from the reinsurance of the overseas captive insurance company. In other words, the insurer will bear credit risk in reinsurance transactions.

Fig. 10.3 shows the insurance channels of reinsurance captive insurance companies established overseas.

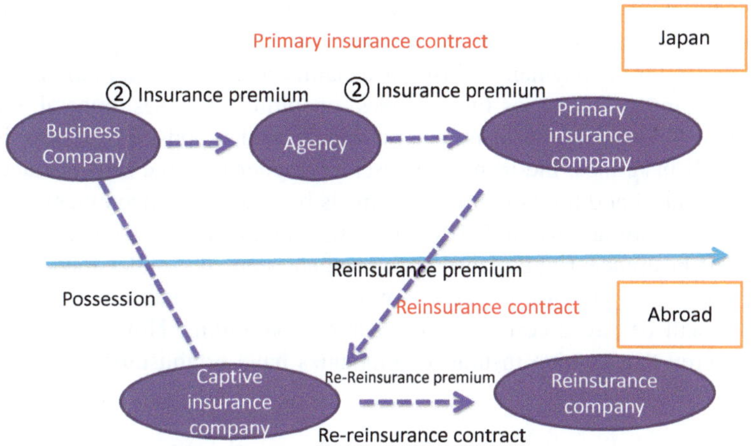

Fig. 10.3 Insurance channels of insurance captive insurance company established overseas (*Source:* Various materials)

On the other hand, many overseas captive insurance companies often cannot meet their solvency conditions on their own. As collateral for solvency in such cases, the domestic primary insurance company requests a debt guarantee from its parent company, a stand-by letter of credit, which is a letter of credit that guarantees payment by the bank or a money trust. An alternative to these guarantees is to obtain a financial rating for the captive insurer. The rating for the captive insurance company varies depending on the rating agency, but in principle it is based on the financial rating of the parent company.

10.1.4 Benefits of Captive Insurance Companies

The advantages of captive insurance companies are as follows.

10.1.4.1 Risk Management

By collecting the risks of a business company in a captive insurance company, it is possible to grasp and quantify the risks of the entire business company. Through this, if the risk is improved and the insurance payment is reduced, the profit of the captive insurance company will increase, and the profit will ultimately belong to the parent company.

10.1.4.2 Cost Optimization

Business companies will be able to understand insurance premiums, which used to be a "black box", and how to arrange overseas reinsurance. Using this information, it is possible to consolidate the risks of group business companies and negotiate with insurance companies in a lump and, based on the strengthened bargaining power, reduce insurance premiums and optimize risk management costs.

In addition, the premium borne by the business company consists of a net premium (risk premium) and an additional premium (loading premium). Net premiums are for the payment of insurance claims, and additional premiums include insurance company expenses (agency fees, operating expenses, general expenses) and profits. Comparing the insurance premiums paid by business companies with those of self-insurance, the insurance costs are higher than the self-insurance costs by the amount of additional premiums. This is because insurance money is the cost of accident occurrence so, in theory, the same amount will be incurred even in the case of self-insurance. Captive insurance companies are also understood as a type of self-insurance so, at least in theory, it is thought that additional premiums in insurance will be saved compared to insurance premiums. However, it must also be considered that captive insurance companies have establishment and operating costs.

10.1.4.3 Risk Financing Means for Risks that Are Difficult to Insure

For risks that are generally difficult to insure, such as environmental pollution risk, it is possible to equalize costs by combining in-house ownership and ceding. By accessing the overseas reinsurance market directly, it may be possible to find more risk underwriters.

10.1.4.4 Leveling Fluctuations in Insurance Premium Rates

Depending on the situation it can be expected that the insurance premium rate will be leveled by controlling the amount of risk holding, such as holding a part within the company group and reinsuring the rest when the insurance premium rate rises.

10.1.4.5 Profit-Center

When a captive insurer becomes able to secure stable profits, it can also become a profit center. It is also possible to grow into a profit center of the parent company by seeking more stable profits, taking risks other than the parent company, or actively conducting insurance business.

10.2 Finite Insurance

Finite means "limited", but finite insurance literally offers only limited risk transfer and compensation compared to traditional insurance. In other words, finite insurance is an insurance in which a company accumulates premiums commensurate with individual risks to an insurance company up to a certain amount over a certain period. Then, in the event of a disaster or the like, the insurance company pays up to a certain limit as insurance money, such as the sum of the insurance premiums accumulated by the company and the risk burden of the insurance company.

For environmental pollution and natural disaster risks, for which the probability of occurrence and the degree of damage are statistically difficult to grasp, the law of large numbers does not work and it is difficult to disperse the risk by traditional insurance. Finite insurance covers these risks and limits the risks transferred to the insurer by making a contract to transfer only the timing risk to the insurer to make it easier for the insurer to take the risk. It is a mechanism in which the insurance company and the policyholder share the risk. This finite insurance is often referred to as finite reinsurance because it is usually a reinsurance policy.

On the other hand, timing risk is a risk that can be dealt with by financing, such as deposits or loans. Insurance that addresses this timing risk has been referred to as financial (re)insurance, but in recent years it has come to be referred to as finite risk insurance, or finite insurance. This finite insurance is a general term for insurance that has a mechanism in which the risk of being transferred to an insurance company is limited to timing risk (finite). This finite insurance has various forms and is classified as retained earnings, which is a type of holding, but it may also be classified as insurance.

In this finite insurance, basically, the insurance company pays the insurance money first, and the premium is paid later, so the insurance company bears credit risk to the company that is the policyholder. Therefore, insurers tend to only cover finite insurance contracts with creditworthy companies that can reliably pay deferred premiums. In the case of finite insurance, if no insurance accident occurs within the contract period, at the end of the contract the policyholder company will receive a refund of the total amount of insurance premiums plus investment income. In addition, in the event of an insurance accident, the total amount of insurance premiums will cover most of the damage.

The relationship between finite insurance and risk transfer is shown in Fig. 10.4.

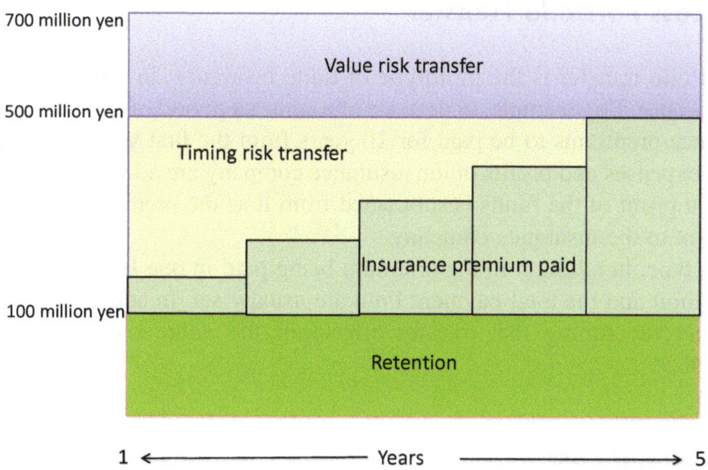

Fig. 10.4 Finite insurance and timing risk transfer (*Source:* Various materials)

Therefore, finite insurance is also said to be a cash flow plan rather than insurance or reinsurance. In this finite insurance, there is no transfer of value risk according to the law of large numbers, which is a characteristic of traditional insurance. However, risk sharing is carried out by the insured company transferring the timing risk to the insurance company.

It is also argued that this finite insurance is not an insurance contract because the risk diversification is not sufficiently performed according to the law of large numbers, which is a characteristic of insurance. For finite insurance, which has limited risk transfer, to be recognized as an insurance product, it is necessary that the transfer of value risk is at a reasonable level. There is a view that timing risk is included in the range of this risk, but there are many views that the insurance premium here is a kind of deposit, so it is "finance" and it is difficult to recognize it as insurance. If it is not recognized as an insurance product, the funds paid to the insurance company are not insurance premiums and cannot be deducted for tax purposes. As a result, recent finite insurance is becoming more and more a combination of traditional insurance in order to increase the level of transfer of value and risk as insurance.

Finite insurance is often used as a method to deal with risks that are difficult to formulate as insurance, such as environmental pollution and PL, and risks that insurance premiums are high. Therefore, in order to make it easier for insurance companies to take on huge risks, finite insurance often sets one or more payment limits per accident, annual payment limits, total payment limits during the period, and so on. This finite insurance is a custom-made contract that suits the circumstances of the contracting company for each contract, and the content of the contract is also highly unique and diverse for each company, but the following three types are typical.

10.2.1 Loss Portfolio Transfer

Loss portfolio transfer is the prototype of finite insurance, in which premiums are paid in advance. For example, in the case of a contract period of 10 years, the amount of insurance premiums to be paid for 10 years from the first year is calculated, the expected expenses and profits of the insurance company are added, and the expected investment profit of the funds is subtracted from it as the premium. It is a one-time prepayment to the insurance company.

In this type, in addition to the premium being paid in one lump sum, the annual payment limit and the total payment limit are usually set. In addition, it can be said that neither the timing risk transfer effect nor the value risk transfer effect is recognized.

10.2.2 Spread Loss

Spread loss pays a fixed amount of insurance premiums that are expected to be paid within a certain period of time, and the premiums are leveled each period. This is finite insurance aimed at stabilizing annual earnings. If it is almost certain that insurance payments will occur over a period of time, but the timing of the payments is undecided, this spread loss will transfer the timing risk of large temporary payments to other insurance companies.

The contract period for this product is generally long, about 5–10 years and cannot be canceled halfway. Annual premiums are usually calculated by dividing the underwriting insurance company's expected payment insurance money with the expected expenses and profits by the insurance period.

As a result, premiums paid will be leveled. In addition, unlike the loss portfolio transfer, even if the damage exceeds the total expected premium for the contract period, the insurance money for excess damage will be paid. There is no transfer of value risk because the amount paid for this excess portion will be returned to the insurance company as a postpaid premium by extending the insurance period. On the contrary, if the total insurance payment for the contract period is less than the total expected insurance premium, there are many contracts in which a refund is generated.

10.2.3 Post-loss Funding Program

The post loss funding program is a finite insurance that receives insurance money after an insurance accident and pays the insurance premiums later. This finite insurance incorporates the concept of a loan line reservation contract (financial product) called the commitment line, which is explained in Chap. 11, into the insurance field.

In this method, the contracting company pays the "commitment premium" to the insurance company and makes an "insurance reservation" contract with the insurance company. Although this commitment premium is in the form of insurance premiums, it is actually a reservation fee for insurance contracts and does not have the nature of a direct consideration for risk transfer.

The commitment premium paid by the contracting company is the sum of the insurance money paid by the insurance company in the event of an insurance accident and the expenses, profits, interests, and so on of the insurance company. The remaining amount will be deferred as insurance premiums in installments over the pre-arranged payment period. This finite insurance also has the effect of transferring timing risk because the insurance money is temporarily replenished by paying the insurance money after the occurrence of the insurance accident, but the insurance money received by the contracting company will be returned as insurance premiums. Therefore, although it has the function of leveling profits and losses, the transfer effect of value risk is not recognized.

Discussion Questions

1. Discuss the strengths and weaknesses of each form of captive insurance company.
2. Describe Japanese business companies and captive insurance companies. In addition, discuss captive insurance companies with business companies in your country.
3. Discuss, with examples, the usefulness and issues of finite insurance.

Contingent Capital

11

This chapter outlines contingent capital, a method of raising funds as a liability and a method of raising funds as capital after a loss occurs.

11.1 Overview

In contingent capital, Contingent means an unexpected or contingent event such as the occurrence of a natural disaster, but in ART the occurrence of an accidental event such as a natural disaster is referred to as an "emergency". In many cases, therefore, contingent capital means capital in case of an emergency, and is a method that enables a company to raise funds in the event of a preset emergency within a certain period of time. Capital here is a concept that includes not only capital that is equity capital but also debt that is capital of others.

Unlike insurance, this contingent capital affects capital or liabilities on the balance sheet, so even if the trigger is triggered, it does not affect the income statement and is not included in the insurance-linked securities. It is generally classified as either a loan contract or an investment contract.

Companies that use contingent capital pay the funder a commitment fee, which is a fee regardless of whether an emergency occurs or not. This commitment fee is like a kind of premium in return for a funding promise in the event of an emergency and will not be refunded in the event of an emergency. This method is arranged before the occurrence of an emergency, and after the occurrence of an emergency becomes clear, the funds are procured at a procurement cost that does not reflect the credit status of the business company, and so on. under predetermined conditions.

If a business company tries to raise funds after an emergency occurs, the credit status will have deteriorated and the cost of raising funds will have increased. Insurers or reinsurers often use this contingent capital instead of risk diversification, such as by reinsurance, in addition to the means of raising funds in an emergency.

The classification of this contingent capital is shown in Fig. 11.1.

H. Lee, *Risk Management*, Springer Texts in Business and Economics,
https://doi.org/10.1007/978-981-16-3468-0_11

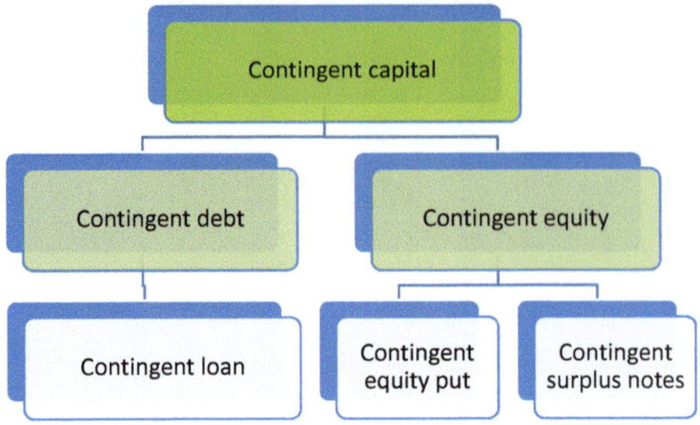

Fig. 11.1 Contingent capital classification (*Source:* Various materials)

Contingent capital can be categorized into contingent debt, which raises funds as debt, and contingent equity, which raises funds as capital. The capital in this contingent capital includes the borrowing of funds from financial institutions and the raising of funds by various securities such as bonds, stocks, or structured products, as well as the capital that is the equity capital. It also includes debt that is the capital of others.

11.2 Contingent Debt

11.2.1 Commitment Line

A commitment line is a contract in which a bank commits a loan to a business company, and so on, and is also called a loan facility reservation or a bank loan facility. It is a contract in which a bank and a company, such as a business company, decide a loan facility in advance and, within a certain period of time, the bank lends the funds to the company without examination regardless of the occurrence of an emergency. Business companies, and so on, can use the loan from the commitment line not only for responding to unforeseen circumstances, such as sudden changes in the market environment, but also for working capital in normal times.

In other words, the commitment line is not a contingent capital that raises funds in an emergency, but a financing method that can be used even in peacetime. As a consideration, the business company pays the bank a commitment fee. Therefore, by setting a commitment line, a bank can receive a commitment fee according to the amount of the credit line, in addition to the normal interest rate when the loan is made.

Commitment lines have traditionally been used in the United States and elsewhere, but were rarely used in Japan by the late 1990s. The possible reasons for this are as follows. First, because of the existence of a main bank system in Japan, in an emergency, the business company received a loan from the main bank as needed. However, in the latter half of the 1990s, the banking industry was reorganized against the backdrop of the disposal of non-performing loans by banks, and lending centered on main banks no longer functioned as before. Second, in the past, commitment fees could be considered as interest, which could result in a violation of the Interest Rate Restriction Act or the Investment Law by exceeding the maximum interest rate. The law stipulates that money other than the principal received by a creditor shall be regarded as interest regardless of its name.

On the other hand, the commitment fee is for the entire loan facility, but if there is no borrowing or a small amount of borrowing, the commitment fee for the borrowed amount may exceed the maximum interest rate. However, in March 1999, the Act on Specified Loan Agreement was enacted, and commitment fees are now excluded from the scope of deemed interest under the Interest Rate Restriction Act and the Investment Law.

There are two types of contracts relating to the commitment line: the bilateral method and the syndicated method. The bilateral method is a method in which a business company makes a contract with an individual financial institution, as shown in Fig. 11.2.

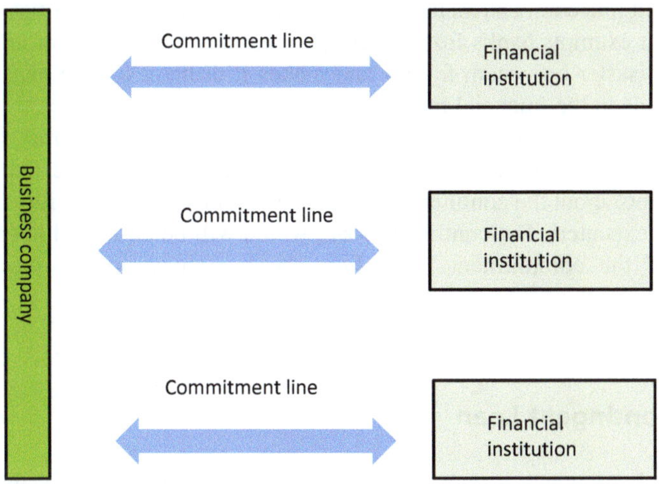

Fig. 11.2 Bilateral (*Source:* Various materials)

On the other hand, the syndicate method is a method in which a secretary financial institution organizes a plurality of financial institutions (syndicates) and sets a commitment line under the same conditions at the plurality of financial institutions, as shown in Fig. 11.3.

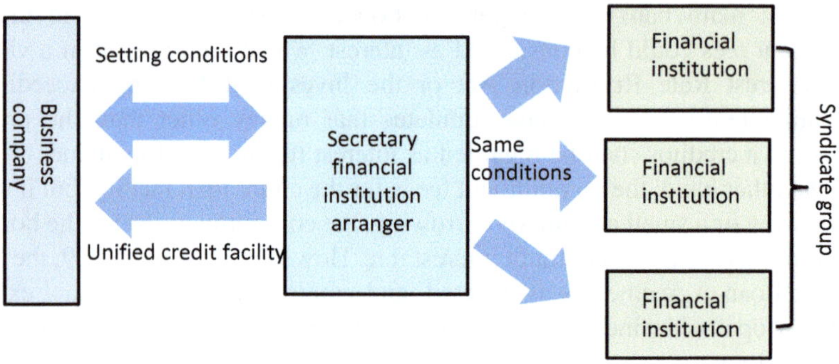

Fig. 11.3 Syndicated method (*Source:* Various materials)

However, the commitment line contract stipulates a condition precedent[1] that allows a bank to decline a loan and, if it is in conflict, the loan will not be executed. Commitment line contracts include a force majeure clause or MAC (material adverse change) that exempts banks from lending obligations in the event of an emergency such as a disaster or system failure that makes it difficult for the bank to raise or transfer funds in the financial markets.

If the bank determines that the loan preconditions are not met because the company suffered enormous damage due to a catastrophe or the like and raised serious doubts about the continuity of the business, there is a possibility that the loan will not be executed. The contingent loan, which will be described later, solves the problem of the commitment line where the loan may not be executed in an emergency.

11.2.2 Contingent Loan

Contingent loan, which is an emergency loan facility reservation, is also known as the contingent commitment line. This is a reservation contract for an emergency loan facility by paying a commitment fee. Among the terms of the commitment line contract is a loan disclaimer.

One of the loan exemption clauses is the "force majeure clause", which is an exemption clause when a loan cannot be executed due to a force majeure such as a

[1]A condition precedent is a condition that the contract becomes effective only when the presupposed condition content is realized. As long as it is a premise, if the content is not realized, the premise that the content written in the contract will be effective will be lacking, so that the content will not be effective in the first place.

A condition subsequent, on the other hand, is called a cancellation condition and refers to a provision that the contract will continue until something happens or something happens. For example, the pension may be canceled under the condition that the pension is continuously paid until the beneficiary dies.

natural disaster that is not the responsibility of the bank. The other is the "financial restriction clause", which is a disclaimer when it is judged that the financial condition of the lender has fallen into a state that is significantly unsuitable for financing. The contingent loan agreement removes these two disclaimers and makes it possible to raise risk response funds from financial institutions in an emergency. Therefore, with a contingent loan, a financial institution cannot refuse to use a loan facility because of the disaster and the resulting deterioration of the financial condition of the business company.

With a contingent loan, a business company or the like can conclude a contingent loan contract with a financial institution such as a bank in advance, and can borrow funds in the event of an emergency such as an earthquake. When a company applies for a loan to a bank in an emergency, it is likely that the loan will be refused or the loan conditions will be stricter than in normal times. However, in the contingent loan contract, the loan conditions in an emergency can be fixed by determining the loan conditions in an emergency in advance. This method allows immediate financing within the loan facility, but it is a liability and requires repayment of principal and interest. In addition, as shown in Fig. 11.4, a contingent loan contract with a SPC intervening is also implemented.

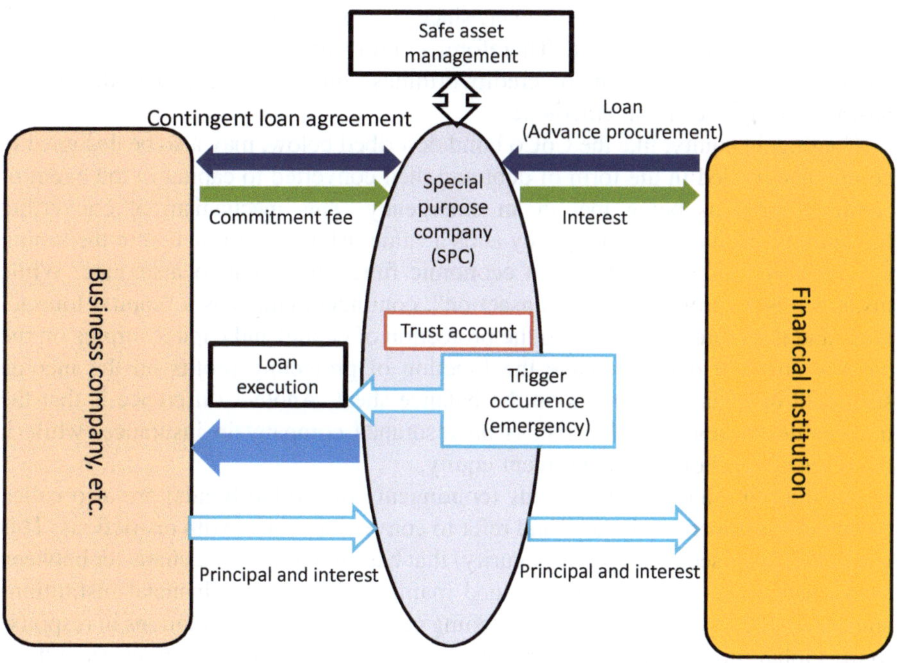

Fig. 11.4 Contingent loan (*Source:* Created with reference to materials from the Ministry of Economy, Trade and Industry)

Fig. 11.4 shows how to raise funds in advance using a SPC so that funds can be raised reliably in an emergency. The SPC concludes a contingent loan contract with a business company, concludes a loan contract with a financial institution, and receives a loan. In normal times, the business company pays a commitment fee to the SPC, and the SPC pays interest to the financial institution with the profit from investing the commitment fee and the loan funds in safe assets. In an emergency, the SPC will cash the assets that were in safe operation and provide funding to the business company through a continuing loan agreement. After the funding is provided, the SPC collects the principal and interest from the business company and repays it to the financial institution.

The mechanism for a contingent loan (emergency loan facility reservation) is as shown in Fig. 11.4.

11.3 Contingent Equity

11.3.1 Contingent Equity (CoCo Bond)

Contingent equity, also translated as "emergency stock issuance", is a contract that reserves the right to issue stock in an emergency in advance. A contingent loan is a liability and must be repaid. However, since contingent equity is funded as capital, there is no need to repay it. Therefore, contingent equity has the function of preventing the deterioration of creditworthiness due to the capital reduction of business companies in an emergency.

Contingent equity, like the CoCo bond described below, may also be designed to be initially funded in the form of debt and then converted to capital in the event of certain conditions being met in an emergency. This mechanism of converting liabilities to capital in an emergency adds a value risk transfer function to the timing risk transfer function, and has an economic function similar to insurance. While insurance is a "profit and loss transaction", contingent equity is a "capital transaction" and therefore contributes to the protection of capital and capital surplus on the balance sheet. It does not have the function of protecting profits on the income statement or retained earnings on the balance sheet. Another difference is that the transfer destination of value risk is an insurance company in insurance, while it becomes a shareholder in contingent equity.

On the other hand, CoCo bonds (contingent convertible bonds) are also called "contingent convertible bonds" and refer to convertible bonds with restrictions. This is a new type of security (hybrid security) that has an intermediate character between stocks and bonds, and has been issued mainly by European financial institutions since around 2010 in the wake of tightening capital adequacy regulations in response to the global financial crisis. After that, it spread to financial institutions around the world, such as Asia and the United States, as one of the means of increasing capital. This CoCo bond has a mechanism in which part or all of the principal is converted into shares when the capital adequacy ratio of the issuing financial institution falls below a predetermined level. This CoCo bond tends to have a higher yield level than straight corporate bonds and subordinated bonds of the same issuer.

The contingent equity (CoCo bond) mechanism is as shown in Fig. 11.5.

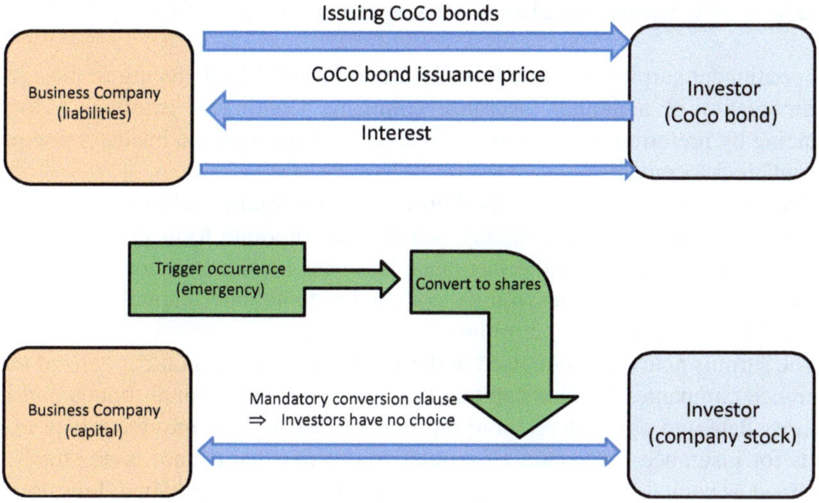

Fig. 11.5 Contingent equity (CoCo bonds) (*Source:* Various materials)

CoCo bonds are called "emergency convertible bonds" because they are corporate bonds that have a mechanism to be converted into capital in an emergency. CAT bond is a mechanism for investors to take on the transfer of risks such as business companies by a mechanism of exemption of principal and interest, while the CoCo bond is a mechanism to reinforce capital by a mechanism of conversion of debt to capital. Investors take risks, and there is a difference in their economic effects.

Business companies issue CoCo bonds to investors and receive payment of the issuance price. The issuance conditions include a "compulsory conversion clause" that stipulates that the conversion to shares will be forcibly executed if certain conditions are met. Then, when this condition is satisfied due to the occurrence of a trigger event, shares in place of corporate bonds are issued at a predetermined rate and delivered to investors. As a result, the issue price of the CoCo bond remains as capital for the company, and the stock of the company that replaces the corporate bond remains for the investor.

The period of the CoCo bond is usually long term, about 10–15 years. In addition, the risk to investors is considered to be high because the issuer has the conversion right for a long period of time and the stock price is expected to be in a declining phase at the time of conversion to shares. For this reason, interest on CoCo bonds is set at a higher level than ordinary convertible bonds. Since the issuance of this CoCo bond has a high risk for investors, negotiations on conditions, such as issuance costs, may become strict. Furthermore, if the converted shares are accompanied by "management participation rights" as shareholders with voting rights, the conversion (issuance) may change the existing shareholder composition and lead to management instability.

11.3.2 Contingent Surplus Notes and Contingent Equity Puts

The contingent surplus note is a form of subordinated debt financing in the event of an emergency of a mutual insurance company. Contingent equity is a form of financing by preferred stocks used by insurance companies and business companies of joint-stock companies.

The contingent surplus note, also known as an emergency subordinated bond, is a means by which a mutual company, which is a corporate form permitted only by insurance companies under the Insurance Business Law, raises funds as a liability. Unlike joint-stock companies, mutual companies do not have capital and are mainly operated by policyholders' premiums.

The surplus note was often used in the 1990s as a way for non-capitalized mutual insurance companies to raise capital. This is similar to corporate bonds and has a maturity date and pays interest, but the funds raised by this provide a way to raise funds for insurance companies of mutual companies that cannot issue shares. It is classified as capital. The reason is that when a company is liquidated, investors, like capital, receive a final allocation of property.

The contingent surplus note is a mechanism for issuing surplus notes to raise funds in the event of an emergency. With contingent surplus notes, insurers such as mutual companies have put options on the assets of their trust accounts to buy subordinated debt in an emergency. The issuance of these subordinated bonds will increase the collateral power (capital) of insurance companies.

The mechanism for contingent surplus notes and contingent equity puts is shown in Fig. 11.6.

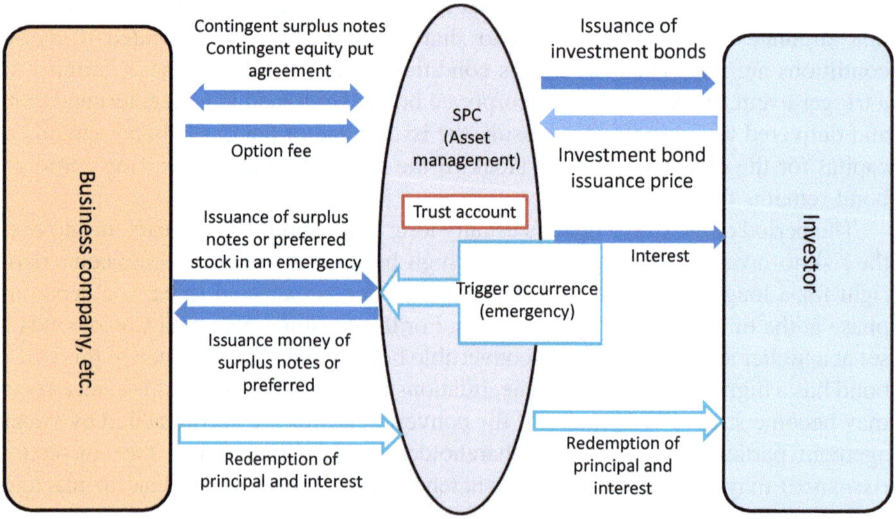

Fig. 11.6 Contingent surplus notes and contingent equity puts (*Source:* Various materials)

From the investor's point of view, the obligation of the investee company to invest even if it is insolvent is regarded as a contingent liability similar to debt guarantee. Therefore, in the contingent capital agreement, the exercise of put options is subject to the condition that the investee company has a sustainable financial condition. On the other hand, in the case of insurance and reinsurance, even if the policyholder company goes bankrupt, the trustee can claim the insurance money as a creditor. Therefore, the consideration for contingent capital is considerably cheaper than the premium for insurance and reinsurance.

In the commitment line mentioned above, from the standpoint of a borrower such as a business company, there is a credit risk that the bank may not provide the loan in an emergency. On the other hand, from the perspective of a bank, it is necessary to lend to an insurance company that has suffered damage such as a huge obligation to pay insurance claims or a business company that has suffered a huge amount of damage and has a credit risk, that is anxiety about its repayment. Contingent equity is also a mechanism for solving problems in such commitment lines.

In the contingent surplus note or contingent equity puts system, business companies raise funds in advance and operate them as trust funds in order to secure funds. In other words, a business company or the like establishes a trust account, solicits funds from investors there, and the funds are invested in government bonds with high liquidity and creditworthiness. The business company (insurance company) has the option of converting the assets in the trust account into surplus notes or preferred stock in the event of a predetermined trigger event. An option fee (stand-by credit fee) paid by the business company (insurance company) to maintain that right is added to the assets under management, and interest is paid to investors with the investment profit. Since the investor invests in a trust account that is separated from the business company (insurance company), it bears almost no credit risk unless a trigger event occurs. In addition, the business company (insurance company) does not bear credit risk because the funds are prepared in the trust account in advance for the financing when the trigger event occurs.

Discussion Questions

1. Explain the concept of contingent capital.
2. Discuss, with examples, the usefulness of and issues with contingent debt.
3. Discuss, with examples, the usefulness of and issues with contingent equity.

Securitization and Insurance-Linked Securities 12

An insurance-linked securities system was created by applying the asset securitization system to insurance risk. This chapter outlines the mechanism of asset securitization and insurance-linked securities.

12.1 Asset-Backed Securities

Securitization is a type of direct finance in which securities are issued with the backing of assets such as monetary claims or real estate, and financing is raised through the sale of securities. This securitization began in earnest in the 1970s with MBS (mortgage-backed securities). After that, ABS (asset-backed securities) were issued with collateral such as car loans, credit card receivables, accounts receivable, and lease receivables. The securitization market in the United States is as huge as the government and corporate bond markets.

ABS is a security backed by real estate or assets. The securitizing company establishes a SPC, a special purpose vehicle (SPV) that has legal personality, and transfers the securitized assets to the SPC. Then, the SPC issues securities backed by the assets and sells them to investors.

ABS has transferred ownership of the underlying asset to the SPC, so even if the company that owned the asset goes bankrupt, the SPC will not be affected and payments to investors will be made. For example, an ABS backed by a loan receivable has the loan receivable transferred to SPC, so if there is no problem with the loan receivable, even if the bank holding the receivable goes bankrupt, the SPC is unaffected and can continue to pay investors.

H. Lee, *Risk Management*, Springer Texts in Business and Economics,
https://doi.org/10.1007/978-981-16-3468-0_12

12.2 Real Estate Securitization

A company that owns real estate establishes an SPC and sells the real estate it owns to the SPC, which issues securities secured by the real estate and sells it to investors. This SPC pays interest and dividends to investors based on real estate income such as rent from tenants.

The mechanism for real estate securitization is shown in Fig. 12.1.

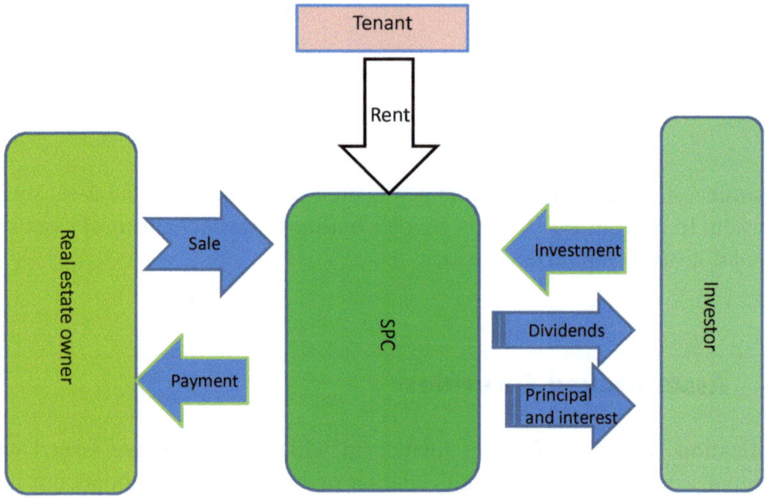

Fig. 12.1 Mechanism of real estate securitization (*Source:* Various materials)

In addition to the method using SPC, there are the following methods for securitizing real estate. The first is a trust method in which a trust bank commercializes assets in small lots in the form of beneficiary rights. Second, there is a method of creating a company-type investment trust (real estate investment trust) and selling its stock.

The following problems are highlighted in real estate investment. First, the liquidity (cashability) is low because it often takes time to buy and sell real estate. Second, the investment scale is relatively large. Third, it is expensive or laborious to manage. However, real estate securitization solves many of these real estate investment problems.

The effects of real estate securitization from the investor's point of view are as follows. First, it has higher liquidity (cashability) than real estate in kind. Second, it is possible to make diversified investments in multiple real estate in small lots.

The effects of real estate securitization from the standpoint of the original owner of the real estate are as follows. First, the original owner of the property has the same effect as selling the target property and can avoid the risk of the price of the property falling in the future. Second, it is possible to improve the financial position of a company by reducing interest-bearing debt with the funds raised by the securitization of real estate. In some cases, even the head office building is subject to securitization.

In addition, REITs (real estate investment trusts) are listed on the stock exchange. This REIT purchases real estate and real estate loans with the funds collected from investors, and pays dividends to investors using the rent and interest generated from them as financial resources.

In Japan, the Investment Trust Law (Law Concerning Investment Trusts and Investment Corporations) was amended in 2000, and real estate was approved as an investment target for investment trusts. As a result, J-REITs were launched in 2001 as two brands.

12.3 Securitization of Receivables

The types of securitization of receivables are as follows.

12.3.1 Commercial Mortgage-Backed Securities

Commercial mortgage-backed securities (CMBS) are a type of asset-backed security (ABS) that are securitized with commercial real estate mortgages, which are loans mainly secured by commercial real estate. With the spread of non-recourse loans (non-recourse debt) in Japan, the use of CMBS has also begun. The first CMBS in Japan was the securitization carried out by Morgan Stanley in February 1999. It was a CMBS funded by the repayment of principal and interest on a non-recourse loan loaned by a foreign bank when it acquired 1200 condominiums from Daikyo.

A non-recourse loan is one in which only the mortgage property is the responsible property. In the event of bankruptcy of a company that is the debtor, even if the mortgage real estate of the loan is sold and used for repayment, the debtor is not liable for the repayment of the remaining amount of the loan. However, with a regular mortgage, if the loan cannot be repaid and the mortgage is sold and used for repayment, the debtor is obliged to repay the balance of the loan. This traditional mortgage can be said to be a loan to "people", while a non-recourse loan can be said to be a loan to "real estate". Unlike commercial mortgages, traditional mortgages are predominantly recourse loans in both Japan and the U.S., since the funds for their redemption come from personal income rather than from real estate.[1]

[1] In some US states, such as California, if you buy a home on a mortgage, the home is owned by a financial institution by the time the loan is repaid. Therefore, if the debtor defaults, the financial institution is granted the right to dispose of the house without going through the court procedure, "foreclosure by power of sale". Instead, banks make it impossible to retroactively trace personal property even if there is a shortage in the disposal of collateral (Masahiro Kobayashi and Yumiko Yasuda (op. Cit.), pp. 150–152). As a result, some states in the United States operate mortgages in a non-recourse manner.

12.3.2 Residential Mortgage-Backed Security

Residential mortgage-backed securities (RMBS) are a type of MBS, namely ones that are issued with the repayment of the principal and interest of the mortgage as collateral. In general, MBS is a security issued with a real estate mortgage loan as collateral.

Another example of mortgage securitization is as follows. The Japan Housing Finance Agency was established on 1 April 2007 as an independent administrative agency that reorganized the former Government Housing Loan Corporation. In October 2003, when the Government Housing Loan Corporation was in existence, a mortgage loan called the "new mortgage loan with securitization support" was started, but fixed-rate mortgage loans up to 35 years were renamed "flat 35" in December 2004. This mortgage is sold by some financial institutions that handle deposits such as banks, credit unions and labor banks, and non-banks such as mortgage banks and companies specializing in housing finance. The flat 35 has a "purchase type" and a "guaranteed type".

Fig. 12.2 shows the purchase type mechanism of flat 35.

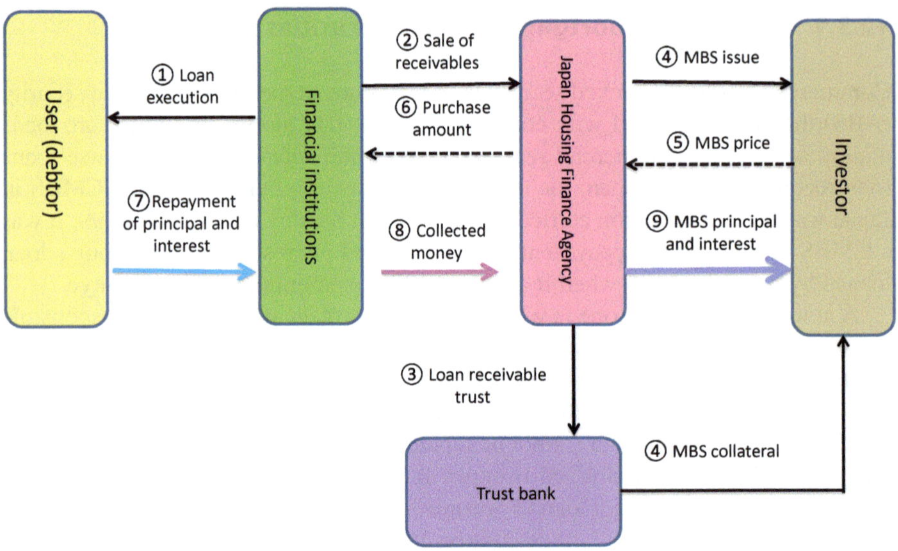

Fig. 12.2 Purchase type flat 35 (*Source:* Various materials)

In the purchase type, the Japan Housing Finance Agency purchases it from a private financial institution that provides flat 35 and securitizes it. The financial institution lends a mortgage to the user (debtor) and, at the same time, transfers the mortgage loan to the Japan Housing Finance Agency.

After that, the Japan Housing Finance Agency entrusts the mortgage loan receivables transferred from the financial institution to a trust bank or the like for the purpose of collateral, issues MBS with the entrusted mortgage loan receivable as collateral, and sells it to investors. The Japan Housing Finance Agency will pay the purchase price of the mortgage loan to the financial institution based on the issue price of MBS. In addition, the debtor repays the principal and interest of the mortgage to the financial institution, and the funds are used to repay the principal and interest to the investor who purchased the MBS through the Japan Housing Finance Agency.

On the other hand, guaranteed mortgage loans are entrusted to a trust bank or the like by a financial institution that handles them and securitizes them. The financial institution has a housing loan insurance (for guarantee type) of the Japan Housing Finance Agency as a guarantee in case the debtor cannot repay the mortgage. When the Japan Housing Finance Agency pays insurance money to a financial institution, the Agency acquires a mortgage loan claim against the debtor owned by the financial institution.

Fig. 12.3 shows the guaranteed mechanism of the flat 35.

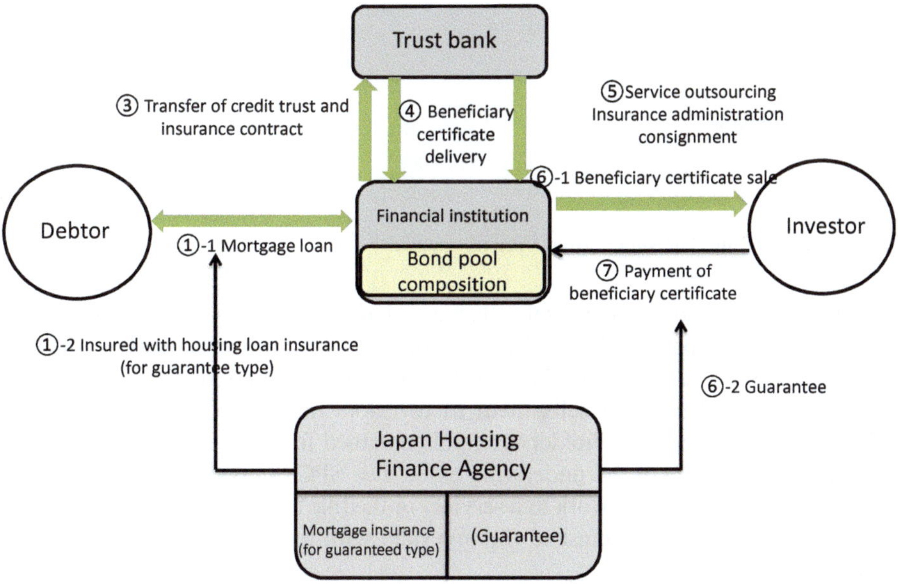

Fig. 12.3 Guaranteed type flat 35 (*Source:* Various materials)

12.3.3 Collateralized Debt Obligation

The collateralized debt obligation (CDO) is also called debt-backed security, and is the case where the underlying assets of ABS are large monetary claims such as loans to the government and companies and public and corporate bonds. In particular, assets that consist only of public and corporate bonds are called collateralized bond obligations (CBOs), and assets that consist only of loan receivables are called collateralized loan obligations (CLOs). Since CDOs are collateralized by public and corporate bonds and monetary claims that have a maturity date, the issued securities also have a maturity date.

The mechanism for a CDO is shown in Fig. 12.4.

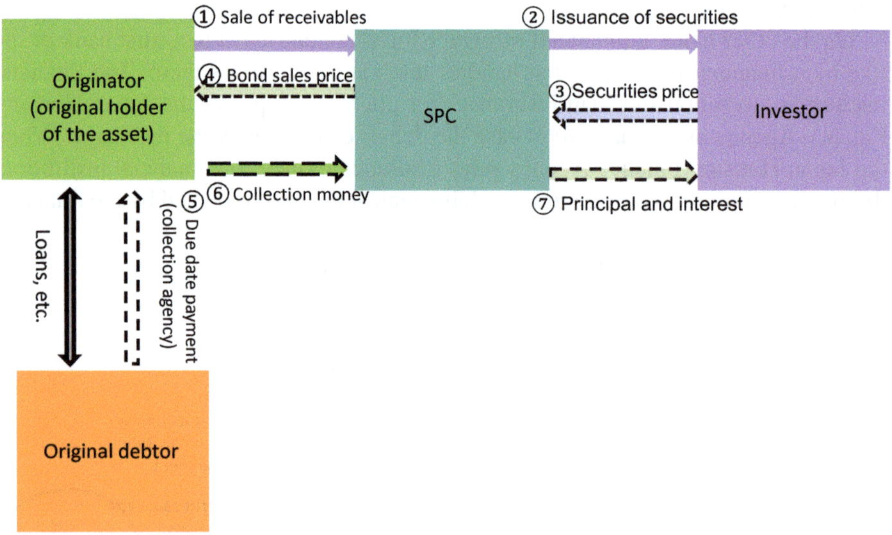

Fig. 12.4 CDO mechanism (*Source:* Various materials)

The original holder of the asset sells the underlying asset (loan assets, public and corporate bonds, and so on) to a SPC established by a securities company or the like. The SPC issues securities backed by the underlying assets and the cash flows generated from them, and sells them to investors through securities companies. The SPC pays the original holder the funds obtained from the sale of the securities as the purchase price of the underlying asset. The SPC holds the underlying assets and entrusts the collection work to a servicer or the like to collect the funds. The SPC pays the principal and interest to the investors with the funds recovered from the underlying assets.

The effects of securitization of receivables from the standpoint of the original holder of the asset are as follows. First, it will be possible to diversify financing methods. Secondly, off-balancing can be achieved. Third, interest-bearing debt can be repaid with the funds raised by securitization to improve the soundness of the financial structure. Fourth, the credit risk of the accounts receivable held can be transferred to investors. Since the risk of receivables is sold to the SPC, it is isolated from the risk of bankruptcy of accounts receivable.

Loans, corporate bonds, ABS, REITs, credit derivative swaps (CDS), and so on are included in this CDO. Due to the subprime loan crisis that started in the United States in 2007, many mortgage loans went bankrupt. As a result, debt-backed securities that were managed as high-rated securities were also damaged, many investors suffered huge losses, and risks such as uncertainty of the assets that were collateralized were exposed.

12.4 Securitization and the Financial Crisis

12.4.1 Subprime Loans

Subprime lending or subprime mortgage is an American high-interest mortgage loan aimed at low-income earners with low creditworthiness, and is a financial product handled by mortgage companies, not banks. Subprime mortgages are mortgages for those below the best customers (prime mortgages)—for low-credit consumers with a history of delinquency or bankruptcy. Those with low creditworthiness do not pass the normal mortgage examination, so the interest rate is accordingly set higher. However, during the first few years of borrowing, subprime is a low interest rate loan because you only have to pay a low interest rate and no repayment of the principal portion. A few years later, interest rates will more than double. The initial interest rate on the actual subprime loan at that time was a little over 8–9%, about 3% higher than the 6% prime loan and about 6% higher than the 3% LIBOR.

Subprime mortgages were a large market with 7.75 million loans at that time, but according to a survey by the Federal Reserve Bank of New York (January 2008), the loan rate was as high as 84.9%. This increased sharply from around 2000, accounting for about 20% of all mortgages from 2005 to 2006. On the other hand, if the house price rose, the collateral value of the purchased house would also increase. In the United States, against the backdrop of rising house prices that continued from 2001 to 2006, refinancing to general mortgages with low interest rates and increasing loans were sometimes used for consumption.

Such subprime mortgages are securitized in the form of a RMBS or MBS, which are then reinstated in the form of CDOs. They were highly rated by rating agencies and sold to investors around the world in combination with other financial products.

Fig. 12.5 shows the mechanism for MBS in the United States.

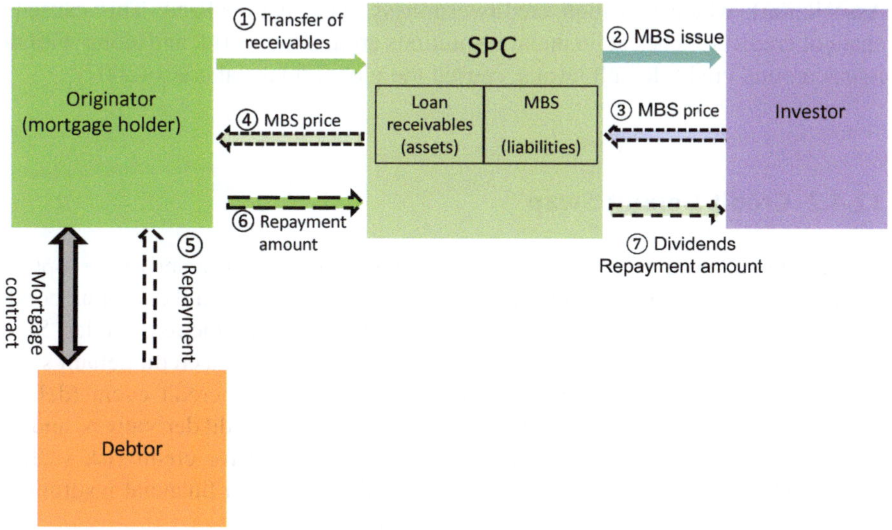

Fig. 12.5 Mortgage securitization in the United States (*Source:* Various materials)

As shown in Fig. 12.5, a financial institution (originator) lends a mortgage to a debtor and sells it to an SPC. The SPC issues MBS and the like with the mortgage loan as collateral. The financial institution (originator) receives the issue price of the MBS and sends it to the next loan. When the mortgage redemption begins, the financial institution (originator) collects the repayment money from the debtor and sends it to the SPC, and the SPC repays the investor. In this scheme, even if the financial institution (originator) goes bankrupt, the interests of the financial institution (originator) as a creditor do not extend to the transferred mortgage loan, which is an asset of the SPC. Therefore, MBS investors can receive cash flow regardless of the bankruptcy of the financial institution.

In the United States, about 60% of the USD 10 trillion mortgage balance at that time was securitized. Also, the mortgage balance was much larger than the banking balance. So, for example, if the banking sector had only USD 5 trillion in deposits and the bank took out a USD 10 trillion mortgage, the difference would have to be securitized.

Under these circumstances, the mortgage delinquency rate began to rise around the summer of 2007, when house prices were said to have fallen for the first time since the Great Depression. As a result, even the credit guarantee of financial products incorporating claims related to subprime mortgages was lost, and the securitized products were sold off in the market. In addition, when the interest rate paid for subprime loans after the low interest rate deferment period exceeded 16%, it became difficult to pay interest rates, and repayment delinquency began to increase sharply.

The mortgage lenders went bankrupt due to the surge in loan delinquency, and the banks that funded the mortgage lenders suffered significant losses. In late 2008, the bankruptcy of Lehman Brothers Holdings Inc., headquartered in New York, caused the Lehman shock. Then, AIG (American International Group), FHLMC (Federal Home Loan Mortgage Corporation), and Fannie Mae (Federal National Mortgage Association), which had high creditworthiness, were nationalized. This caused a chain of credit crunches at financial institutions around the world, and along with the issues around credit default swaps, caused the global financial crisis (2007).

12.4.2 Credit Default Swap

A credit default swap (CDS) is a guarantee transaction, but it is a derivative (option) that buys and sells (transfers) the credit risk of loan receivables and corporate bonds, and it is possible to transfer only the credit risk while holding the receivables. Since this option is often traded by the swap method, it is also called a credit default swap, but it is an option that payment is made in the event of a credit event (default, bankruptcy, and so on). CDS is a representative product of credit derivatives, and is a derivative (financial derivative product) contract prepared for credit risk such as default. This is mainly done in bilateral transactions between financial institutions, similar to credit insurance, and is also called protection.

In exchange for regular monetary payments, CDS purchases credit risk protection for a certain principal amount (notional principal) of a particular country or company's debt, called a "reference entity". The buyer of this CDS transfers credit risk to the seller of the CDS.

A financial institution that wants to avoid credit risk becomes a protection buyer and pays a fixed guarantee fee to the protection seller for a certain period of time. In the event of a credit event over a period of time, the buyer of protection will get a guarantee of repayment of the loan bond. The payment methods include cash payment and physical payment. In cash settlement, the loss amount is paid in cash. In physical settlement, the buyer of protection transfers the receivable to the seller, and the seller pays the cash of the total notional amount. Among these, physical settlement is the mainstream.

If no credit event occurs during a period of time, the protection seller will not pay the buyer, and the protection buyer will only pay a fixed guarantee fee to the seller to terminate the contract.

Fig. 12.6 shows the mechanism for a CDS transaction (in-kind settlement).

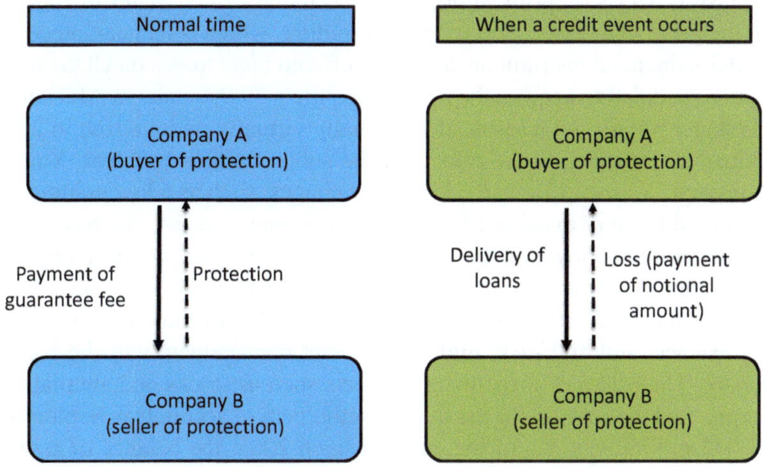

Fig. 12.6 CDS trading mechanism (in-kind settlement) (*Source:* Various materials)

CDS is a contract in which the seller of the guarantee receives the guarantee fee and promises to pay a fixed amount in case the reference company goes bankrupt, and the buyer of the guarantee pays the guarantee fee and receives a fixed amount in case the reference company goes bankrupt. Since this CDS allows transactions between entities that do not have corporate bonds of the reference company, it is possible to place a bet by setting a company with a high possibility of bankruptcy as the reference company.

12.4.3 CDS and Subprimes

AIG is a global insurance and financial services group based in New York. As a leader in the global insurance and financial services industry, the AIG Group has expanded its business to more than 130 countries and territories. AIGFP (AIG Financial Products), a subsidiary of AIG, provided guarantee services similar to those of monoline insurers, which specialize in guarantee insurance services. The guarantee was that instead of the financial institution paying a guarantee fee to AIG (AIGFP), AIG promised to pay the principal if the mortgage could not be redeemed.

The market size of CDS, which was USD 100 billion in 2000, reached about USD 62 trillion at the end of 2007. At that time, AIG's CDS guarantee balance had reached USD 440 billion. According to the New York Times, 17.5% of AIG's overall profits in 2005 came from CDS guarantee fees. However, the collapse of the housing bubble caused mortgages to be overdue all at once, and securitized mortgage products went into default one after another. As a result, claims for guarantees that exceeded AIG's ability to pay occurred at once, and the payment of CDS, which reached USD 14 billion, was stalled.

As a result, AIG's subprime mortgage crisis in the United States in 2007 brought to light the great risks associated with CDS trading, which is its guaranteed product. Then, AIG's financial instruments division suffered huge losses on CDS, and the US government decided to acquire the right to acquire a 79.9% stake in AIG and finance up to USD 85 billion. As a result, it was finally virtually nationalized in 2008.

In Japan as well, due to the effects of the subprime loan problem, Yamato Life went bankrupt. Yamato Life had a lot of advantages, such as a low assumed interest rate compared to other existing life insurance companies due to the past bankruptcy process that forcibly lowered the an assumed interest rate of the company's life insurance contract. However, dangerous asset management was carried out, and foreign securities and other ratios accounted for 42.2% of the company's securities holding balance, and high-risk, high-return asset management was the cause of the bankruptcy. The prices of investment products such as stocks and alternative assets fell sharply, and the net loss for the interim settlement of accounts in September 2008 was 11,043 million yen. As of the end of March 2008, the balance of assets under management was approximately 280 billion yen, of which alternative investment accounted for approximately 30%. The specific content of the alternative investment were real estate-related investment such as structured bonds, hedge fund investments, CLOs, and REITs.

12.5 Insurance-Linked Securities

12.5.1 The Emergence of Insurance-Linked Securities

Insurance-linked securities (ILS) is a general term for securitized products of insured risks that transfer insured risks to investors. ILS include CAT bonds, industry loss warranties (ILW), sidecar, collateralized reinsurance, and so on, depending on the type of transaction.

The different types of insurance link securities are shown in Fig. 12.7.

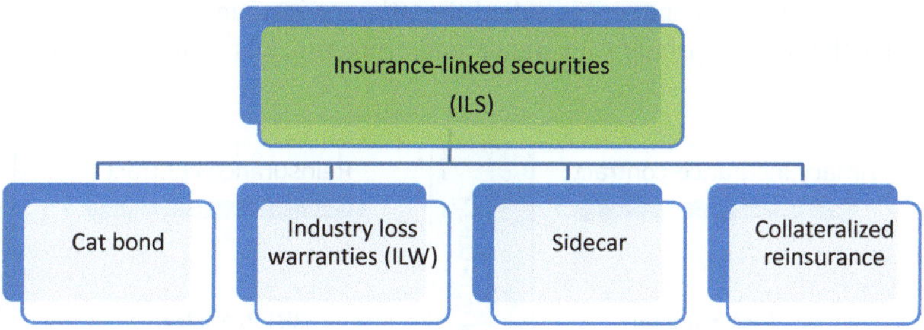

Fig. 12.7 Types of insurance-linked securities (*Source:* Various materials)

Insurance companies may face a shortage of underwriting capacity when underwriting an abnormal disaster where the law of large numbers is difficult to work, and it is necessary to increase the capital to reinforce the underwriting capacity. Insurers have also used reinsurance to take risks that exceed their underwriting capacity. In recent years, insurers have been able to use ILS in addition to these capital increases and reinsurances as a means of supplementing their underwriting capacity.

ILS was developed in the United States in 1992 as a means of transferring insurance risk to the capital markets due to the lack of underwriting capacity of insurance companies when Hurricane Andrew occurred.

On the other hand, the risk diversification of insurance companies is traditionally done by reinsurance. For example, if a non-life insurance company underwrites a huge risk insurance contract such as an oil refinery, the amount of the insurance money paid may exceed the solvency in the event of an insurance accident. Non-life insurance companies reinsure some or all of the risks they assume to reinsurers, and so on, so that even the payment of such a large amount of insurance money does not have a significant impact on their financial condition. Risk diversification is carried out. With this reinsurance, the insurance industry has diversified risks within the insurance industry and effectively utilized the underwriting capacity of the entire insurance industry.

However, its underwriting capacity is limited by the total capital of the non-life insurance industry as a whole. Therefore, the underwriting capacity of the insurance industry is limited by its total equity capital, and the insurance industry faced a lack of underwriting capacity when the insurance company suffered great damage due to a catastrophe or financial crisis. In such a situation, the insurance market became hard and the insurance premium rate soared. To make up for the lack of underwriting capacity of insurance companies against this abnormal disaster, the capital market, which has more funds than the insurance market, has attracted attention as a risk transfer destination.

The reinsurance for risk diversification of this insurance company is called "reinsurance" because it is "insurance of insurance". This reinsurance against reinsurance is called retrocession. On the other hand, primary insurance may refer to an insurance contract that an insurance company concludes with an individual policyholder, but if a reinsurance contract is concluded for "a certain insurance contract", the "certain insurance contract" is called the primary insurance.

The mechanism of primary insurance and reinsurance is as follows (Fig. 12.8).

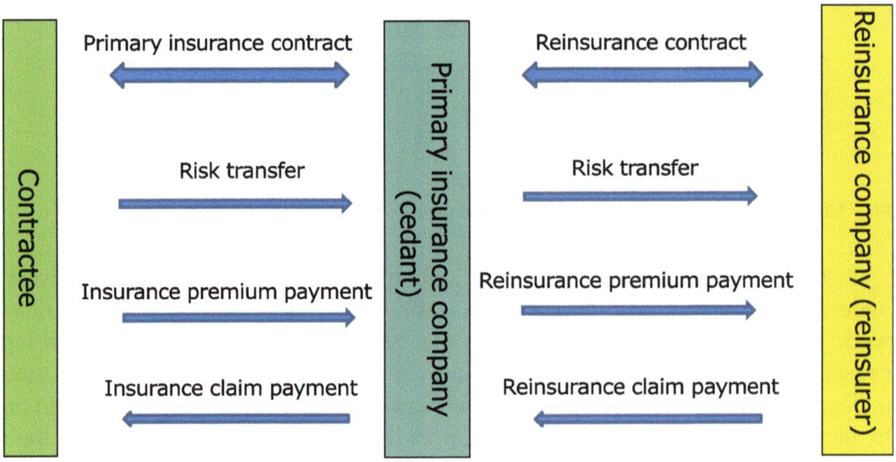

Fig. 12.8 Primary insurance and reinsurance (*Source:* Various materials)

This reinsurance is a type of non-life insurance and is provided by most non-life insurance companies, but there are also companies specializing in reinsurance. In Japan, the Toa Reinsurance Co Ltd. and the Japan Earthquake Reinsurance Company are reinsurance specialists. Life insurance reinsurance is permitted not only by non-life insurance companies but also by life insurance companies.

The reinsurance contract is a contract independent of the primary insurance, and the primary insurance company is responsible for paying the insurance money under the primary insurance contract regardless of the receipt of the reinsurance from the reinsurance company. In addition, the policyholder of the primary insurance has no right to the reinsurance company, not the party to the reinsurance policy, and cannot directly claim the insurance money.

This reinsurance diversifies risk within the insurance industry and contributes to the expansion and stabilization of the insurance market by stabilizing the earnings of the primary insurer and securing additional underwriting capacity. However, due to the reinsurance chain, the more reinsurers that are involved, the greater the credit risk of those insurers. There is the possibility that in the event of an insurance accident, the reinsurer may not be able to pay the reinsurance money, but the insolvency of one company in the reinsurance chain causes an insolvency chain.

An example of an insolvency chain is the LMX (London Market Excess of Loss) spiral, an excess of loss cover that occurred in the London reinsurance market in the 1980s. An excess reinsurance contract is a type of reinsurance contract, and when the amount of damage caused by an accident exceeds the amount determined by the reinsurance contract, the excess portion is compensated. London's reinsurance market syndicate underwriters repeatedly signed the reinsurance agreement and took on the risk of reinsurance. In this state, many syndicates collapsed due to a series of unprecedented catastrophes such as typhoons and earthquakes that occurred between 1987 and 1990.

However, ILS transactions are becoming established as a new risk transfer alternative to reinsurance, without the possibility of such insolvency chains. The spread of this ILS has forced the insurance industry to seek out new business models.

12.5.2 The Mechanism of Insurance-Linked Securities

ABS and MBS are all securitizations of assets, while ILS is the securitization of liabilities. This insurance-linked security raises funds from the capital market using the mechanism of "securitization", which is a financial method, but in an emergency the mechanism of "reduction of principal or interest" of the bond is activated. In particular, when certain conditions are met in the event of a catastrophe such as an earthquake, hurricane, or typhoon, the principal or interest of the bond is exempted, and the amount equivalent to the exemption is paid to the company like insurance money. Those that have such a mechanism are called "catastrophe bonds".

On the other hand, the National Association of Insurance Commissioners (NAIC) defines ILS as "securitized products that have a track record of being linked to the damage record of a particular insurance risk".[2] This insurance-linked security is often used by insurance companies in addition to or in place of reinsurance.

With insurance-linked securities, investors receive a premium (commission) as consideration for taking the risk of paying compensation to insurance companies, reinsurance companies, and so on. The risk of compensation payments undertaken by investors is the risk of exemption from redemption of part or all of the investment principal in the event of a risk such as a disaster. This is the mechanism by which the investment principal is paid to the insurance company or reinsurance company in the event of a disaster and is the source of insurance money for the insurance company or reinsurance company. The relationship between insurance-linked securities and the secondary market is shown in Fig. 12.9.

[2]NAIC, Capital Markets Special Report: Insurance Linked Securities: Recovering Slowly After the Crisis (February 2011).

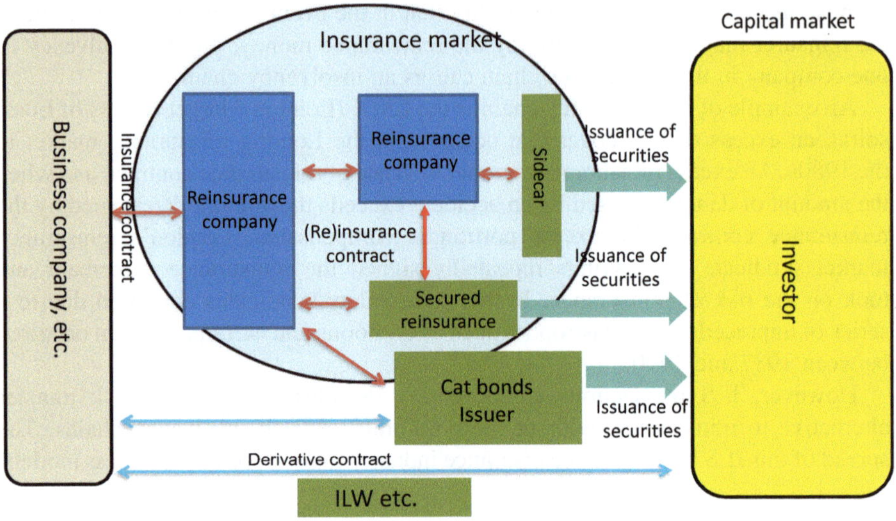

Fig. 12.9 Relationship between insurance-linked securities and secondary market (*Source:* Various materials)

It is said that the five major risks in the world are hurricanes and earthquakes in the United States, storms in Europe, and typhoons and earthquakes in Japan, and many CAT bonds target these five major risks. Most of the risks covered by insurance-linked securities are the risks of catastrophes represented by CAT bonds. However, ILS have emerged that cover risks related to mortality or longevity (increased mortality, risk of longevity, and so on) and medical billing.

This ILS dramatically expands the transfer destinations of insurance risks because insurance companies and the like are seeking transfer destinations of risks in the capital market. In addition, the ILS mechanism allows insurance companies to avoid the credit risk of insurance companies in reinsurance. In the case of reinsurance, when a huge risk occurs, the credit risk that the reinsurance money may not be paid due to the lack of solvency of the reinsurance company becomes a problem.

However, in ILS credit risk is not a problem because the funds are procured from investors from the beginning for SPCs. On the other hand, from the investor's point of view, ILS has the advantage of obtaining high yields. In addition, since natural disasters do not correlate with economic fluctuations, ILS has the characteristic of having risks and returns that are independent of economic trends. Therefore, investors can increase risk diversity and make diversified investments by adding ILS to their investment portfolio.

Traditional ILS investors have been insurers and reinsurers because of their esoteric nature and inherent risks. It is the insurance fund that has expanded the investment of general investors in this ILS. The first insurance fund was established in 1997 by Nephila Capital, a subsidiary of Willisk, a leading UK insurance broker. Since then, in addition to insurance companies, major asset management companies have also set up insurance-specialized funds.

12.5.3 Trigger

The payment terms (events) for compensation specified at the time of issuance of ILS are called "triggers". When this trigger occurs, the bond will default and some or all of the investment will be used to pay the sponsor. By reducing or exempting the redemption to the investor, the investor bears the risk of reducing or exempting the principal and interest.

Various types of trigger are laid out in Table 12.1.

Table 12.1 Types of trigger

Trigger		Content
Indemnity		Compensation will be based on the damage actually caused. Damage compensation method similar to insurance contract or reinsurance contract
Index	Modeled loss index	A method of estimating the amount of damage that will occur by inputting wind speed, rainfall, and so on into a predetermined individual model
	Industry loss index	Method based on industry-wide damage forecast
	Parametric index	A method based on observation indicators such as hurricane wind speed and earthquake magnitude, regardless of the amount of damage

Source: Created by excerpting from various materials

If part or all of the principal and interest of a bond is exempted in the event of a disaster, investors will suffer damage. In the past, the index type of trigger was the mainstream, but in recent years the actual loss compensation type has increased. In the actual loss compensation type trigger, payment is not made only by the occurrence of a specific event, such as an earthquake, but is paid when the amount of insurance money paid by the insurance company reaches a certain amount.

Index-type triggers include the modeled loss index, which calculates an index using an individual estimation model, and the industry loss index, which calculates an index based on the estimated amount of damage for the entire industry. In addition, there is a parametric index type that calculates an index based on observation indexes such as hurricane wind speed and earthquake magnitude.

In the financial markets, the difference between the spot price and the futures price is called "basis". When futures are sold to hedge the risk in kind, the risk that profit or loss fluctuates significantly due to this basis is called basis risk. If there is a basis risk, hedging will be inadequate. The term basis risk in the financial markets has been diverted to the insurance sector and is used to mean the difference between the actual amount of damage and compensation. In the actual loss compensation type trigger, the insurance company's insurance payment amount is the trigger, so the insurance company's basis risk does not occur.

However, from the investor's point of view, moral hazard has been pointed out as the actual loss compensation trigger. That is, in the event of a catastrophe, insurance companies tend to pay unreasonably large amounts of insurance money due to their reputation. Therefore, this trigger requires the objectivity of calculating the damage amount. In addition, it is difficult for investors to accurately grasp the details of the risks assumed by insurance companies, and it is pointed out that there is adverse selection to securitize those with poor quality of risk. Furthermore, from the standpoint of a CAT bond issuer, such as an insurance company, it takes time to determine the amount of damage for determining the actual loss compensation type trigger, so it takes time to receive payment.

Index-type triggers are said to be suitable for securitization because they are easy to standardize and have relatively low transaction costs. From an investor's point of view, index-type triggers are less likely to be adversely selected from moral hazard, which is set in favor of insurance companies, and are highly transparent.

12.6 Japan's Earthquake Insurance and ILS

Japan's fire insurance exempts earthquake risk and does not cover damage caused directly or indirectly by an earthquake/eruption or a tsunami caused by them. Therefore, to cover earthquake risk with insurance it is necessary to purchase earthquake insurance separately. Japan's earthquake insurance was established based on the Earthquake Insurance Law 1966, which was triggered by the 1964 Niigata earthquake, and means that the government will underwrite reinsurance. Earthquake insurance under this law covers residential buildings for households and personal property (excluding precious metals, jewelry, fine arts, and so on) up to a certain amount. However, buildings, fixtures, and machinery dedicated to factories and offices for companies were also excluded. This earthquake insurance for households is not aimed at rebuilding homes, to fund the reconstruction of houses, but at securing funds for rebuilding lives and contributing to the stability of the lives of disaster victims. To this end, Japanese earthquake insurance includes earthquake insurance for households that has government reinsurance within a certain amount, and earthquake insurance that exceeds the limit and does not have government reinsurance for companies.

The relationship between Japan's earthquake risk and ILS is shown in Fig. 12.10.

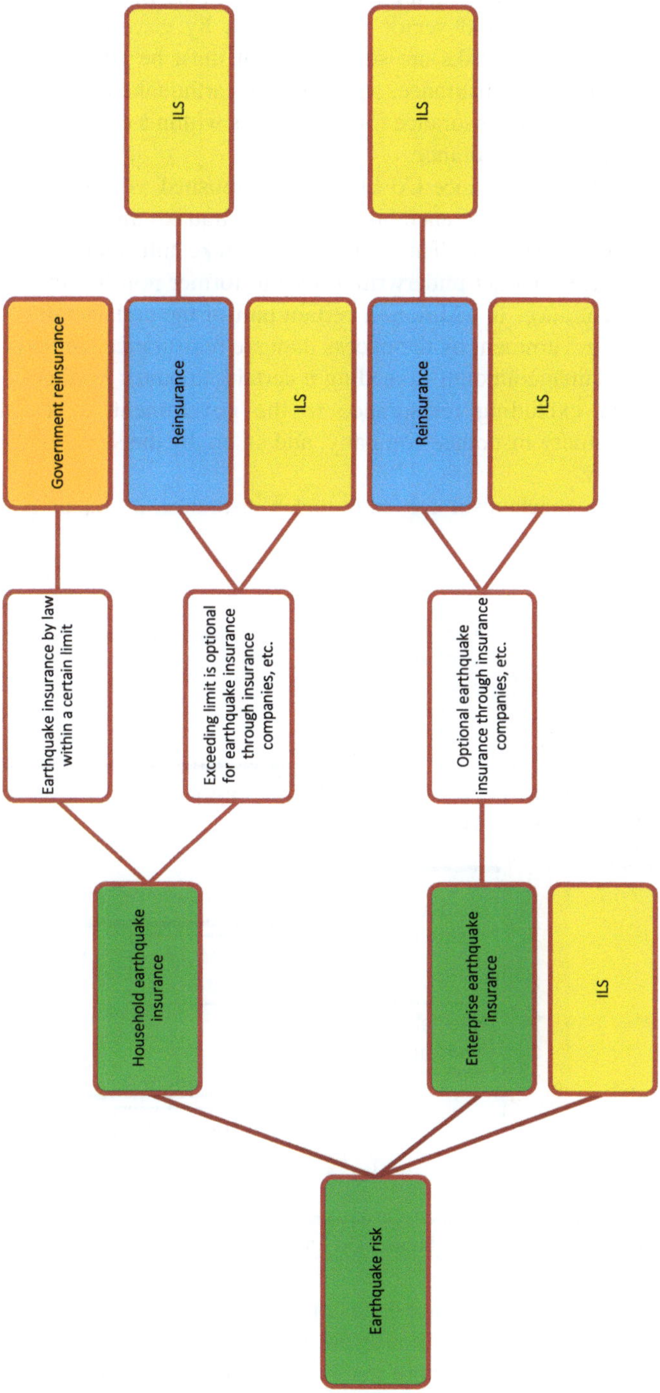

Fig. 12.10 Earthquake risk in Japan and ILS (*Source:* Created by the author)

As shown in Fig. 12.10, among the earthquake risks, the earthquake risk within a certain limit in the household sector is dealt with by government reinsurance. However, other earthquake risks are situations that must be addressed by private earthquake insurance and reinsurance, and ILS. The earthquake insurance described in this chapter is earthquake insurance for households within a certain limit, which is covered by government reinsurance.

Japan Earthquake Reinsurance Co Ltd. was established as a non-life insurance company engaged in the reinsurance business of earthquake insurance stipulated in the Earthquake Insurance Law. The company will take full responsibility for the earthquake insurance contract underwritten by the former non-life insurance company through reinsurance. In addition, a certain part of the underwriting liability is reinsurance to the government by the excess damage reinsurance method (a method of reinsuring the damage amount exceeding a certain amount). Furthermore, of the insurance liability excluding reinsurance to the government, a certain part is reinsured to the primary insurance company, and so on, by the same excess damage reinsurance method.

The reinsurance mechanism for earthquake insurance in Japan is shown in Fig. 12.11.

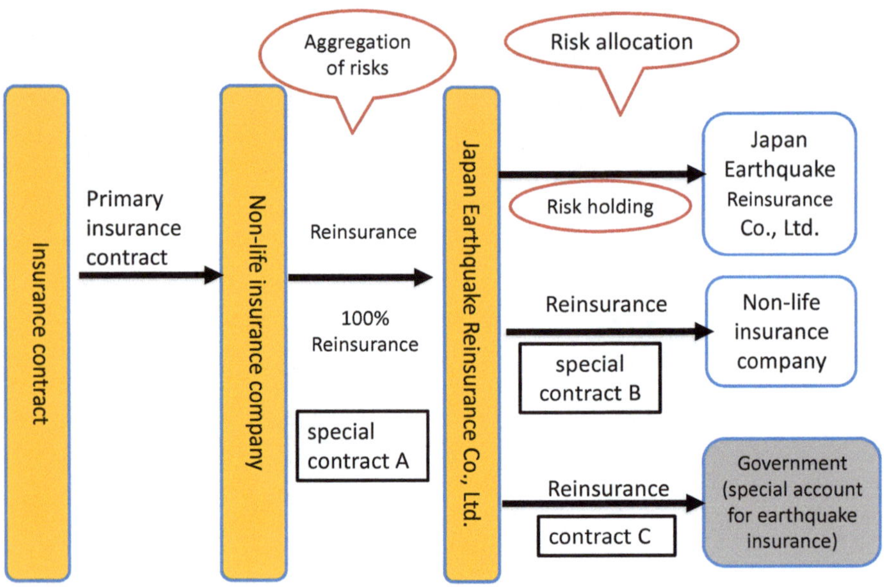

Fig. 12.11 Japan's earthquake insurance reinsurance mechanism (*Source:* Created by referring to the materials of Japan Earthquake Reinsurance Co Ltd.)

This earthquake insurance cannot be taken out independently, but is attached as a special contract to fire insurance (house fire insurance, general housing insurance, ordinary fire insurance, general store insurance, and so on). This is to reduce the contract cost of the insurance company and reduce the insurance premium by that amount. If you do not wish to attach earthquake insurance, you are required stamp the earthquake insurance confirmation column of the fire insurance contract application form to confirm your intention not to take out earthquake insurance. However, if you wish to attach earthquake insurance, you should not seal it.

The amount of earthquake insurance is set within the range of 30–50% of the amount of fire insurance that comes with earthquake insurance, but it is limited to 50 million yen for buildings and ten million yen for household goods. This earthquake insurance is reinsured by the government to ensure payment of insurance in the event of a major earthquake. In addition, in the event of a large earthquake, the amount of damage will be huge and there is a possibility that the reserve fund for earthquake insurance will be insufficient, so the total amount of insurance money paid by the government and non-life insurance companies due to one earthquake and so on is limited. This total payment limit is set based on the statistical results of insurance payments for earthquake disasters of the Great Kanto Earthquake scale, which is the largest earthquake that has occurred in the past. That earthquake was a M7.9 earthquake that occurred on 1 September 1923, and the damage was aggravated by the fire that occurred after the earthquake.

If the insurance claims exceed this total payment limit, the earthquake insurance claims paid in each contract will be reduced by the ratio of the total insurance claims payment limit to the total insurance claims to be paid. Here, one earthquake collectively refers to two or more earthquakes that occurred within 72 hours, but if the affected areas do not overlap, it is considered as a separate earthquake, and the reduction provision applies to each.

Due to the revision of the Earthquake Insurance Law Enforcement Ordinance, the damage classification will be revised for earthquake insurance contracts whose insurance start date is 1 January 2017 or later. In other words, the "half loss" in the previous three categories (total loss, half loss, partial loss) was divided into two, and the damage categories became four categories (total loss, large half loss, small half loss, partial loss). In this way, the damage classification is divided into four according to the degree, and the certification criteria described later are simplified. The reason is that the damage caused by the earthquake is considered to occur in large quantities, so the efficiency of the payment operation is improved and the payment is dealt with promptly. The market value here is the value obtained by making a deduction corresponding to the number of years of use from the new construction price.

Table 12.2 shows the insurance claims for each degree of damage in earthquake insurance.

Table 12.2 Insurance claims by degree of damage in earthquake insurance

Degree of damage	Insurance payment amount
Total loss	100% of insurance amount (market value is the limit)
Large half loss	60% of insurance amount (up to 60% of market value)
Small half loss	30% of insurance amount (up to 30% of market value)
Partial loss	5% of insurance amount (up to 5% of market value)

Source: Ordinance for Enforcement of Law Concerning Earthquake Insurance

Table 12.3 shows the damage certification criteria for earthquake insurance.

Table 12.3 Damage certification criteria for earthquake insurance

Degree of damage	Building		Household goods
	Damage amount of main structural parts	Floor area burned down or washed away (partial loss is flooding on the floor, and so on)	Damage to household goods
Total loss	50% or more of the market value of the building	70% or more of the total floor area of the building	80% or more of the market value of household goods
Large half loss	40% or more and less than 50% of the market value of the building	50% or more and less than 70% of the total floor area of the building	60% or more and less than 80% of the market value of household goods
Small half loss	20% or more and less than 40% of the market value of the building	20% or more and less than 50% of the total floor area of the building	30% or more and less than 60% of the market value of household goods
Partial loss	3% or more and less than 20% of the market value of the building	When the building is damaged by flooding on the floor or flooding more than 45 cm from the ground surface, and it does not result in total loss, majority loss or minor loss	10% or more and less than 30% of the market value of household goods

Source: Earthquake insurance damage certification criteria

Table 12.4 shows "total loss", "large half loss", "small half loss", and "partial loss" in the case of damage caused by the tsunami and damage caused by ground liquefaction.

Table 12.4 Criteria for certifying damage caused by tsunami and damage caused by ground liquefaction in earthquake insurance

Degree of damage	Damage caused by tsunami		Damage caused by ground liquefaction caused by "earthquakes", and so on	
			Inclined	Maximum subsidence
Total loss	Other than the following	When flooded on the floor of 180 cm or more or when flooded 225 cm or more from the ground surface	When exceeding 1.7/100 (about 1°)	If it exceeds 30 cm
	One-story building	When flooded on the floor of 100 cm or more or when flooded 145 cm or more from the ground surface		

(continued)

Table 12.4 (continued)

Degree of damage	Damage caused by tsunami		Damage caused by ground liquefaction caused by "earthquakes", and so on: Inclined	Damage caused by ground liquefaction caused by "earthquakes", and so on: Maximum subsidence
Large half loss	Other than the following	When flooded on the floor of 115 cm or more and less than 180 cm, or when flooded 160 cm or more and less than 225 cm from the ground surface	When it exceeds 1.4/100 (about 0.8°) and is 1.7/100 (about 1°) or less	If it exceeds 20 cm and is 30 cm or less
	One-story building	When flooded on the floor of 75 cm or more and less than 100 cm, or when flooded 80 cm or more and less than 145 cm from the ground surface		
Small half loss	Other than the following	When flooded on the floor less than 115 cm or when flooded more than 45 cm and less than 160 cm from the ground surface	When it exceeds 0.9/100 (about 0.5°) and is 1.4/100 (about 0.8°) or less	If it exceeds 15 cm and is 20 cm or less
	One-story building	When flooded on the floor less than 75 cm or when flooded more than 45 cm and less than 80 cm from the ground surface		
Partial loss	When flooding above the height of the foundation does not result in total loss, majority loss or minor loss		When it exceeds 0.4/100 (about 0.2°) and is 0.9/100 (about 0.5°) or less	If it exceeds 10 cm and is 15 cm or less

Source: Earthquake insurance damage certification criteria

As shown in Table 12.4, if the inclination of the building exceeds 1° or the maximum amount of subsidence exceeds 30 cm, it is recognized as a total loss. Table 12.5 shows the magnitude and level of magnitude of several earthquakes since 1900.

Table 12.5 Large-scale earthquakes that occurred after 1900

Rank	Date of occurrence	Earthquake (source)	Magnitude
1	23 May 1960	Chile	9.5
2	28 March 1964	Gulf of Alaska	9.2
3	26 December 2004	Off the western coast of northern Sumatra, Indonesia	9.1
4	11 March 2011	Off Sanriku, Japan (the 2011 Tohoku-Pacific Ocean earthquake)	9.0
	5 November 1952	Kamchatka Peninsula	9.0

(continued)

Table 12.5 (continued)

Rank	Date of occurrence	Earthquake (source)	Magnitude
6	27 February 2010	Off Mauri, Chile	8.8
	1 February 1906	off the coast of Ecuador	8.8
8	4 February 1965	Aleutian Islands, Alaska	8.7
9	29 March 2005	Northern Sumatra, Indonesia	8.6
	15 August 1950	Assam, Tibet	8.6
	9 March 1957	Aleutian Islands, Alaska	8.6

Source: Japan Meteorological Agency

As shown in Table 12.5, the Tohoku-Pacific Ocean earthquake that caused the Great East Japan earthquake in 2011 ranked fourth."Seismic intensity" represents the strength of shaking caused by an earthquake at a certain location, and magnitude (M) represents the magnitude of the earthquake itself. The relationship between the two may be explained by the relationship between the brightness of a light bulb and the brightness of the surroundings, and if the value representing the brightness of the light bulb is magnitude, the brightness of a place away from the light bulb corresponds to the seismic intensity. In other words, just as a light bulb is bright but dark at a distance, seismic intensity is small at a distance from the epicenter even if the magnitude is large. By contrast, even in an earthquake with a small magnitude, if the distance from the epicenter is small, the ground will sway more and the seismic intensity will increase. In addition, even in an earthquake with a large magnitude, if the distance from the epicenter is great, the shaking of the ground will be small, so the seismic intensity will be small. Fig. 12.12 shows the relationship between magnitude and seismic intensity.

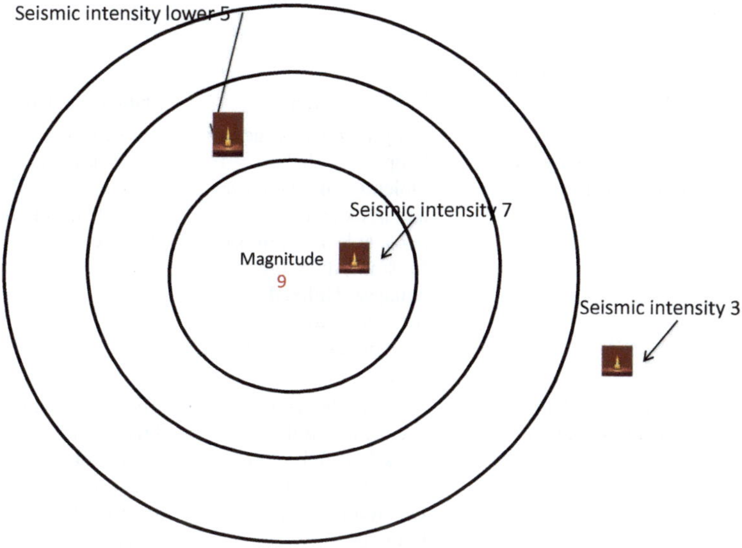

Fig. 12.12 Relationship between magnitude and seismic intensity (*Source:* Various materials)

Seismic intensity is expressed in ten stages, as shown in Table 12.6.

Table 12.6 Seismic intensity and shaking strength

Seismic intensity class	Human experience/ behavior	Indoor situation	Outdoor situation
0	People do not feel shaking, but they are recorded on the seismograph	–	–
1	Some people who are quiet indoors feel a slight tremor	–	–
2	Most people who are quiet indoors feel shaking. Some sleeping people wake up	Hanging objects such as lamps shake slightly	–
3	Most people indoors feel shaking. Some people who are walking feel shaking. Most sleeping people wake up	Tableware on the shelves may make noise	Overhead electric cables shake a little
4	Most people are surprised. Most people walking feel shaking. Most sleeping people wake up	Hanging objects such as lamps shake greatly, and tableware on the shelves make noise. Unstable figurines may fall over	Overhead electric cables shake greatly. Someone driving a car may notice the shaking

(continued)

Table 12.6 (continued)

Seismic intensity class	Human experience/ behavior	Indoor situation	Outdoor situation
5 weak	Most people are frightened and want to grab something	Hanging objects such as lamps may shake violently, and tableware and books on the bookshelf may fall off. Most unstable figurines collapse. Unfixed furniture may move and unstable ones may fall over	In rare cases, the window glass may break and fall. You may see utility poles sway. Roads may be damaged
5 strong	Most people find it difficult to walk unless they hold on to something	Much of the tableware and books on the bookshelf fall off. The TV may fall off the table. Unfixed furniture may fall over	The window glass may break and fall. Unreinforced block walls may collapse. Inadequately installed vending machines may fall over. Some cars stop because it becomes difficult to drive
6 weak	It becomes difficult to stand	Most of the loose furniture will move and some will fall over. Doors may not open	Wall tiles and windowpanes may break or fall
6 strong	You cannot stand and you cannot move. You can be shaken, unable to move, and even blown away	Most of the unfixed furniture moves and much falls over	Many buildings have damaged wall tiles and windowpanes and fall. Most of the unreinforced block walls collapse
7		Most non-fixed furniture may move, fall over, and even fly through the air	More buildings will have their wall tiles and windowpanes damaged and fall. Some of the reinforced block walls are also damaged

Source: Japan Meteorological Agency.

Thus, seismic intensities 5 and 6 have strong and weak, respectively.

The 1995 Hyogo-ken Nanbu earthquake was an earthquake that occurred at 5:46 a.m. on 17 January 1995, and caused great damage mainly in the southern part of Hyogo prefecture. This earthquake is the first major earthquake in Japan with an epicenter directly under a large city, and the first earthquake with a seismic intensity of 7 (magnitude 7.2) recorded since the introduction of seismic intensity 7 into the Japan Meteorological Agency seismic intensity class.

Fig. 12.13 shows the damage caused by the Hyogo-ken Nanbu earthquake.

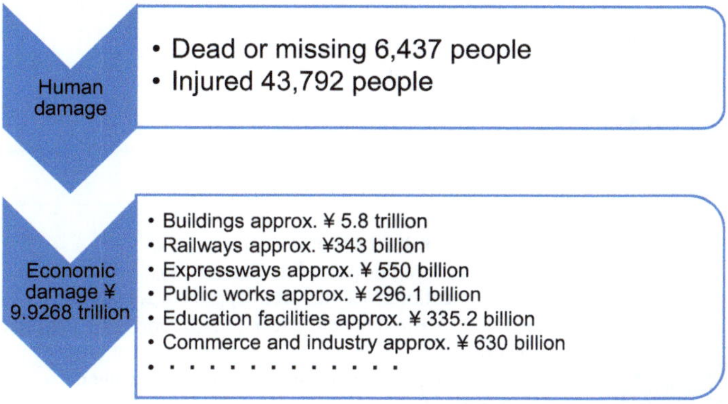

Fig. 12.13 Damage caused by the 1995 Southern Hyogo Prefecture earthquake (*Source:* General Insurance Association of Japan)

Table 12.7 shows the payment of insurance and mutual aid due to the Hyogo-ken Nanbu earthquake.

Table 12.7 Payment of insurance and mutual aid related to the 1995 Hyogo-ken Nanbu earthquake

Type	Amount
Household earthquake insurance	78.3 billion yen
JA Mutual Insurance	118.8 billion yen
Zenrosai	18.5 billion yen

Source: General Insurance Association of Japan, JA Mutual Aid, Zenrosai

Furthermore, the Great East Japan earthquake was caused by the 2011 earthquake off the Pacific coast (with the largest magnitude in Japan's observation history of 9.0), the tsunami caused by it, and the aftershocks that occurred after that.

As mentioned above, the Great East Japan earthquake was the fourth largest earthquake in world history, and caused enormous human and property damage. Due to this earthquake, the TEPCO Fukushima Daiichi Nuclear Power Station lost all power due to a power outage, resulting in a serious nuclear accident in which the reactor could not be cooled and a large amount of radioactive material was released.

The damage caused by the Great East Japan earthquake is shown in Fig. 12.14.

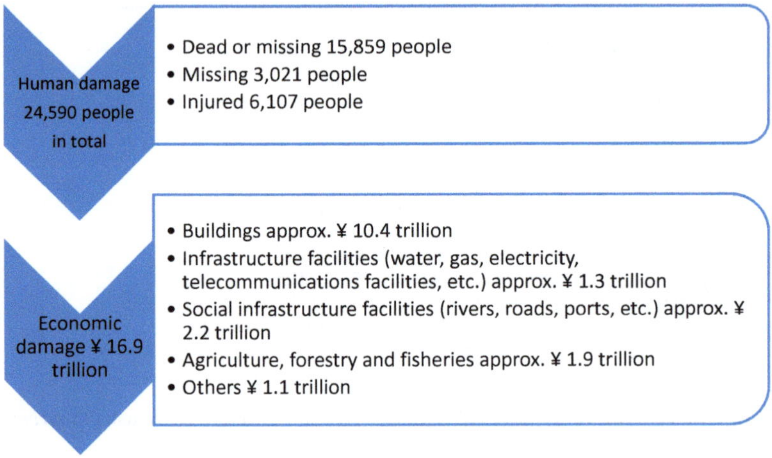

Fig. 12.14 Damage from the Great East Japan earthquake of 2011 (*Source:* Cabinet Office, among others (excluding damage caused by the nuclear accident))

Table 12.8 shows the payment of insurance and mutual aid due to the Great East Japan earthquake.

Table 12.8 Payment of insurance and mutual aid related to the Great East Japan earthquake

Type		Amount
Non-life insurance	Household earthquake insurance	1,234.6 billion yen
	Non-life insurance other than household earthquake insurance (after reinsurance collection)	600 billion yen (200 billion yen)
Mutual aid	Building system	1,053.7 billion yen
	Life system	64.5 billion yen
Life insurance	Death insurance	159.9 billion yen

Source: The Life Insurance Association of Japan, General Insurance Association of Japan, General Insurance Association of Japan, Financial Services Agency

Earthquake victims often have double mortgage problems. When borrowing a mortgage from a bank, the debtor is required to take out fire insurance in order to maintain the mortgage value of the house set by the mortgage, but not to take out earthquake insurance. Therefore, if a house is damaged by an earthquake, it cannot be covered by fire insurance, which is exempt from earthquake risk, and the mortgage remains. Victims will have to take out a loan again from a bank or the like in order to rebuild their home while holding a mortgage, and will be in a state of a double loan with two mortgages, and will suffer from higher repayment. Even if you take out earthquake insurance, the insurance amount, which is the limit of compensation, is 30–50% of the market value of the building, so you may not be able to pay off your mortgage with the insurance money. However, earthquake insurance is effective to a certain extent in preventing the occurrence of double mortgages.

On the other hand, insurance companies and the like take on disaster risks (catastrophe risks) such as earthquakes and hurricanes that are not covered by the government's earthquake insurance reinsurance from policyholders. Insurance companies issue CAT bonds, a type of ILS, to transfer this disaster risk to investors.

Earthquake risk and ILS in Japan are shown in Fig. 12.15.

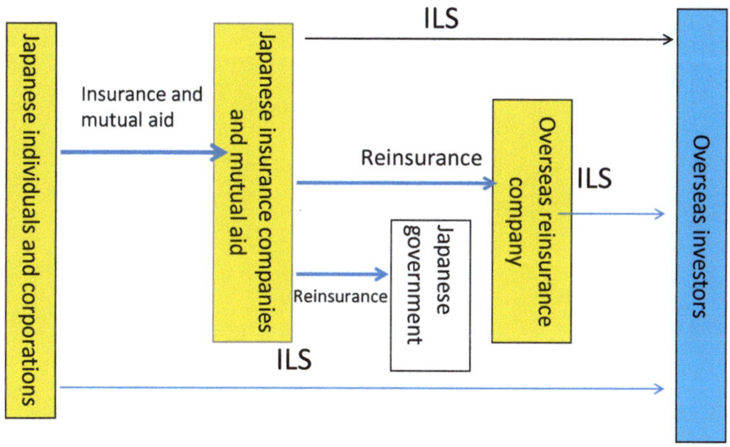

Fig. 12.15 Japan earthquake risk and ILS route (*Source:* Various materials)

The mechanism is that a risk-hedging policyholder or insurance company issues securities as an ILS issuer and is exempt from paying principal and interest to investors when a pre-specified risk arises. The interest rate of the bond is set higher than that of a general bond in proportion to the risk of the investor's exemption from principal and interest. Bonds issued in this way will be redeemed in full in principal if no particular risk arises by maturity. However, in the event of certain risks, all or part of the principal will be paid to sponsors such as insurance companies like reinsurance claims, and the amount of reimbursement to investors will be partially or wholly reduced.

Discussion Questions

1. Explain, with examples, securitization and the financial crisis.
2. Explain, with examples, the usefulness and issues of ILS.
3. Explain the mechanism of principal insurance and reinsurance. Also, discuss the roles and limitations of primary insurance and reinsurance in risk management.
4. Explain, with examples, Japan's earthquake risk and ILS. Also, find out if there are such cases in your country. If there are no such cases, discuss the possibility of disaster risk securitization.

Insurance-Linked Security Types 13

The ILS system was created by applying the asset securitization system to insurance risk. This chapter outlines the types of ILS and how they work.

13.1 CAT Bonds

13.1.1 CAT Bond Mechanism

The CAT bond (catastrophe bond) is a type of ILS. With a CAT bond, insurance companies or business companies transfer the risk of natural catastrophes to investors in financial markets. The world's five largest risks in the non-life insurance industry, in descending order of magnitude, have been said to be American hurricanes, American earthquakes, European windstorms, Japanese typhoons, and Japanese earthquakes. CAT bonds are often issued triggered by any or a combination of these five major risks. They have been issued by many national and international insurance companies since Hannover Re issued the first CAT bond in 1994. In April 1999, Oriental Land Co Ltd., which operates Tokyo Disneyland, issued the world's first "earthquake bond" of about 20 billion yen.

The mechanism of the CAT bond is as follows. An insurance company that has assumed the risk of a major disaster or a business company that has the risk of a major disaster will establish a special purpose insurance company (SPI) as a sponsor. They will then pay the premium to the SPI and transfer the risk to the SPI. This SPI issues CAT bonds using insurance premiums received from sponsors as a source of funds and sells the CAT bonds (bonds) to investors.

The mechanism of the CAT bond is shown in Fig. 13.1.

H. Lee, *Risk Management*, Springer Texts in Business and Economics,
https://doi.org/10.1007/978-981-16-3468-0_13

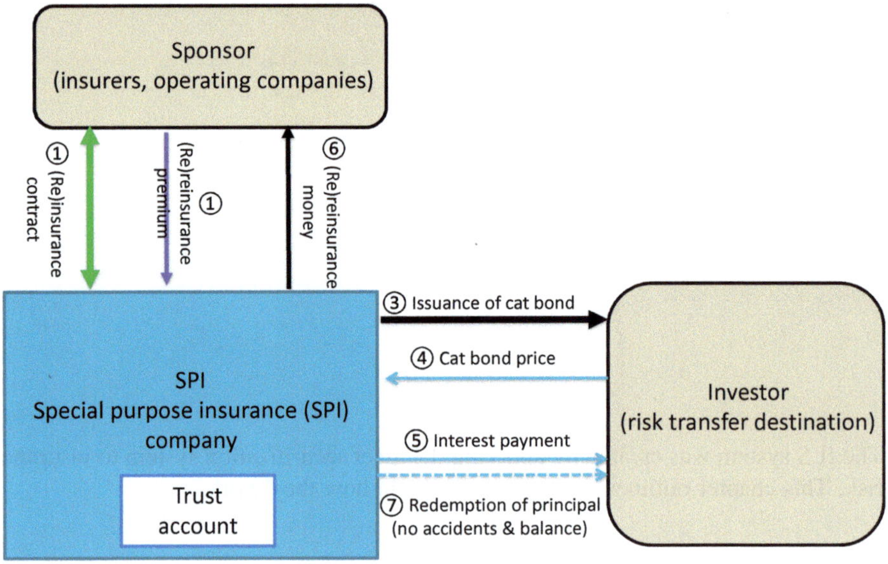

Fig. 13.1 CAT bond mechanism (*Source:* Various materials)

The issuance price of CAT bonds from investors is managed as a highly secure asset in the trust account of the SPI. With this asset management income and (re) premiums from sponsors as financial resources, interest on CAT bonds is paid to investors on a regular basis. In addition, the funds in this trust account will be the source of insurance money paid to the sponsor in the event of a trigger event. If a trigger event occurs by the redemption period, which is generally set to 2–5 years, the proceeds from investors through the sale of CAT bonds will be used to pay insurance money to sponsors. In that case, the repayment of principal and interest to the investor will be reduced or exempted, but the principal will be returned to the investor if the period has passed without any accident.

The investment yield of funds in the trust account is generally LIBOR, and for interest payments an additional interest rate (premium) of about 2% per year is added to LIBOR. This premium is an expense from the sponsor's point of view and is also an insurance premium for risk transfer. The sponsor pays about 2% of the annual cost and, in the event of a catastrophe, the sponsor can receive all or part of the predetermined issuance amount from SPI. On the other hand, the investor receives the total amount of the LIBOR interest rate and the premium as investment income.

Non-life insurance companies issue CAT bonds to pass on the risk of insurance claims due to the catastrophe of their insurance to investors. For example, a non-life insurance company issues a CAT bond with a reinsurance character in preparation for the payment of earthquake insurance claims it has underwritten. Then, in the event of an earthquake, the principal redemption amount of the CAT bond will be reduced, and the non-life insurance company will receive it and use it as a source of funds for the payment of earthquake insurance.

13.1.2 CAT Bond Effects

The effects of CAT bonds from the issuer's point of view are as follows.

13.1.2.1 Long-Term Cover

Earthquake insurance usually has an insurance period of about 1 or 2 years. However, since the issuer can set the period of a CAT bond relatively freely, it is possible to set a long redemption period of up to about 10 years.

13.1.2.2 Fixed Cost

As mentioned above, earthquake insurance has a short insurance period, so each time a contract is renewed, the insurance premium rate fluctuates according to the situation of the insurance market at that time, but the insurance premium may rise two to three times. However, with CAT bonds, the redemption period can be set for a long period of time, and the fixed interest rate can be set within that period, so the cost can be fixed for a long period of time.

13.1.2.3 Reinforcement of Underwriting Capacity of Insurance Companies

By transferring the risk of natural disasters to investors, the underwriting capacity of insurers can be reinforced.

13.1.2.4 Immediateness of Funds

In insurance, when damage occurs, the amount of the damage is determined through a damage investigation. This is because insurance has the principle of compensation for damages and the principle of prohibiting gains, and it is not possible to cover more than the actual amount of damages. This damage investigation can take months or years. However, with a CAT bond, a trigger is set, and when the condition is met, a predetermined amount is immediately paid to the issuer.

13.1.2.5 Neutrality from Credit Risk

In the event of a catastrophic disaster, the damage may exceed the solvency of the insurer or reinsurer, and the insurer or reinsurer may not always be able to pay the full amount. However, in CAT bonds, when a bond is issued, SPI has the investment from investors paid in, and the funds are managed in the trust account of SPI. The CAT bond has the funds to pay the issuer in the event of a catastrophe from the beginning, so there is no credit risk that investors will not be able to pay in the event of a disaster.

13.1.2.6 Flexible Response to Issuance Conditions

Issuance conditions such as trigger settings, payment conditions, and interest rates can be set according to the issuer's situation.

On the other hand, the merits of CAT bonds from the investor's point of view are as follows.

13.1.2.7 Rating

CAT bonds are exempt from redemption in part or in whole in the event of a natural disaster, depending on the trigger conditions. To set this trigger condition, an international risk assessment company evaluates the probability of the exemption condition through past meteorological statistics and geological analysis. For example, the CAT bond issuance conditions specify that probability, such as "the probability that an investor will be fully exempt from paying principal by maturity is 1%". Based on this, international rating agencies such as Moody's, Standard & Poor's, and Fitch rate CAT bonds (for ratings) (see Chap. 1). Therefore, investors can easily investigate the credit risk for the redemption of CAT bonds.

13.1.2.8 Risk Independence

Since the redemption risk of CAT bonds is a risk related to natural disasters, it is not linked to the economic activities of each country and has almost no correlation with the financial markets and real estate markets of corporate bonds and stocks.

For example, suppose you invest 100 million yen each in three types of the same double A-rated corporate bond.

First, when investing in the bonds of three Japanese companies, the investment risk is linked to the risk of economic fluctuations in Japan.

Second, when investing in bonds of Japanese, American, and European companies, the economic risk of each country is diversified, but in the case of a global financial crisis, all three types of corporate bonds losses can occur.

Third, when investing in the bonds of two Japanese companies and the "earthquake bond" in Japan, let us assume that the occurrence of a major earthquake in Tokyo is a condition for exemption from redemption of the earthquake bond. In the event of the Great Tokyo earthquake, the principal of the earthquake bond will not be redeemed but, at the same time, many Japanese companies are likely to go bankrupt.

Fourth, let us assume the case of investing in one Japanese company, the "earthquake bond" in the United States, and the "earthquake bond" in Europe. There is almost no risk correlation between the risk of bankruptcy of Japanese companies, the earthquake in the United States, and the earthquake in Europe.

For this reason, pension funds, life insurance companies, reinsurance companies and others continue to increase the proportion of CAT bonds. If the ratings are the same, one of the attractions is that the yield of CAT bonds is higher than that of ordinary corporate bonds (around 1%).

13.1.3 CAT Bond Issuance Example

13.1.3.1 Case of Oriental Land (Issued by the Company)

Earthquake insurance covers the collapse of buildings, but does not cover the resulting loss of income. In addition, damage investigation is required for payment of earthquake insurance, and it takes time from the occurrence of an earthquake to payment of insurance money. The premium for this earthquake insurance is relatively high compared to other insurance. Many companies do not have earthquake insurance due to the problems of earthquake insurance and the lack of underwriting capacity of non-life insurance companies. Oriental Land Co Ltd., the operator of Tokyo Disneyland (TDL), did not have earthquake insurance because of the facilities' sufficient earthquake resistance.

However, the company was concerned about the risk of a decrease in visitors in the event of an earthquake. The company's total revenue for the fiscal year ended March 1999 was 187,772 million yen, all of which came from one TDL. If the business is closed due to an earthquake disaster, the amount of this income may be completely lost because the business establishments are concentrated.

TDL established a SPC overseas in June 1999 to prepare for this possibility of operating loss. Through this, TDL issued a CAT bond "earthquake bond" totaling USD 200 million (about 24 billion yen) in the US market.

There were two types of CAT bonds issued. One was the "principal risk type", which was exempt from repayment of part or all of the principal, for USD 100 million. The other was a "credit risk switch type" of USD 100 million, in which the principal was repaid but interest payments were exempted for 3 years. This CAT bond is known as the first business company in the world.

The CAT bond was as follows. If an earthquake with a magnitude of 6.5 or more occurs within a TDL radius of 75 km in Urayasu City, Chiba Prefecture, Oriental Land Co Ltd. will be exempt from repayment depending on the magnitude of the earthquake. In that case, TDL would receive funding from CAT bond funds. If a direct earthquake of magnitude 6.5 or greater occurs within a TDL radius of 10 km in 5 years, TDL will receive 25% of the principal, and if an earthquake of magnitude 7.5 or greater occurs, it will receive the full amount of the principal. Investors, on the other hand, are at risk of losing all of their principal if a magnitude 7.5 earthquake occurs within a TDL radius of 10 km within 5 years. However, if an earthquake does not occur within 5 years, the principal will be redeemed and the investment yield will be as high as 8% per year.

13.1.3.2 JA Mutual Aid CAT Bond "Muteki" (Reinsurance Company Intervention)

Munich Re established SPC MUTEKI Ltd in the Cayman Islands in May 2008 to issue CAT bonds for earthquakes in Japan. The SPC issued a CAT bond with a three-year maturity, a coupon (interest rate) of LIBOR + 4.4%, and a face value of USD 300 million denominated in US dollars, with "Zenkyoren" as the beneficiary.

In this CAT bond "Muteki", the entire amount of the issue amount of USD 300 million (about 24 billion yen) was recovered by the Great East Japan earthquake that occurred in March 2011. This was the first CAT bond to recover reinsurance from an earthquake disaster. It was the first time in history that a CAT bond was exempt from 100% principal redemption. In earlier cases, hurricane Katrina forced Zurich Financial Services (ZURN.VX), a leading Swiss insurance company, to pay insurance claims. As a result, Kamp Re 2005 bonds (USD 190 million) had a partial reduction in principal.

13.1.3.3 Typhoon Risk Securitization (Reinsurance Company Intervention)

On 16 April 2012, Mitsui Sumitomo Insurance Company issued a typhoon risk securities "AKIBARE II" with a redemption period of 4 years through the SPC "AKIBARE II Limited". The CAT bond typhoon risk securities calculated the estimated damage based on the observation data of the Japan Meteorological Agency in the event of a large typhoon. The condition was that if the estimated damage amount exceeded a certain level, the principal redemption to investors would be partially or wholly exempted according to the excess amount, and the exempted amount would be paid to Mitsui Sumitomo Insurance Company.

The mechanism of the typhoon risk securities "AKIBARE II" is shown in Fig. 13.2.

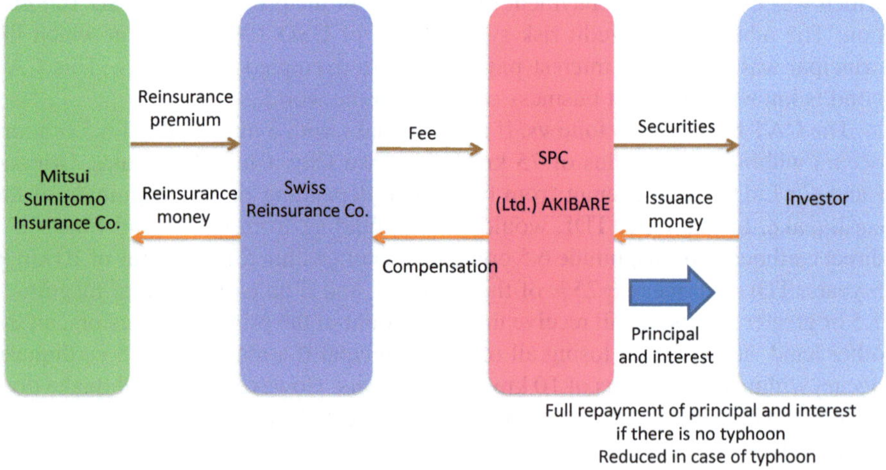

Fig. 13.2 Typhoon risk securities AKIBARE II (Mitsui Sumitomo Insurance Co Ltd) (*Source:* Various materials)

Typhoon risk securities "AKIBARE II" assumed that the scale of a typhoon for which a part of the principal is reduced is approximately once every 60 years, and that the total amount is reduced once every 200 years. This is the first securities targeting disaster risk in Japan to use the estimated damage of a typhoon based on the observation data of the Japan Meteorological Agency as an index.

Furthermore, in March 2018, MS & AD Insurance Group's Mitsui Sumitomo Insurance Company and Aioi Nissay Dowa Insurance Co Ltd jointly issued a CAT bond "Akibare Re 2018-1" targeting domestic natural disaster risks. Mitsui Sumitomo Insurance Company is the fourth issue, and Aioi Nissay Dowa Insurance Co. is the first issue. In addition to domestic typhoon risk, this CAT bond is the first in the non-life insurance industry to cover flood risk, and the CAT bond issued by Mitsui Sumitomo Insurance Company also covers the risk of earthquake and fire costs. The yield for the fixed portion was set at 1.90%. The risk of earthquake fire costs is insurance money paid in the event of a certain percentage of damage caused by an earthquake or eruption or a fire caused by a tsunami.

Table 13.1 shows the outline of "Akibare Re 2018-1".

Table 13.1 Outline of "Akibare Re 2018-1"

Classification	Class A	Class B
Target company	Mitsui Sumitomo Insurance Co.	Aioi Nissay Dowa Insurance Co.
Issuer	Akibare Re Ltd.	
Issuance time	March 2018	
Maturity	End of March 2022 (4 years)	
Target risk	① Domestic typhoon risk ② Domestic flood risk ③ Domestic earthquake fire cost risk	① Domestic typhoon risk ② Domestic flood risk
Issue amount	USD 220 million (approximately 23.3 billion yen): 1 dollar = 106 yen conversion	USD 100 million (approximately 10.6 billion yen): USD 1 = 106 yen conversion
Yield	Yield on collateral bonds + 1.90%	Yield on collateral bonds + 1.90%

Source: The company's news release

The mechanism (at the time of issuance) of "Akibare Re. 2018-1" is as shown in Fig. 13.3.

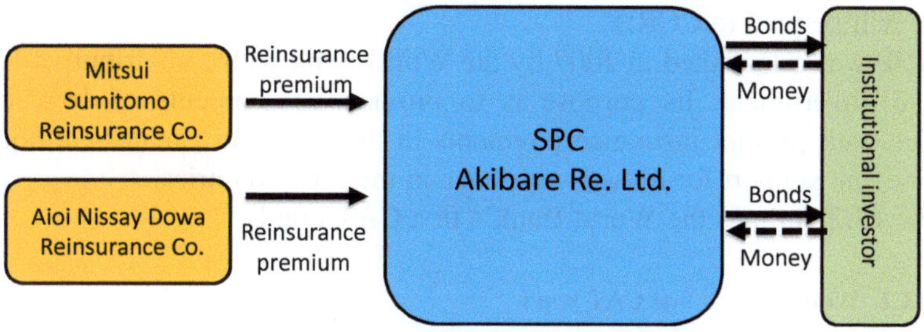

Fig. 13.3 Structure of "Akibare Re. 2018-1" (at the time of issuance) (*Source:* The company's news release)

As shown in Fig. 13.3, both companies have established the SPC "Akibare Re. Ltd." and issued CAT bonds.

The mechanism of "Akibare Re. 2018-1" (when a disaster occurs) is as shown in Fig. 13.4.

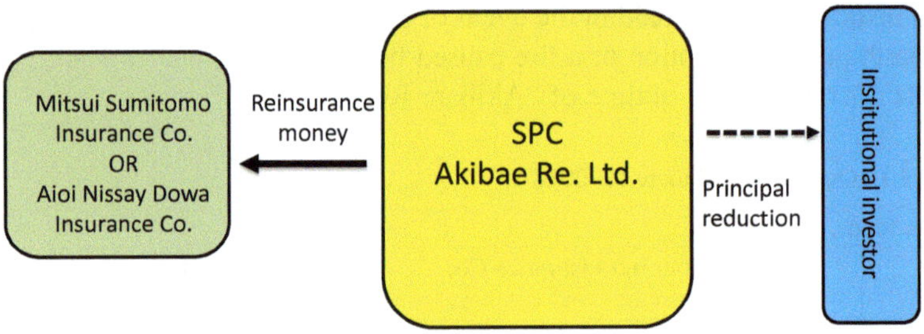

Fig. 13.4 Structure of Akibare Re. 2018-1 (at the time of a disaster) (*Source:* The company's news release)

In this CAT bond, when a trigger occurs, the principal is reduced, which is the source of insurance money for both insurance companies.

13.1.3.4 World Bank CAT Bond

On 30 June 2014, the World Bank issued the first CAT bond for a period of 3 years totaling USD 30 million. CAT bond interest payments and principal redemptions are made through an insurance swap agreement with the World Bank of the Caribbean Disaster Risk Insurance Organization (CCRIF). In the event of a natural disaster that exceeds a certain scale, the CAT bond principal will be exempt from redemption according to the scale of the disaster, and the principal of the exempted redemption amount will be paid to CCRIF.

CCRIF was established in 2007 by the World Bank with a contribution from the Japanese government. Its purpose is to provide governments of 16 Caribbean countries with prompt insurance payments in the event of a major earthquake or hurricane and support for disaster response in member countries.

Table 13.2 outlines the World Bank's first CAT bond.

Table 13.2 World Bank's first CAT bond

Classification	Contents
Issuer	World Bank (International Bank for Reconstruction and Development: IBRD)
Issue amount	USD 30 million
Redemption amount	If the cyclone and earthquake that occur in the Caribbean countries exceed a certain scale, the principal will be used for insurance payment according to the scale of the disaster, and the amount after deducting that amount will be the reimbursement amount
Date of issue	30 June 2014
Interest rate	Six months LIBOR + 6.30% (however, the minimum interest rate is 6.50%)
Interest payment	Every 3 months
Redemption date	7 June 2017

Source: World Bank

13.2 Sidecar

As shown in Fig. 13.5, a sidecar is the name of a tricycle with another wheel installed next to a two-wheeled vehicle such as a motorcycle or bicycle, or a part installed next to it.

Fig. 13.5 Sidecar (*Source:* Various materials)

On the other hand, sidecar or reinsurance sidecar in ART is a mechanism in which investors share a certain percentage of the risk of reinsurance of an SPI. The insurance company becomes the sponsor cedant and the administrator of the reinsurer SPI. It is a risk-sharing mechanism—an insurance company drives a motorcycle and the SPI is in a side car installed next to it.

Instead of diversifying risks through reinsurance contracts or retrocession contracts with existing reinsurance companies, insurance companies (reinsurance companies) establish SPIs as reinsurance companies and reinsure to this SPI. This SPI underwrites a certain percentage of the reinsurance contract of the insurance company (reinsurance company) and receives the reinsurance premium. In addition, the SPI transfers risk to investors by raising funds from them in the form of equity or debt (loans).

The basic structure in which a sponsor (insurance company or reinsurance company) transfers risk to an SPI and then the SPI transfers that risk to investors is similar to ILS such as a CAT bond. This sidecar differs from a CAT bond in that the transfer of risk to the SPI of the sponsor (insurance company or reinsurance company) is full in a CAT bond, but is a proportionate share in sidecar.

The sidecar has spread since three hurricanes (KRW: Hurricane Katrina, Rita and Wilma) struck the United States in August–October 2005 as a combined insurance (reinsurance) and CAT bond mechanism.

The mechanism of the sidecar is shown in Fig. 13.6.

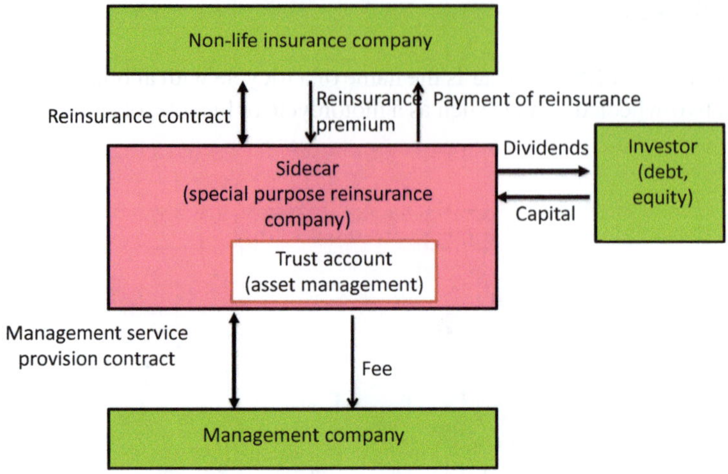

Fig. 13.6 Sidecar mechanism (*Source:* Various materials)

In the case of equity, by investing in a sidecar, investors also take on insurance risk, which is a business model that aims at both insurance underwriting profit and investment fund management profit. However, investors are worried about the adverse selection of the non-life insurer, who is both the cedant and the sidecar manager, to choose a poor-quality risk and reinsure the sidecar. Therefore, the relationship of trust between the non-life insurance company and the investor is important.

13.3 Industry Loss Warranties

Industry loss warranties (ILW) are an ILS, and are a form of reinsurance or insurance derivative contract in which an insurance company or the like pays insurance money based on the total amount of damage experienced by the entire non-life insurance industry. The main seller of ILW is the reinsurance company. The main buyers are non-life insurance companies, but the ties between the insurance and financial markets are not very strong as they are used as a complement to reinsurance. In addition, it is possible that an investor in the financial market who purchased a CAT bond or the like will purchase this ILW as a hedging instrument but, in this case, the risk in the financial market will be transferred to the insurance market.

Traditional ILWs are in the form of reinsurance contracts, but some are in the form of derivatives or swaps.

The mechanism of the reinsurance type ILW is as shown in Fig. 13.7.

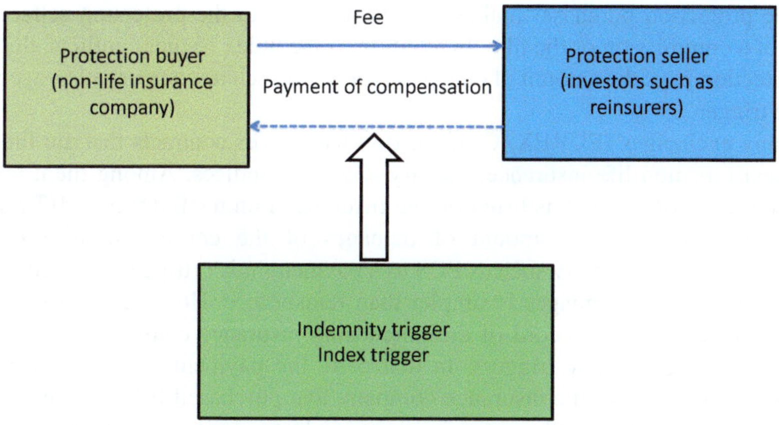

Fig. 13.7 Reinsurance type ILW (*Source:* Various materials)

Two triggers are set for the ILW trigger. For example, the condition for triggering is that the insurance money paid by the non-life insurance company that purchased the ILW exceeds a certain amount and the reference index also exceeds a certain value. The most frequently used reference index in the ILW is the insurance industry-wide loss index calculated by the Property Claims Service (PCS), which is a statistical organization of the US insurance industry. Here, the actual loss compensation trigger means that the ILW purchaser bears the damage until the trigger is reached, which means that the ILW purchaser has an insured interest that is a potential damage. Therefore, in the United States and other countries, that part is classified as a reinsurance contract. When ILW is classified as a reinsurance contract, if the insurance company is the purchaser, the obligation to reserve reserves is exempted.

Swap-type insurance derivatives are over-the-counter products that imitate CDS, and are also called event loss swaps.

The mechanism of swap-type ILW is as shown in Fig. 13.8.

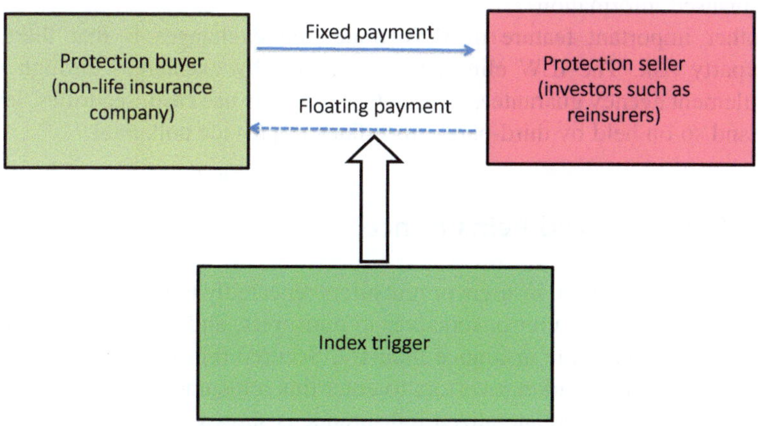

Fig. 13.8 Swap type ILW (*Source:* Various materials)

The protection purchaser makes a fixed payment to the protection seller in the form of a commission or the like. In addition, if the index trigger conflicts, the seller of protection pays the amount of change in the form such as compensation according to the trigger.

Many exchanges (EUREX, CME, IFEX) list futures contracts that are linked to parametric or non-life insurance industry-wide loss indices. Among them is event link futures (ELF), which is listed on the Insurance Futures Exchange (IFEX).

Since ILW uses the amount of damages of the entire insurance industry announced by a third party such as PCS as a payment index (trigger), the mechanism for determining the damages is simpler than reinsurance. However, in some cases, the insurance payment record of the purchasing insurance company is added as a trigger to make multiple triggers. In that case, the payment condition is that the amount of damages of the insurance company that purchased ILW and the damage index (industry index) of the entire insurance industry exceed a certain value at the same time. However, the insurer who bought the ILW is at risk of failing to meet the industry trigger, although its damages are touching the trigger. In this way, the loss index of the entire insurance industry and the loss index of the ILW purchasing insurance company may be different, so that the purchasing insurance company may have a basis risk in which the amount of damage and the amount of payment received are different.

The non-life insurance industry's loss index is so transparent that the underwriting process is easy to carry out. Although usually not customized for individual transactions, ILW has standardized contracts. Standardized contracts are easier to trade in the secondary market and easier to claim payments. This ILW is considered to be the most liquid ILS because of its standardized terminology and transparent pricing.

ILW is unlikely to cause moral hazard issues, as payments are calculated based on independent third-party indicators rather than buyer-reported damages. For example, an individual company's loss index can be a moral hazard because the company can affect its own damage. In addition, ILW is less likely to be adverse selection because its payments are based on widely available information and there is little asymmetry in the misused information.

Another important feature of ILW traded on exchanges is that there is no counterparty risk. The ILW eliminates credit risk by exchanges through margin and settlement agency guarantees. Derivative products use cash, securities, letters of credit, and so on held by third-party custodians to provide collateral.

13.4 Collateralized Reinsurance

In the reinsurance market, insurers or reinsurers repeatedly transfer some or all of the risks assumed by the insurer or reinsurer to reinsurers, and so on, and the risks are diversified throughout the insurance industry. Secured reinsurance has been developed to allow capital market investors to enter this reinsurance market.

The mechanism for collateralized reinsurance is shown in Fig. 13.9.

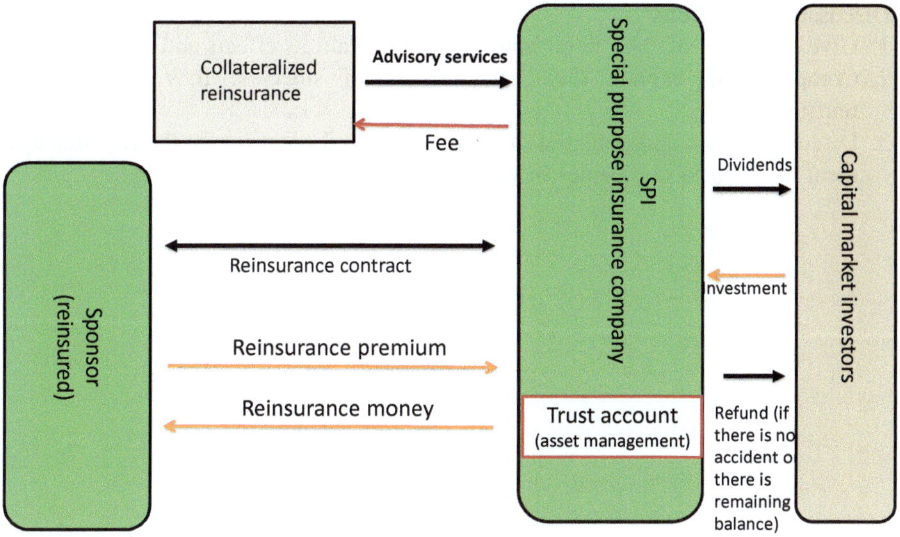

Fig. 13.9 Mechanism for collateralized insurance (*Source:* Various materials)

A sponsor such as an insurance company pays a reinsurance premium to a SPI and transfers the risk. Insurance premiums from sponsors such as insurance companies are deposited in a trust account. Investors invest in a SPI by purchasing stocks or bonds such as preferred stocks, and the funds are deposited in a trust account together with reinsurance premiums as a source of insurance payments. This trust account is managed with safe assets such as US Treasuries, and serves as repayment funds for principal and interest to investors in normal times, and as collateral for insurance payments in the event of damage.

In addition, collateralized reinsurers play an important role in collateralized reinsurance, such as designing mechanisms and negotiating reinsurance and trust contracts. This secured reinsurer is the entity that installs, provides, and manages the SPI in consideration of the fee. However, it is not necessarily a traditional reinsurance company, but an ILS fund or a specialized company that provides collateralized reinsurance transaction affairs and advisory services. The secured reinsurer provides underwriting and negotiation services, but does not underwrite risk transfer. Secured reinsurers need specialized knowledge of risk assessment and modeling and an understanding of the complex contractual language of reinsurance transactions.

Secured reinsurance is the fastest growing form of transaction in the ILS market in recent years. The background to this expansion is that for compensation buyers, secured reinsurance has the same structure as traditional reinsurance, offering wider coverage and lower costs than CAT bond. However, it is pointed out that the actual risk underwriter is an unrated and fragile capital-based SPI, and the certainty of the collateral assets provided depends on the trust contract that supports it.

Discussion Questions

1. Give examples of CAT bond issuance and explain its effects and issues.
2. Compare and explain the characteristics of sidecars, ILW, and secured reinsurance.
3. Discuss the role and potential of insurance-linked securities in the risk management of business companies in your country.

Derivatives and Insurance Derivatives 14

Insurance derivatives were created by applying the derivatives mechanism to insurance risk. This chapter outlines how derivatives and insurance derivatives work.

14.1 Derivatives

14.1.1 Overview

Derivatives, or financial derivatives, are a general term for transactions that are derived from existing financial products such as stocks, bonds, foreign exchange, deposits, and loans called underlying assets. Derivative here means "derivative" or "secondary" in English.

It is said that the history of derivatives dates back several thousand years, but the origin of derivatives in Japan was the futures trading among rice merchants, buying and selling rice before harvesting, in the Edo period in the eighteenth century in Dojima, Osaka. It is said to be a "choai rice transaction" in which the price is decided in advance. The price of rice is constantly changing due to weather and natural disasters. Therefore, rice merchants set the selling price of rice before harvesting in order to stabilize the price, thereby eliminating the possibility of damage from fluctuations in the price of rice. In addition, some people used it to predict a price increase of rice and buy it, while others predicted a price decrease and sell it. However, the use of derivatives in the modern sense is said to have come from foreign exchange derivatives in the mid-1980s. Interest rate derivatives began to be used in the 1990s.

There are a variety of assets that are subject to derivative transactions, such as individual stocks (equities), currencies, and commodities, which can be referred to as underlying assets or underlying securities. Derivatives (financial derivatives) are generally transactions that index the price of the underlying asset and exchange the

H. Lee, *Risk Management*, Springer Texts in Business and Economics,
https://doi.org/10.1007/978-981-16-3468-0_14

profit or loss of that value in the future. Derivatives traded in the market include "standard products" and "indexes". Derivatives include futures, options, and swaps.

The various types of derivatives are as outlined in Table 14.1.

Table 14.1 Types of derivatives

Underlying asset/type	Futures	Option	Swap
Stock	Stock index futures	Individual stock options, stock index futures options	–
Interest rate	Interest rate futures, bond futures	Interest rate futures options, bond futures, caps, and so on	Interest rate swap
Currency	Currency futures, exchange contracts	Currency options	Currency swap

Source: Various materials

The characteristics of derivatives are as follows. First, derivatives are off-balanced and therefore do not appear on the balance sheet. The value of the derivative at the time of contract is zero. Secondly, derivatives are leveraged transactions, which allow you to trade large amounts with a small amount of margin. Since the derivative is a reservation transaction, a large amount of funds is not required for the transaction, and the settlement is the delivery of only the difference portion. Thirdly, since derivatives are risk transactions, profits and losses fluctuate due to uncertainty such as future price fluctuations.

There are three main purposes of using this derivative. The first is risk hedge, used to offset the profit or loss of the hedged item. The second is speculation, to obtain a large profit with a small investment. Third, arbitrage aims to earn profits through the buying and selling of overpriced or undervalued financial products compared to market value.

The various purposes of using derivatives is shown in Fig. 14.1.

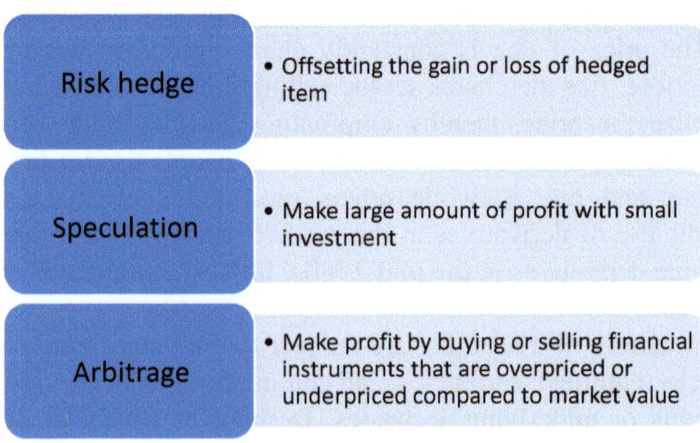

Fig. 14.1 Purpose of using derivatives (*Source:* Various materials)

Hedges include price fluctuation risks such as stocks and bonds, interest rate fluctuation risks such as deposit interest rates and bond interest rates, and exchange rate fluctuation risks. Hedging is also called "insurance connection" or "hanging connection", and there are "selling connections" and "buying connections". For example, if you actually own a financial product, you may transfer the risk of suffering damage due to a subsequent decline in the price of the financial product using futures trading.

If you have a physical position, you can reserve the same quantity for sale in futures trading. Therefore, if the price of this futures falls, profits will be generated, so there is a case where the risk of the fall in the spot price is covered by the profit from the closing of the open interest of the futures sales contract.

Open interest refers to the total number of unsettled contracts that are left unsettled or unsettled in margin trading, futures contractors, and so on. The unsettled portion of the buy is called the open interest (long position), and the unsettled portion of the sell is called the open interest (short position).

Speculation is a transaction that purely anticipates a rise or fall in the derivative price and seeks to make a profit from it. Arbitrage is a transaction that uses interest rate differences and price differences between commodities or markets to earn margins.

The derivatives trading market has the following characteristics. First, the market in which the derivatives are traded depends on the type of underlying asset. Second, Japanese futures trading is listed on the Osaka Securities Exchange and the Tokyo Financial Futures Exchange. Third, swaps are traded bilaterally over the counter due to the nature of the transaction, which is an exchange. Fourth, currency options are often over-the-counter, while interest rates and equity derivatives are traded on exchanges.

The trading market for derivatives is shown in Table 14.2.

Table 14.2 Derivatives trading market

Classification	Futures	Swap	Option
Exchange	Listed	Over the counter	Over the counter
Interest rate	Listed	Over the counter	Listed
Stock	Listed	–	Listed

Source: Various materials

14.1.2 Futures

Futures are transactions in which a price, quantity, trading date, and so on are executed at the present time for a specific financial product, and when the trading deadline is reached the trading is carried out. This futures are a reservation transaction for standard commodities on an exchange and is a transaction in which an opposite transaction is made within the deadline (contract month) for the initial buy reservation or sell reservation, and only the profit and loss is settled by difference. The opposite concept to futures is spot trading. In this futures trading, since the trading price at the time when the contract date arrives is determined in advance, it is used for hedging the price fluctuation risk of commodities whose prices fluctuate.

The characteristics of futures trading are as follows.

14.1.2.1 Exchange Transactions

Futures are traded on exchanges.

14.1.2.2 Standardization

The standardized products are called "standard products", and the trading units such as foreign exchange and government bonds to be reserved and the trading conditions such as the delivery date are fixed.

14.1.2.3 Margin System

Only margin is required when booking futures, but since this margin is around 3% of the reservation amount, there is a leverage effect that allows you to trade a large amount with a small margin.

14.1.2.4 Difference Settlement

The difference settlement is a system peculiar to the futures trading of the exchange, in which the profit and loss in the futures trading is settled by the opposite trading to the trading of the original reservation before the maturity. For example, if you initially purchased futures, you sell the futures and settle the profit or loss of the transaction by the difference. Specifically, if you buy a futures contract for 150 yen and the price rises to 200 yen, you can sell the futures contract for 200 yen and you will get a profit of 50 yen. With the difference settlement that gives and receives only the difference between the bid price and the ask price, it is not necessary to deliver the goods and the price of each transaction of the initial transaction and the counter-trading.

Futures trading is characterized by being traded on exchanges and standardizing transaction units and settlement dates. When the seller and the buyer freely negotiate the transaction conditions such as the due date and the amount of money, they are not called futures but forwards even if they are supposed to be delivered in the future. Forward exchange contracts are typical of forwards and are sometimes called futures exchanges, but they are officially forward transactions.

Exchange futures are exchange trading. Foreign exchange futures are transactions in which an unspecified number of people participate and reserve a specific currency at a specific price at a specific date in the future, and transaction conditions such as transaction units and settlement dates are standardized.

On the other hand, a repurchase transaction is a transaction in which a bond or the like is promised in advance to be bought back (sold back) at a certain price after a certain period of time. It is a transaction in which the seller and the buyer agree and determine the yield for a certain period in advance regardless of fluctuations in the market interest rate. From the bond seller's point of view, it is a short-term fund raising, a "selling repurchase", and from the buyer's point of view, it is a short-term fund management, "buying repurchase".

This futures contract is also used as a means of hedging. This is because, at a specific point in the future, even if the price rises, it can be purchased at the price reserved by futures trading. For example, if you plan to purchase a product in the future and the price is expected to rise, you may decide the price at this point and make a reservation to purchase it on a fixed day in the future. Predetermining the purchase price of a commodity on a future fixed day and avoiding the risk of price increase through futures trading is called a buy hedge. In addition, if there is a plan to sell a product in the future and there is a possibility that the price will fall, determining the selling price of the product at the present time by trading futures and avoiding the risk of price decline is called a sell hedge. Pursuing profits by using price fluctuations for this hedge is called speculation.

14.1.3 Options

14.1.3.1 Outline

An option is the buying and selling of options that allows you to buy or sell foreign exchange, stocks, bonds, and so on at a specific price on a fixed day in the future or within a certain period of time. There are two types of options: a call option, which is the right to buy the underlying asset (stocks, interest rates, and currency), and a put option, which is the right to sell the underlying asset.

The planned trading price of the underlying asset, which is the target product of the option, is the exercise price or the strike price, and the option right can be exercised at this price. In actual option trading, when the underlying asset is foreign exchange, it is called a currency option; when it is a bond, it is called a bond option; when it is an interest rate, it is called an interest rate option; and when it is a stock index, it is called a stock index option. In addition, the price of an option is called an option premium or an option price.

In order to acquire the right, the buyer of the option pays the seller (setter) of the option a consideration called an option fee or an option premium and obtains a call or put. The option is for the buyer to pass on the risk of future price fluctuations to the seller.

The buyer of the call option predicts that the underlying asset may rise, so the risk is transferred to the seller by paying a premium, and the seller predicts that the price will fall or will not rise. Therefore, it means that the seller decides that it is relatively safe to take the premium and take the risk.

In addition, put options buyers are transferring the risk by paying a premium to the seller because they anticipate that the underlying asset may fall. The seller predicts that the price will rise or not fall, which means that he decides that it is relatively safe to take the premium and take the risk.

This premium is similar to insurance premiums in terms of risk pass-through consideration and fluctuates depending on the price of the underlying asset of the option, volatility, maturity and other factors. Volatility is the possibility of price fluctuations of the underlying asset, that is the risk of price fluctuations. The option premium of the underlying asset with high volatility is high, and the option premium of the underlying asset with low volatility is low.

Option buyers may exercise their rights only at their convenience. That is, the call buyer can purchase the target product at the exercise price by selectively exercising the right in a situation that is advantageous to them. Put buyers may sell their goods at the exercise price by selectively exercising their rights in their own favor. The seller of the option is obliged to buy or sell at the exercise price if the buyer exercises the option in consideration of receiving the premium from the buyer. Options that can only be exercised on the maturity date are referred to as the European type, and options that can be exercised at any time until the maturity date are referred to as the American type.

Options trading is similar to futures trading in that it reserves for future trading. However, as mentioned above, futures buyers do not have the option of trading options, and are obliged to make a "promise" to buy or sell in the future or to settle the difference through counter-trading. Therefore, futures buyers have the potential for both profits and losses due to fluctuations in futures prices. On the other hand, the buyer of the option can choose to exercise the right only if it is profitable and waive it if it is a loss.

14.1.3.2 Profit and Loss of Call Options

In a call option, if the actual market price at the time of purchase of the goods is higher than the exercise price, by exercising the right, the purchaser can purchase at the exercise price lower than the market price. Also, if the actual market price at the time of purchase of the item is lower than the exercise price, the purchaser of the call option can waive the right because it can be bought at a price lower than the exercise price in the market. Fig. 14.2 shows the profit and loss of this call option.

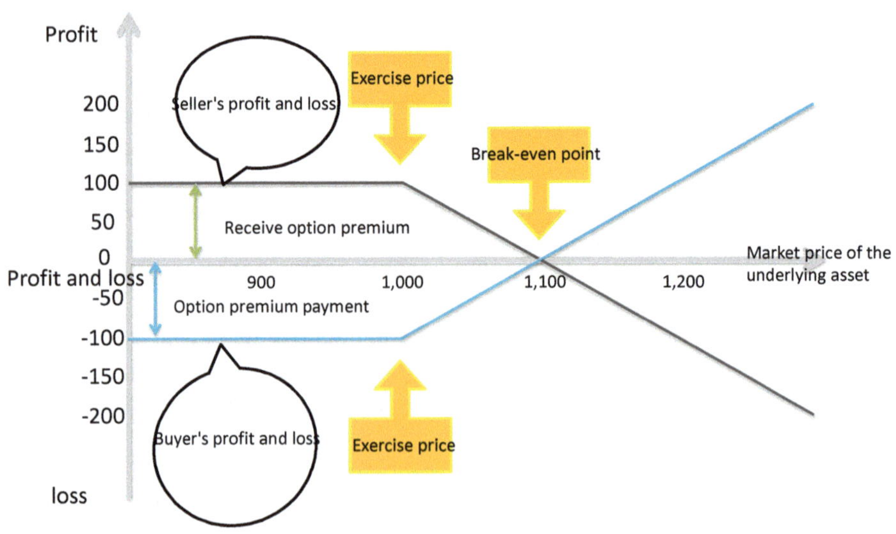

Fig. 14.2 Profit and loss of call options (Example of exercise price 1000 yen, premium 100 yen) (*Source:* Various materials)

As shown in Fig. 14.2, call option buyers are limited to loss on option premium payments, but profits increase indefinitely as prices rise. Call option sellers, on the other hand, are limited in profits by receiving option premiums, but losses increase indefinitely as prices rise.

14.1.3.3 Profit and Loss of Put Options

Put options allow the purchaser to sell at an exercise price higher than the market price by exercising that right if the actual market price at the time of sale of the goods is lower than the exercise price. In addition, if the actual market price of the product at the time of sale becomes higher than the exercise price, the purchaser can sell the product at a price higher than the exercise price in the market, and thus can waive the right. Fig. 14.3 illustrates the profit and loss of this put option.

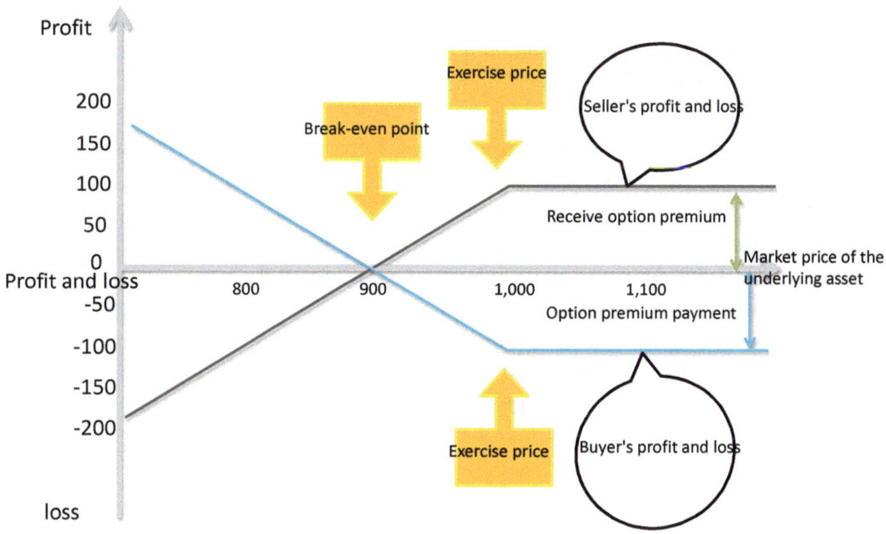

Fig. 14.3 Gains and losses on put options (Example of exercise price 1000 yen, premium 100 yen) (*Source:* Various materials)

As shown in Fig. 14.3, put options buyers are limited to loss on option premium payments, but profits increase as the price goes down until the price goes to zero. Put options sellers, on the other hand, are limited in profits by receiving option premiums, but losses increase as the price goes down until the price goes to zero.

14.1.3.4 Offsetting Transaction

For option trading, the difference between the bid price and the selling price is delivered by the offsetting transaction or reversing trade, at which point the option contract is extinguished. This offsetting transaction can also be used to make a transaction to earn profits due to fluctuations in option premiums. This is because if you buy an option and then sell it when the premium rises, the difference will be profitable. By contrast, if you sell the option and buy it back cheaply later, you can make a profit. For example, if you buy when the premium of the call option is 100 yen and then sell it when the price rises to 150 yen, the difference of 50 yen will be a profit. If you buy or sell in the opposite direction, the call option contract you originally bought will be extinguished. In this way, if there is a possibility that the price of the underlying asset will rise, you can buy a call option and make a profit when the market price rises. However, if the price of a call option drops unexpectedly, the damage is limited to the premium paid, as the exercise of that right can be waived.

14.1.3.5 Loan with Cap

A loan with a cap is a floating interest rate loan with a cap on the interest rate. The capped loan has an interest rate call option built in, so if the interest rate level exceeds a certain level, you will receive interest from the option seller. Since the amount of money supplements the interest rate that exceeds a certain level of interest rate, that interest rate level becomes the actual upper limit of the interest burden. The interest rate borne by consumers in capped loans is as high as the payment of option premiums compared to the normal floating interest rate type, but it can hedge the risk of rising interest rates.

Examples of capped loans are as follows. When a business company borrows from a bank under the condition of "six months LIBOR + loan spread", it can enjoy the benefits of low interest rates while LIBOR is low, but if LIBOR rises the procurement cost will increase infinitely. If you purchase a cap with a maximum interest rate of 1.5% for a period of 5 years, the burden on the premium will increase, but the procurement cost for the next 5 years can be kept to "1.5% + loan spread" at the maximum, and you can also enjoy the benefits of low interest rates. Premium payments can be made in a lump sum at the time of contract or in installments over the contract period, and can be operated according to the financial situation.

The mechanism for a loan with a cap is shown in Fig. 14.4.

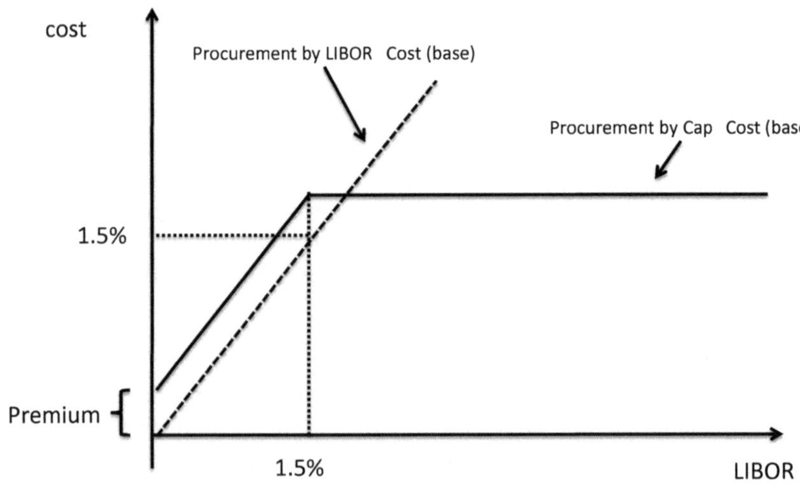

Fig. 14.4 Mechanism of a loan with a cap (*Source:* Various materials)

14.1.4 Swap

Swap is a general term for transactions that have the meaning of exchange and exchange equivalent cash flows. This swap transaction is a bilateral transaction between one seller and one buyer, and is a transaction in which two parties exchange a "future series of money flows" having the same value. In the swap contract, the timing of exchange and the calculation method of the exchange amount are specified.

Swap transactions include interest rate swaps and currency swaps.

14.1.4.1 Interest Rate Swap

Interest rate swaps are transactions that exchange different types of interest rates between the same currency. Interest rate swap transactions were developed in the early 1980s and began to be used by major business companies for interest rate risk management in the mid-1980s. By the 1990s, they were also actively used by small and medium-sized enterprises.

Interest rate swaps usually do not exchange principal, but determine the notional principal, which is the nominal principal for interest rate calculation. Specifically, the two parties determine a certain notional amount, period, interest exchange date, and so on, and exchange fixed interest rates with floating interest rates, and floating interest rates with different types of floating interest rates. The exchange of fixed and floating LIBOR is the most used.

In addition to LIBOR, the exchanged floating interest rates include TIBOR (Tokyo Interbank Offered Rate), long-term prime rate, short-term prime rate, and so on, and are used properly according to the type of interest rate for procurement and operation owned by the business company. LIBOR is the lending rate between London banks offered by the funding bank in the London market and is used as the base interest rate for international financial transactions. The British Bankers' Association (BBA) aggregates the offered rate, which is the rate offered by the sellers of each bank at 11:00 a.m. London time, and publishes the average value. On the other hand, the rate offered by the buyer is called the bid rate.

On the other hand, TIBOR is an interbank lending rate in the Tokyo offshore market presented by a bank that lends funds in the Tokyo market, and it has been used as a base interest rate for financial transactions between financial institutions. The Japanese Bankers Association aggregates the offered rates of specific banks at 11:00 a.m. Japan time and publishes the average value.

For example, it is assumed that the financing costs of the major excellent company A and the medium-sized company B are as shown in Table 14.3.

Table 14.3 Financing costs for companies A and B

Classification	Short-term funds	Long-term funding
Company A	TIBOR + 0.25%	3%
Company B	TIBOR + 0.5%	3.75%
Cost difference	0.25%	0.75%

Source: Various materials

This procurement cost is advantageous for company A, which is a large and excellent company in both long and short terms, but the difference in procurement cost for long-term funds is 0.75%, and the difference in short-term funds is 0.5% larger than 0.25%.

Here, Company B originally needed long-term funds, but it decided to procure short-term funds and asked Company A to procure long-term funds with a larger difference in funding costs. The two companies then decided to perform an interest rate swap to exchange interest payment obligations. Company A secured a margin of 0.25% by raising long-term funds at a fixed interest rate of 3% and providing it to Company B at 3.25% via a financial institution. On the other hand, Company B raises short-term funds with a floating interest rate at TIBOR plus 0.5% and provides it to Company A at TIBOR plus 0.25%. The flow of funds from this swap is shown in Fig. 14.5.

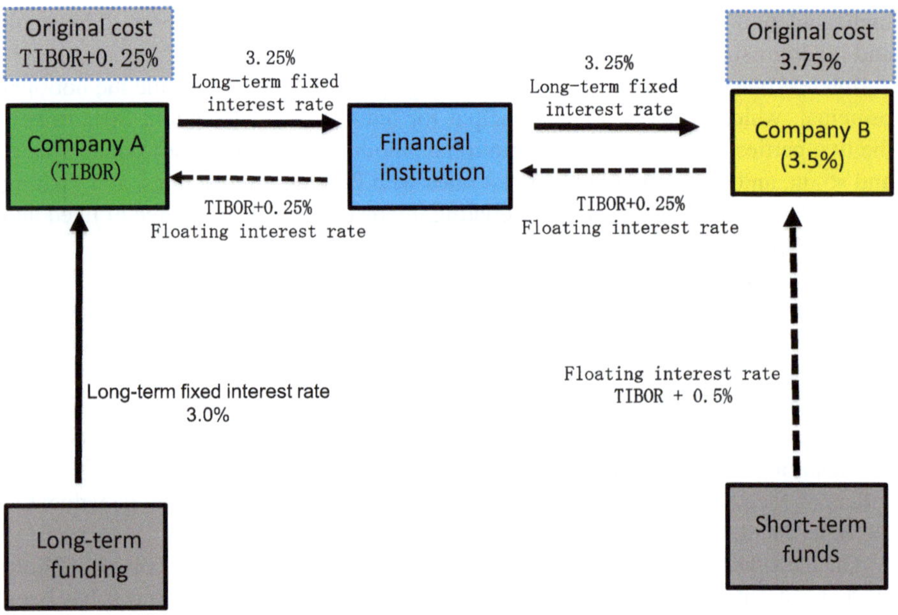

Fig. 14.5 Interest rate swap mechanism (*Source:* Various materials)

With this swap, Company A will pay 3%, which is the real TIBOR. This is because the floating interest rate TIBOR plus 0.25% (floating interest rate) paid to Company B minus the margin of 0.25% (3.25–3.0%) from the exchange of long-term fixed interest rates with Company B is 3%.

On the other hand, Company B's actual funding cost is 3.5%, which is the sum of 3.25% (long-term fixed interest rate) paid to Company A and 0.25% of the shortfall due to the exchange of floating interest rates. Company B pays a floating interest rate of TIBOR plus 0.5% for short-term funds, but the interest rate received from Company A is TIBOR plus 0.25%, so 0.25% is insufficient.

By this swap transaction, Company A had a single short-term financing cost of TIBOR plus 0.25% (3.25%), but now it can be procured at 3%, which is TIBOR itself. Company B had a single long-term funding cost of 3.75%, but was able to raise it at a fixed interest rate of 3.5%. As a result, both companies A and B were 0.25% less expensive than if they were raising their own funds.

14.1.4.2 Currency Swap

Currency swap is a transaction in which two parties exchange different types of interest rates between different currencies, and exchange principal. For example, if you issue a dollar-denominated corporate bond and exchange the payment for yen by currency swap, future interest payments and principal redemption will be yen. In currency swaps, in addition to exchanging interest rates, the principal is generally exchanged at the start and end of the transaction, but currency swaps that exchange only interest rate without exchanging principal is known as "coupon swap". Similar to interest rate swaps, currency swaps are carried out through over-the-counter transactions, and conditions such as the period are determined through negotiations between the parties.

Since the principal of a currency swap is exchanged between the start date and the maturity date, the "notional principal amount" in the interest rate swap is not set, and the term "principal amount" is simply used. On the other hand, the "currency swap agreement" is an agreement between the central banks of each country, unlike the currency swap of derivatives. The content stipulates that in the event of a currency crisis in one's own country, the currency of the partner country of the agreement should be exchanged at a predetermined rate for depositing and exchanging the currency of one's own country.

Currency swaps are as follows. For example, the principal of 100 million dollars is exchanged for yen under the condition of 100 yen per dollar, which is the current exchange rate, and the annual interest rate is also exchanged from 4% for the dollar interest rate to 3% for the yen interest rate. In addition, the conditions for repayment of 10 billion yen for the principal of 100 million dollars will be exchanged on the redemption date.

14.2 Insurance Derivatives

The term "insurance derivatives" is a concept that is not used in positive law, and although its definition has not been established, it is a derivative that covers the risks traditionally covered by insurance. This insurance derivative is a general term for weather derivatives, earthquake derivatives, credit derivatives, and the like. This insurance derivative is a type of derivative, not insurance, but is sold by insurance companies and banks.

If insurance derivatives can be used to transfer insurance risk to financial markets, it will complement the underwriting capacity of the insurance market and dramatically increase risk underwriting capacity. Insurance derivatives use observed values such as earthquake magnitude or seismic intensity, temperature and precipitation as conditions for invoking payment. In that case, if a certain value specified in the activation condition is observed, payment will be made according to the predetermined condition regardless of the actual occurrence of damage. Therefore, in that case, the amount of payment may exceed the actual amount of damage. However, since payment is automatically executed according to a certain numerical value specified in the triggering conditions, the period from the occurrence of the accident event to payment is extremely short.

There are two types of derivative technologies used for insurance derivatives: options and swaps. In other words, it applies the function of transferring price fluctuation risk to others and exchanging it with others in derivatives to transfer and exchange insurance risk. The option transaction type contracts the payment of the amount calculated by the difference between the value contracted in advance and the actual value at a certain time in the future, based on the numerical value of meteorological observation. It is an image of exercising the right when it exceeds or falls below the standard value (exercise price).

In the swap transaction type, business companies exchange different risks and pay compensation to each other for the occurrence of the risks. The swap transaction type includes credit default swaps, which are credit derivatives (CDS). Credit derivatives are a form of swap or option of credit risk such as bonds. This credit derivative is a derivative that will be delivered in the future using the creditworthiness of the issuer, which is the debtor, as an index. However, this targets credit risk, whereas other derivatives target market risk of price fluctuations.

This insurance derivatives are understood to be a type of derivatives, not insurance, but it is different from a regular derivative. Insurance derivatives and regular derivatives differ in the following ways. First, the risks targeted are different. Derivatives are primarily targeted at market risk, and insurance derivatives are targeted at insurance risk (pure risk). Second, the presence or absence of underlying assets is different. Insurance derivatives do not have financial products as underlying assets and are subject to fluctuations in indicators based on insurance risk. Therefore, the sale of derivatives can hedge the risk of the underlying financial asset, but the sale of insurance derivatives cannot hedge the risk of the underlying asset. That is, the seller of an insurance derivative cannot use the insurance derivative as a means of hedging because it has no underlying asset. As a result, the seller of the insurance derivative remains at risk, such as weather risk, and adds that amount to the weather derivative price as a risk premium.

This insurance derivatives and insurance differ in the following ways. First, insurance derivatives are a type of derivatives, not an insurance product. Secondly, insurance derivatives are not based on actual damage compensation (indemnity base) but are paid according to objective indicators (index base). Therefore, since it is not a requirement that "actual loss" has occurred, the damage investigation necessary for insurance payment is not conducted. As a result, there is a basis risk that can result in a difference between the actual amount of damage and the amount paid. Third, since there is no concept of insured interests, there is no concept of partial insurance, full insurance, or excess insurance. Therefore, there is no principle of prohibiting gain. Fourth, the premium rate of insurance is calculated by a statistical method based on the law of large numbers, while the premium of insurance derivatives is calculated by a financial engineering method.

The criminal law does not define "gambling", but in general gambling is "by chance victory or defeat" competing for the gains and losses of property and other property benefits. Such gambling is prohibited in principle by Article 185 of the Criminal Code unless it is a legitimate act by law, and anyone who gambles can be punished by imprisonment with work of up to 3 years.

Insurance derivatives are similar to gambling, in that property is exchanged by accident. Therefore, "derivative transactions" were positioned as "ancillary business" under the Insurance Business Law by the amendment of laws and regulations related to the Financial System Reform Law that came into effect in December 1998 (Article 98 of the Insurance Business Law). In addition, credit derivatives are regarded as "financial derivatives transactions", which are ancillary businesses of banks and insurance companies. Insurance derivatives are thus separated from gambling.

On the other hand, Japanese non-life insurance companies do not sell insurance derivatives that they intend to purchase for speculative purposes. In addition, the inspection manual of the Securities and Exchange Surveillance Commission stipulates that the use of weather derivatives for speculative purposes has a problem with the suitability of the purchaser of the product. Therefore, insurance derivatives cannot be purchased or sold for speculative or investment purposes.

Discussion Questions

1. Compare the areas of application of risk management using financial derivatives and risk management using insurance and discuss why each is applied.
2. Compare and explain the differences between options and insurance.
3. Compare and explain insurance derivatives and options.

Weather Derivatives Trading 15

For many business companies, performance depends on the weather risk. This chapter outlines typical weather derivatives of insurance derivatives.

15.1 Weather Risk and Companies

"Weather" and "climate" are the meteorological conditions in a specific area—such as fine weather, temperature, and wind. The "weather" represents meteorological conditions that occur in hours, weeks, up to a month. The climate is a long-term meteorological condition of more than a month. Meteorology is a term that expresses changes in the state of the atmosphere as a physical phenomenon.

In recent years, extreme weather events such as typhoons and floods have occurred frequently, and the profits or sales volumes of many companies are affected by extreme weather events. This abnormal weather is a weather phenomenon that deviates greatly from the average weather phenomenon in the past and occurs rarely. Extreme weather includes short-term heavy rains and strong winds, long-term droughts, and extremely cold summers and warm winters. In principle, abnormal weather is judged by the Japan Meteorological Agency based on "a phenomenon that occurs at a certain place (region) and at a certain time (week, month, season) with a frequency of once or less every 30 years". In addition, the World Meteorological Organization defines "a phenomenon in which the deviation of average temperature and precipitation occurs only once every 25 years or more" as abnormal weather.

The El Nino, or La Nina, phenomenon occurs in cycles of several years and is not itself considered extreme weather. The El Nino phenomenon is one in which the sea surface temperature is higher than normal for about a year in the cold water area off Peru. The La Nina phenomenon is the opposite of the El Nino phenomenon, and refers to a phenomenon in which the sea surface temperature near the equator of the eastern Pacific continues to be lower than normal for a long period of time. When the

H. Lee, *Risk Management*, Springer Texts in Business and Economics,
https://doi.org/10.1007/978-981-16-3468-0_15

El Nino phenomenon occurs, there is a cold summer in the vicinity of Japan because the temperature is low and the sunshine hours tend to be short in the summer, but it is a warm winter. When the La Niña phenomenon occurs, the temperature tends to be high in summer near Japan, so it becomes a hot summer, but in winter it becomes cold.

Corporate profits are greatly affected by such extreme weather. Here are some excerpts from past newspaper articles on the relationship between weather and corporate interests:

- Domestic shipments of oil heaters in January surged five times from the same month of the previous year. Due to the continuing severe cold, such as heavy snowfall in various parts of the Kanto region, manufacturers are pleased with the special demand “thanks to the arrival of the cold wave” (*Mainichi Shimbun*, 9 February 2001).
- Jusco will sell vegetables at low prices for 3 days from the tenth, when the store price is rising due to poor harvest due to unseasonable weather such as heavy snow. Jusco purchases a large amount from contract farmers and sells radish, domestic cabbage, and so on at a discount of 30–50% of the current store price (*Nikkei Shimbun*, 9 February 2001).
- Due to the record heavy snowfall, the use of ski resorts in the Tohoku region has dropped significantly. Lift passenger revenues in 2000 fell by double digits. The bad weather caused by heavy snow hit the market and the number of customers was greatly reduced from the lack of snow in the previous season (*Nikkei*, 28 April 2001).
- Summer products are selling well due to the intense heat every day. Sales of air conditioners, beverages, frozen desserts, and daily necessities have increased significantly from the previous year. The heat wave effect has spread to materials such as containers, and more and more companies are preparing to increase production. The intense heat stimulates personal consumption and supports the economy (*Nikkei*, 25 July 2001).
- At the rooftop beer garden of the building in the center of Sendai city, the heat wave continued in July and it was busy every day, but the number of visitors since the beginning of August is about half of last year. According to the Sendai District Meteorological Observatory, the average temperature in July in Sendai was 24.7 °C, which was 2.6 °C higher than normal, but in early August it was 21.0 °C, which is 3.5 °C lower than normal (*Nikkei Shimbun*, 15 August 2001).

The weather risks that affect a company’s profit and loss are shown in Table 15.1.

Table 15.1 Weather risk of reduced profits and industry

Weather risk (decrease in profits)	Business type
Cold summer	Power companies, beverages, air conditioner makers, pools, seaside houses, swimwear makers, beer gardens
Heavy rain	Amusement parks, restaurant industry, fresh food sales, golf courses, department stores, namagashi manufacturing and sales, construction companies
Typhoon	Event companies, transportation (ships, aviation), agriculture, local government pools, seaside houses, theme parks
Warm winter	Gas companies, kerosene sales, heating equipment manufacturing, winter clothing manufacturing, ski resorts (light snow)

Source: Various materials

It is said that three-quarters of companies are affected by the weather. Such weather risks need to be dealt with by changing the product mix or the input market based on the management strategy for long-term climate changes. However, it is effective to deal with risks such as weather change that temporarily deviates from the average by risk financing, such as weather derivatives explained in this chapter.

The first weather derivative transaction to address this weather risk was in September 1997 between the comprehensive energy companies ENRON and Koch. It covered winter temperatures in the Wisconsin region between 1997 and 1998. ENRON, headquartered in Houston, Texas, had lower revenues during the cold summer due to lower demand for air conditioning and so lower electricity usage. On the other hand, the demand for gas used for heating decreases in the warm winter. Therefore, ENRON has begun to hedge the risks of both parties by using a derivative contract with Koch, a northern energy company whose profits decline in the warm winter. In the United States, the liberalization of electricity is progressing, and it is difficult to pass on the decrease in revenue to electricity charges when profits decline in the cold summer, which has led to weather derivative transactions.

15.2 Weather Derivatives

15.2.1 Features of Weather Derivatives

A weather derivative is a transaction in which the settlement amount is determined based on the average weather data for a certain period and the difference between the actual weather data for that period and the standard. Companies whose performance is affected by extreme weather events can avoid that risk with weather derivatives. In weather derivatives, standard conditions are set based on meteorological phenomena such as temperature, humidity, rainfall, snowfall, frost, wind speed, and typhoons. It is a weather derivative that promises the right to pay the amount calculated based on the difference between this condition and the actual value. The purchaser of the weather derivative pays the option fee, and the seller pays the purchaser compensation depending on the result of the weather.

The characteristics of weather derivatives are as follows.

1. The reference meteorological data is various weather data such as temperature, wind, precipitation, and snowfall, but usually, meteorological data that combines several meteorological events is used instead of a single data.
2. Weather derivatives target weather risks that have a high probability of occurrence but a small amount of damage, such as cold summer, rather than major damage that has a low probability of occurrence but a large amount of damage, such as an earthquake.
3. For weather derivatives, payment is decided only by the realized weather events, regardless of the amount of damage actually incurred by the contractor. The criteria for payment is called a trigger event, but in weather derivatives payment is made when indicators such as temperature reach a predetermined criterion.
4. Since payment is made regardless of whether or not actual damage has occurred, there is a possibility that basis risk will occur, which will cause a difference between the receipt of the contractor and the actual amount of damage. Therefore, the amount received may be less than the amount of damage to the contractor.
5. The index data is objective meteorological data from a neutral third party, such as the Japan Meteorological Agency. The Japan Meteorological Agency's Amedas Data has been observed since 1976 at approximately 1300 locations nationwide. Recently, there have been cases where weather derivatives are sold to overseas companies using satellite observation data, such as that from NASA.[1]

The conditions for determining weather derivatives are as follows.

1. *Target risk.* The target risk is a meteorological phenomenon that affects the profits of each company. The target risks include maximum temperature, minimum temperature, average temperature, precipitation, snowfall, snow depth, wind speed, and sunshine duration, and these may be combined.
2. *Observation point.* This observation point is generally selected as the point most affected by climate change.
3. *Exercise value (strike).* The exercise value is a numerical value at which payment is started, and this exercise value is determined.
4. *Payment period.* The payment period depending on the target weather is generally several weeks to several months.

[1]In December 2016, Mitsui Sumitomo Insurance Co Ltd. launched a weather derivative using satellite observation data from NASA and others to compensate for the risk of damage to mine development due to heavy rain and damage to aquaculture business due to rising seawater temperature.

5. *Payment method.* Based on the exercise value, if it exceeds or falls below it, the method of calculating the payment amount is determined, such as XX yen per day.
6. *Maximum payment amount.* The set payment limit per contract.

15.2.2 Types of Weather Derivatives

There are two types of weather derivatives: the option type and swap type. The option type is a form in which a business company pays a premium to an insurance company in advance and receives a certain amount of compensation if a meteorological event, such as temperature exceeds, or falls below a certain level within a certain period of time. There are two types of options trading: a "call option" transaction in which the contractor receives a larger amount as the index becomes larger, and a "put option" transaction in which the contractor receives a larger amount as the index becomes smaller.

The profit and loss of the call option transaction of the weather derivative is illustrated in Fig. 15.1.

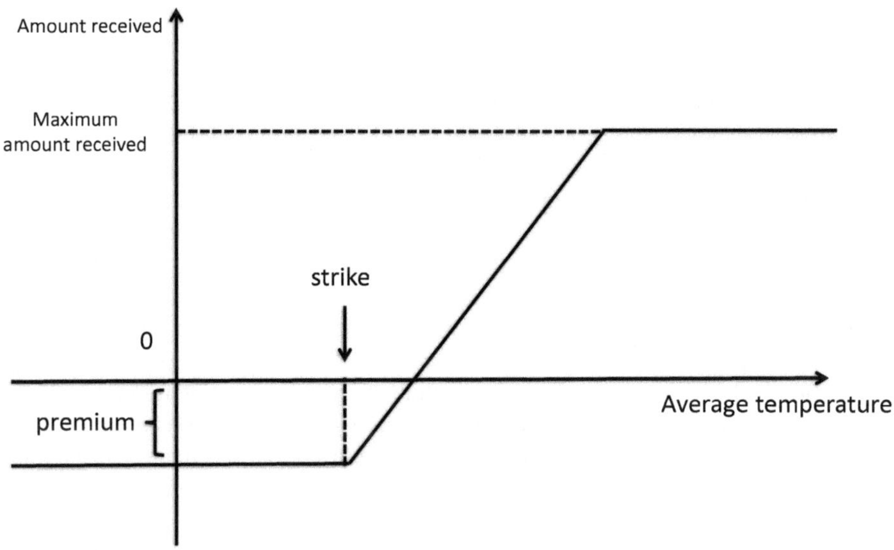

Fig. 15.1 Weather derivative call options trading (*Source:* Various materials)

The profit and loss of put options trading of weather derivatives is shown in Fig. 15.2.

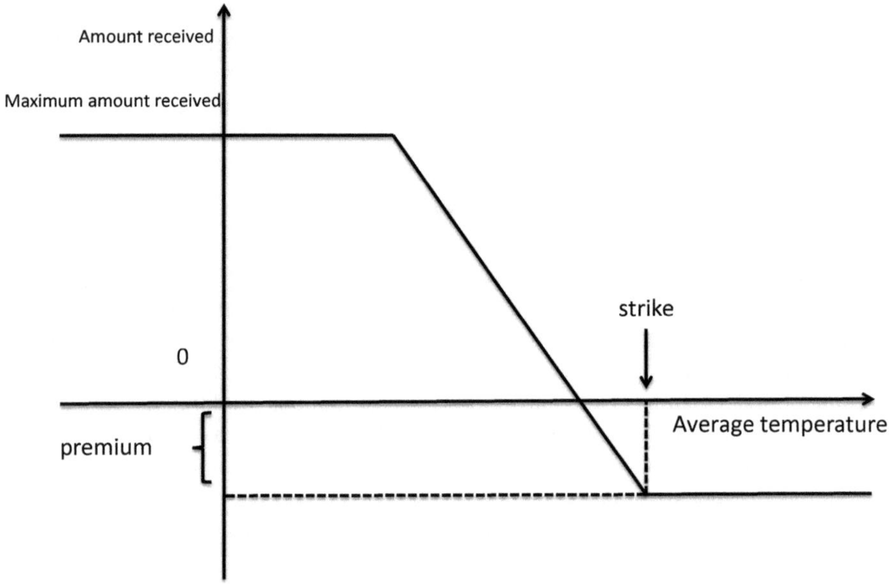

Fig. 15.2 Gains and losses on put options transactions for weather derivatives (*Source:* Various materials)

Insurance derivatives, including weather derivatives, have no underlying assets. Therefore, the underlying asset cannot be traded in insurance derivatives. However, it separates call options and put options based on the shape of the fund transfer curve of the option with the underlying asset. That is, when the index increases beyond the strike value, the amount received increases is called a call option, and when the index decreases below the strike value, the amount received increases is called a put option. In both transactions, the financial burden on the contractor who is the buyer of the option is limited to the premium paid to the seller at the time of contract.

In addition, the swap form is a method in which business companies exchange different weather risks. Swap-type transactions do not require a premium to be paid in advance between contracting operators. If the weather conditions are conditions that increase the company's profits during a certain period, the funds will be paid, and if the weather conditions are conditions that the company's profits will decrease, the funds will be received.

Fig. 15.3 illustrates the profit and loss of the weather derivative swap transaction.

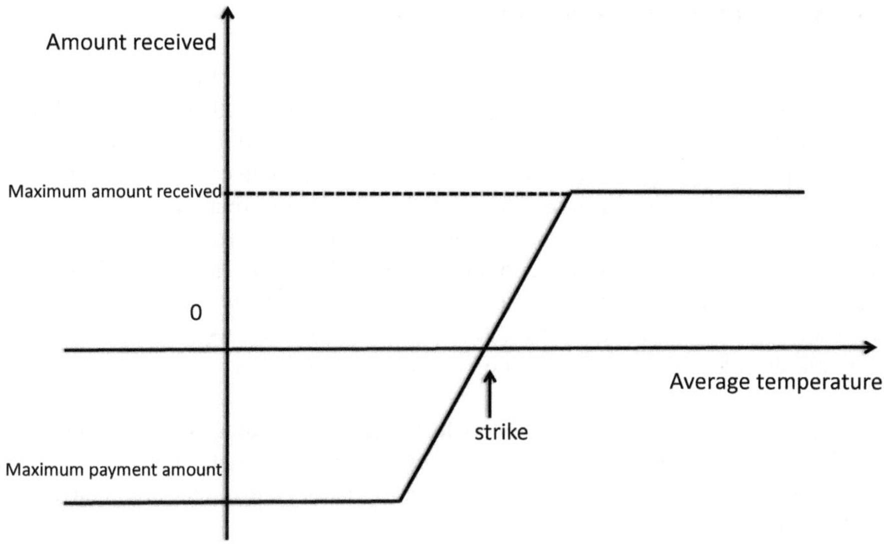

Fig. 15.3 Gain/loss of swap transactions of weather derivatives (*Source:* Various materials)

A variant of this swap is called a collar. In collar trading, if the weather conditions during the observation period are within a certain range, such as ±1 °C of the average temperature funds will not be exchanged with each other, and if it exceeds that range funds will be exchanged. It is called a collar transaction because the curve that represents the transfer of funds in this form of transaction resembles a collar.

The profit and loss of the collar transaction of the weather derivative is shown in Fig. 15.4.

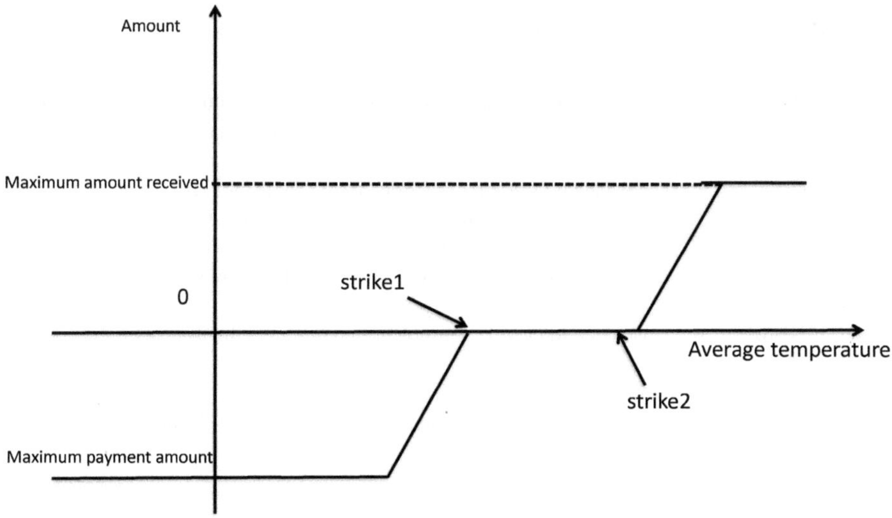

Fig. 15.4 Gain/loss of collar transaction of weather derivative (*Source:* Various materials)

15.2.3 Effects of Weather Derivatives

The effects of purchasing weather derivatives are as follows. First, it will stabilize management because it will be a countermeasure against weather risks. It will be a means of risk management for weather risks and will be a countermeasure against a decrease in corporate profits (decrease in sales and increase in costs) due to abnormal weather. Secondly, it is effective in terms of the IR (investor relations) of a company. In other words, it is possible to explain to business partners and investors the proactive risk management efforts of companies. Thirdly, in the event of abnormal weather, cash back using the payment of weather derivatives can be implemented and used as a means of promoting sales of services or products.

Examples of the use of weather derivatives are as follows.

1. Company A, which operates a soccer team, has a large sales of tickets on the day of the match, and purchased a weather derivative for the match date as a measure against the risk of a decrease in the number of visitors due to rainfall on the day of the match.
2. Company B, which operates an ice breaker garinko ship (sightseeing ship) in Hokkaido (Monbetsu), has a decrease in the number of passengers on the ship due to delays in the berthing of the ice breaker and earlier departure of shore due to the direction and strength of the wind.
3. Company C, which manufactures pickles, purchased a weather derivative in order to deal with the risk that the price of raw vegetables will rise due to lack of sunshine.

The added value (purchase effect) to the weather derivative service is set out in Table 15.2.

Table 15.2 Added value to weather derivative services (purchase effect)

Business type	How to use
Air conditioner	Cash back to contractors who purchased air conditioners in cold summer
Golf course	Cash back a part of the play price to the contractor who played on a hot day
Leasing business	Cash back part of the lease price to the contractor who leased the natto manufacturing equipment in the event of intense heat that affects the fermentation conditions of natto
Automobile supplies sales	Cash back to snow tire buyers in case of light snow
Sales of heating equipment	Cash back to heating equipment purchasers in the event of a mild winter
Japanese hotel	Abalone provided to guests on rainy days
Wedding hall	Wedding reception held on rainy days. Accommodation vouchers provided to couples

Source: Various materials

On the other hand, the amount of prizes such as cash back in the case of selling products is limited to 2% or less of the total planned sales or 100,000 yen by the Act against Unjustifiable Premiums and Misleading Representations.

15.3 Weather Derivatives Trading

15.3.1 CDD and HDD

Cooling degree days (CDDs) and heating degree days (HDDs) have traditionally been used as indexes for weather derivatives in the United States since the time of over-the-counter (OTC) transactions, and are also widely used in listed weather derivatives. Since fireplaces were ignited when the temperature reached 65 °F (18.315 °C), it is assumed that below this level ordinary households will start using heating appliances, and above this level they will start using air conditioners. For convenience, it has come to be used in the calculation of weather derivatives. The greater the deviation from 65 °F, the greater the energy consumption.[2]

HDD is the calculation of the frequency below 65 °F in winter and CDD is the calculation of the frequency above this in summer. Degree day means the difference between the average daily temperature, which is the sum of the maximum and minimum temperatures between 0:00 and 24:00 divided by 2, and 65 °F. The National Climate Data Center (NCDC) in the United States has announced HDDs and CDDs throughout the United States.

The daily HDD is expressed by a formula as follows.

$$\text{Daily HDD} = \text{Max}\left(0^{\circ} \text{ or } 65^{\circ} F - \text{daily average temperature}\right).$$

If the average daily temperature is 40 °F, then 65–40 = 25, so the daily HDD is 25. If the average daily temperature is 67 °F, 65–67 = −2 is less than zero, so the daily HDD is zero. CME Group's HDD index is the daily accumulation of HDDs in a month (calendar), and the final cash settlement is done for USD 100 per HDD. For example, if the average daily HDD in November in a city is 25 (65 °F − 40 °F), then November has 30 days, so the HDD index is 750 (daily HDD 25 × 30 days). If the HDD index in November is 750, the nominal price of the futures market in the city will be USD 75,000 (HDD index 750 × USD 100).

The daily CDD is expressed by the following formula. Calculated with daily CDD = Max (0, or daily average temperature − 65 °F). If the average temperature on a summer day is 85 °F, then 85–65 = 20, so the CDD is 20. If it is 62 °F, 62–65 = −3, so the CDD is 0. Like the HDD index, the CDD index is a daily

[2]The formula for converting Fahrenheit to Celsius is "(Fahrenheit F − 32) × 0.555 = C". On the other hand, the formula for converting Celsius to Fahrenheit is "1.8 × Celsius °C + 32 = °F". Celsius is a unit of temperature where the freezing point of water is 0° and the boiling point is 100°. Fahrenheit, on the other hand, is a unit of temperature with a freezing point of water of 32° and a boiling point of 212°, separated by 180°.

collection of CDDs in one (calendar) month, with a final cash settlement of USD 100 per CDD. For example, if the average daily CDD in June for a city is 10 (75 °F – 65 °F), then June has 30 days, so the CDD index is 300 (daily CDD 10 × 30 days). Assuming a June CDD index of 300, the city's futures market has a nominal price of USD 30,000 (CDD index 300 × 100).

15.3.2 Listing of Weather Derivatives

Weather derivatives were listed on the Chicago Board of Trade (CBOT) after the outbreak of Hurricane Andrew in 1992. It started with the trading of anomalous disaster futures linked to the index provided by the Insurance Services Office, and then options trading (both put and call). After that, the index of futures and options was changed to PCS (Property Claims Service) because ISO could not fully reflect the damage caused by the 1995 California Northridge earthquake. However, due to the small volume of transactions, it was delisted in 2000. CBOT was acquired by CME Group in 2007.

In addition, an option was listed on the Bermuda Commodities Exchange, which was established in 1996, to cover personal property damage caused by extreme weather events in the United States. For this, the index by GCCI (the Guy Carpenter Catastrophe Index), which is calculated based on the amount of insurance claims paid by a specific insurance company (around 40 companies in total) and the premium income, was used. However, due to the small volume of transactions, the transaction was stopped after 2 years. The transactions of insurance derivatives as listed products did not grow sufficiently because the volume of transactions was small and the emphasis was on reinsurance transactions between insurers and reinsurers, but there was a basis risk.

The Chicago Mercantile Exchange (CME), the largest financial and commodity derivatives exchange in North America, listed the world's first weather derivative futures, futures options, and swaps on 22 September 1999. This was due to the liberalization of electricity in the United States and the surge in OTC weather derivatives due to the record warm winter caused by the El Nino phenomenon in 1997. At the beginning of the listing, it targeted four US cities (Atlanta, Chicago, Cincinnati, and New York) that targeted HDDs. Later, other regions were added, and CDD was also added as a target index. However, this weather derivative was delisted in 2000 due to sluggish trading.

The CME weather derivative is a monthly temperature futures and options contract with a cumulative index of CDDs or HDDs. For listed weather derivatives, CDD is targeted for the 5 months (summer) from May to September, and HDDs are targeted for the 5 months (winter) from October to March.

The characteristics of weather derivatives listed on CME are as follows. (1) Since it is an exchange transaction, there is no credit risk of the trading partner. In the case of OTC transactions, there is a credit risk of defaulting on the counterparty. However, in exchange transactions, the funds of market participants are settled by the exchange clearing house. (2) Trading participants need to deposit a certain amount of margin. (3) Transactions have been standardized and made smaller. Since the index has been standardized to CDD/HDD and the unit is USD 100, not only large-lot transactions but also small-lot transactions have come to be carried out. (4) With CME, 24-h trading is possible using a dedicated electronic trading system. In transactions via exchanges, market prices are formed.

In addition, three giant hurricanes, collectively known as KRW (Katrina, Rita, and Wilma), which struck America in 2005, listed US hurricane risk futures and options on CME in 2007. Transactions at CME use an index called the CMI (the CME Hurricane Index), which measures the amount of potential damage caused by hurricanes, based on data from the National Weather Service's National Hurricane Center.

15.4 Weather Derivatives in Japan

In Japan, the Insurance Business Law, which came into effect in December 1998, allowed insurance companies to sell weather derivative products. However, none have been listed and are sold OTC. On 25 June 1999, the first weather derivative contract was signed between Mitsui Sumitomo Insurance Company (currently Mitsui Sumitomo Insurance Co Ltd.) and Himalayan Co Ltd. (a major general sports retailer focusing on skiing and snowboarding). It was a premium fee of ten million yen for the risk of low rainfall. In the end, because it snowed, the settlement amount was not paid to Himalayan Co Ltd.

The characteristics of weather derivatives traded in Japan are as follows.

First, since the buyers of weather derivatives in the United States are mainly energy companies, many of them use HDD and CDD as indexes and temperature as the target risk.[3] However, the buyers of weather derivatives in Japan are diverse, such as department stores, trading companies, restaurants, construction companies, retail companies, travel companies, and apparel companies, in addition to energy companies.

Second, since the buyers of weather derivatives in Japan are diverse, the target risks are also various meteorological phenomena such as temperature, humidity, rainfall, snowfall, frost, wind speed, and typhoons. At present, it seems that there are many targets for temperature, rainfall, snowfall, and typhoons. However, as the production of renewable energies such as wind and solar power is expected to increase, weather derivatives using sunshine hours and wind as an index are also expected to increase.

Third, weather derivatives in the United States are listed on exchanges. However, weather derivatives in Japan have never been listed and are traded through OTC transactions.

Fourth, product development and risk underwriting of weather derivatives in Japan are mainly carried out by non-life insurance companies and major banks.

[3]In some cases, the target risk in weather derivatives is called the underlying asset.

The non-life insurance company and major banks also sell directly, but regional banks and credit unions have joined as agents. In addition, major banks hedge some of the risks they take on non-life insurance companies. The reason is that insurance companies have traditionally assumed the risk of natural disasters such as storms and floods. In addition, the market for weather derivatives is not well developed, and the calculation of the premium is a specialty of insurance companies that use statistical methods to calculate insurance premiums.

Fifth, energy companies such as electric power companies and gas companies have a large impact on the profits of weather risk. Energy companies tend to prefer the exchange of risk through swaps between energy companies.

The sales channels for weather derivatives in Japan is illustrated in Fig. 15.5.

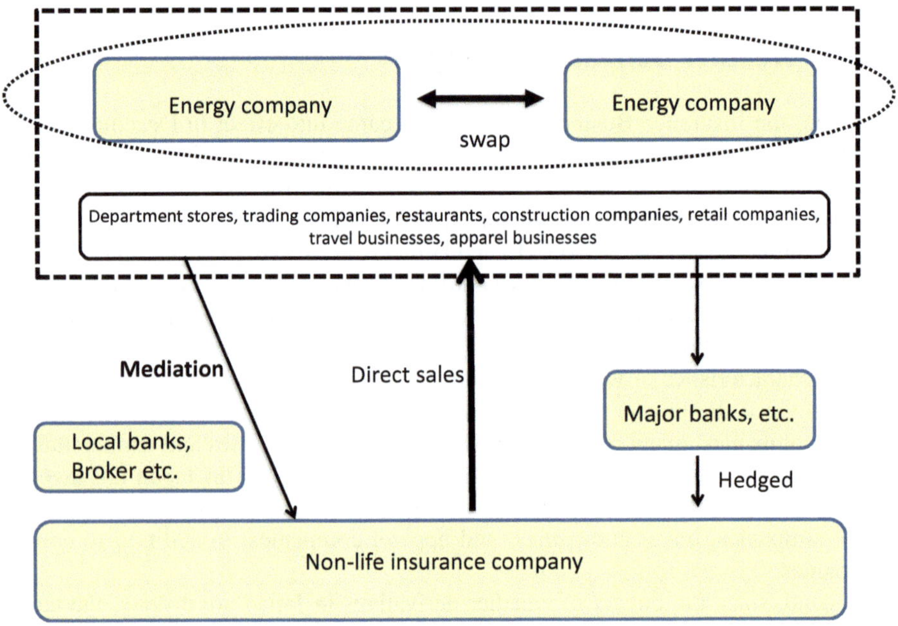

Fig. 15.5 Sales channels for weather derivatives in Japan (*Source:* Various materials)

15.5 Examples of Weather Derivative Products

15.5.1 Risk Exchange Transactions

The Chugoku Electric Power Co Inc. and Hiroshima Gas Co Ltd. signed an agreement to exchange the risk of temperature fluctuations in the summer of 2003. There is an inverse correlation between Chugoku Electric Power and Hiroshima Gas in summer temperature and profits. In other words, the profit of Chugoku Electric Power increases during the heat wave when the demand for air conditioning increases, but the profit decreases during the cold summer because the demand for air conditioning decreases. However, the profit of Hiroshima Gas decreases in the hot summer when the demand for hot water supply for households decreases, and increases in the cold summer because the demand for hot water supply for households increases. The exchange means that Chugoku Electric Power will pay Hiroshima Gas a part of the increase in sales during a hot summer, and Hiroshima Gas will pay a part of the increase in sales to Chugoku Electric Power in a cold summer. The conditions for risk exchange transactions are as follows:

1. *Target period*: 1 July 2003 to 30 September 2003 (92 days)
2. *Transaction index*: average temperature during the target period with the Hiroshima Local Meteorological Observatory as the observation point
3. *Standard temperature*: the temperature agreed upon by both companies. Set the transactions of both companies to be equal based on the temperature of the same period in the past
4. *Transaction details*: when the actual average temperature during the target period exceeds the standard temperature of +0.8 °C, Chugoku Electric Power will pay Hiroshima Gas a pre-arranged amount according to the temperature above the standard temperature. In the cold summer when the actual average temperature during the target period falls below the standard temperature of −0.8 °C, Hiroshima Gas will pay Chugoku Electric Power a pre-arranged amount according to the temperature below. However, the maximum amount of money that can be exchanged is approximately 50 million yen when the standard temperature is ±2.0 ° C.

An outline of the temperature risk exchange between Chugoku Electric Power and Hiroshima Gas is given in Fig. 15.6.

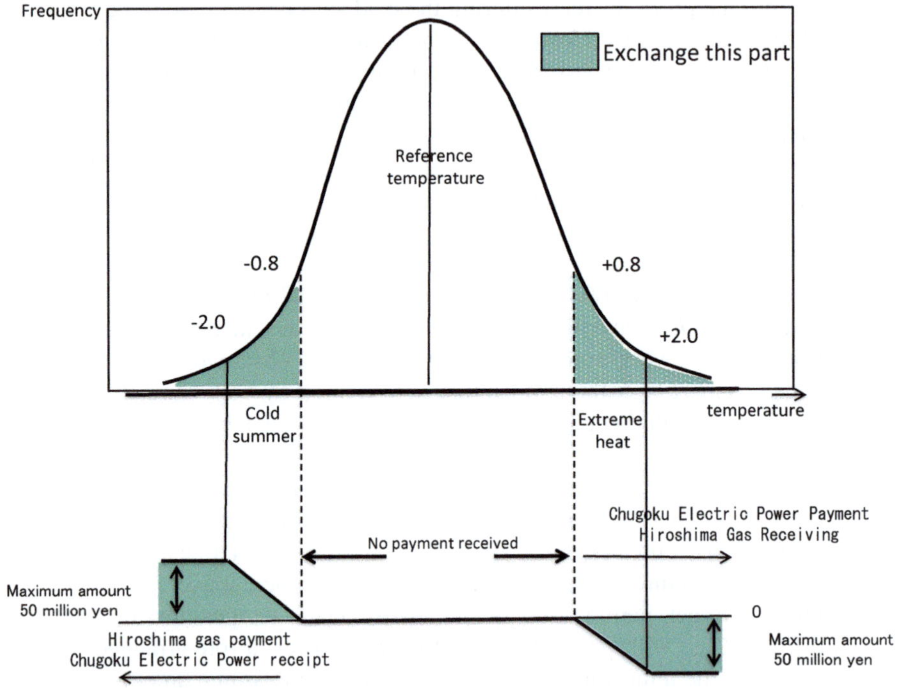

Fig. 15.6 Outline of temperature risk exchange between Chugoku Electric Power and Hiroshima Gas (*Source:* The news release of the Chugoku Electric Power and Hiroshima Gas)

15.5.2 Non-life Insurance Company Products

It is known that the sales of weather derivatives of non-life insurance companies are steadily increasing every year because the occurrence of abnormal weather, which is said to be caused by global warming, is increasing.

The weather risks by industry are given in Table 15.3.

Table 15.3 Weather risk by industry

Industry	Weather risk
Leisure (theme parks, golf courses, ski resorts, hotels, travel halls)	Visitors decrease due to rainfall, typhoons, earthquakes, snowfall, light snowfall, and so on
Retail/food and drink	Hedge the risk of a decrease in visitors due to rainfall, typhoons, snowfall, and so on
Beverages, apparel, heating and cooling equipment, kerosene, LP gas	Sales decrease due to cold summer and warm winter
Energy (electricity, gas, oil)	Risk of decreased sales due to cold summer or warm winter
Construction, transportation	Work delay due to rainfall, typhoon, snowfall, and so on

Source: Various materials

An example may be considered. The contractor is an outdoor beer restaurant that is open for a limited time. The risks are low temperature and rain and, when the temperature is low, the number of visitors drops sharply. In addition, although there is a rain shield, if it rains heavily, the store will be closed. The purpose is to hedge the risk of low temperature and heavy rain.

In this example, a weather derivative contracts might appear as in Table 15.4.

Table 15.4 Examples of low temperature and heavy rain

Transaction form	Low temperature or rainy days call option (European)
Target period	1 July–10 August 2002
Observation site	Sapporo, Hokkaido
Index	The number of days with a daily rainfall of 10 mm or more, or the total number of days with a maximum temperature of 22 °C or less
Exercise value	Fifth
Amount of payment	2 million yen per day
Maximum payment amount	20 million yen

Source: Various materials

This is an example of a weather derivative that prepares for rainfall. Since the premium equivalent to the insurance premium is set at a relatively small amount, 250,000 yen per unit, the number of subscription units can be selected from a small amount. During "Golden Week", which is a long holiday in May, if it rains more than 5 mm for a certain number of days (for example, 3 days in Tokyo), 500,000 yen per bite, up to three million yen will be paid.

Table 15.5 presents an example of the "If type", for businesses that want to prepare for long-term rainfall. The premium is 250,000–450,000 per unit and, if it

Table 15.5 Former Nissay Dowa damage

<table>
<tr><th colspan="2">Classification</th><th>Standard type</th><th>If type</th></tr>
<tr><td colspan="2">Meteorological observation site</td><td colspan="2">Ten areas of Sapporo, Sendai, Tokyo, Yokohama, Nagoya, Kyoto, Osaka, Kobe, Hiroshima and Fukuoka</td></tr>
<tr><td colspan="2">Meteorological observation period</td><td colspan="2">27 April–6 May 2002 (10 days)</td></tr>
<tr><td rowspan="3">Payment</td><td>Conditions</td><td colspan="2">Depending on the number of days of rainfall above a certain amount (daily precipitation of 5 mm) during the observation period, the following amount will be paid for each type for each day that exceeds the exemption days</td></tr>
<tr><td>Amount (per population)</td><td>Up to 500,000 yen and three million yen per day</td><td>Up to five million yen and ten million yen per day</td></tr>
<tr><td>Disclaimer days</td><td>Second for Sapporo/Tokyo, fourth for Nagoya, third for other meteorological stations</td><td>Five days at all meteorological sites</td></tr>
<tr><td colspan="2">Premium</td><td>250,000 yen per unit at all meteorological stations</td><td>250,000 yen for Sapporo/Tokyo, 450,000 yen for Nagoya, 300,000 yen for other meteorological observation sites</td></tr>
</table>

Source: The company's news release

rains 5 mm or more for 6 days or more during Golden Week which are consecutive holidays from the end of April to early May containing a number of Japanese holidays, five million yen per day, and up to ten million yen, will be paid. This is less likely to be received than the "standard type", but in the unlikely event the amount received will be larger than the standard type.

Discussion Questions

1. Explain, with examples, the impact of weather risk on businesses.
2. Give an example of a weather derivative and explain its characteristics and effects.
3. Explain, with examples, the actual situation of weather derivative transactions in the United States.
4. Explain the case and distribution of weather derivatives in Japan.

16 Risk Management in China

China is a large country with a population of about 1.4 billion people. Natural disasters such as earthquakes, typhoons, and floods occur frequently in China, and there is an insurance system in place to protect against these natural disasters. In addition, measures are being taken against cyber risks and pandemics. This chapter outlines the risk management in China.

16.1 Earthquake Risk

16.1.1 Characteristics of Earthquakes in China

Earthquakes in China can be characterized in the following way.

The first is the frequent occurrence of earthquakes. China is sandwiched between two major seismic zones, the Pacific Rim and the Europe-Asia seismic zone. It is also surrounded by the Pacific Plate, Indian Plate, and Philippine Sea Plate, and is located in an area where faults are active.

The second is the magnitude of the earthquakes. This includes not only the seismic intensity and magnitude, but also the large number of victims and economic loss due to the collapse of houses. The 1920 and 1932 Gansu earthquakes killed more than 170,000 people in total. More than 200,000 people were killed in the 1927 Nanchang earthquake. So, earthquakes in China are frequent and the amount of damage is enormous. In the twentieth century, three magnitude 8.5 class earthquakes were observed in the world—two of them occurred in China. It can be said, therefore, that the large scale of earthquakes in China is a major feature.

Third is the wide geographical spread of the earthquakes. Earthquakes of M5 or higher have occurred in a wide range of provinces and municipalities throughout China, and earthquakes with a seismic intensity of 7 or higher have been observed in 70% of medium- and large-sized cities with a population of one million or more.

H. Lee, *Risk Management*, Springer Texts in Business and Economics,
https://doi.org/10.1007/978-981-16-3468-0_16

China has 12 seismic floors, and M5 is equivalent to a seismic intensity of about 4 on the Japanese seismic intensity scale.

Fourth, most of the earthquakes that occur in China are direct earthquakes. Earthquakes that occur in China are not plate-type earthquakes that occur frequently in Japan and have relatively deep epicenters. The epicenter is shallow, and there are many earthquakes that cause great damage locally.

16.1.2 Large-Scale Earthquakes

The following are the past large-scale earthquakes that have occurred in China in recent years.

16.1.2.1 Tangshan Earthquake

On 28 July 1976, there was a M7.8 earthquake, with its epicenter near Tangshan City, Hebei Province, located in northeastern China. At that time, Tangshan, one of the leading industrial cities in China, was severely damaged, killing nearly 150,000 out of a population of about one million and destroying 94% of all buildings. According to official records, the death toll, including outside Tangshan, was about 240,000, most of which were caused by crushing under collapsed buildings. Additionally, 800,000 were injured.

Tangshan City had few seismic facilities in place against earthquakes, for two reasons.

First, the residents who lived in the eastern region at that time had low awareness of disaster prevention against earthquakes. In 1920, there was a major earthquake with a seismic intensity of 8.5 in Ningxia Haiyuan in western China. However, since then, there had been several earthquakes in the western region, but no severe earthquakes in the east. Therefore, it is presumed that the citizens of Tangshan in northeastern China had low awareness of disaster prevention against earthquakes and had not taken any defense measures.

Second, the seismic code did not require disaster prevention measures against earthquakes. Since the establishment of the People's Republic of China, the Ministry of Construction focused on earthquakes. However, it was in areas where earthquakes with a seismic intensity of 9 or higher could occur that the seismic standards were set in detail. The seismic intensity classification of Tangshan City was designated as 6°, and it was thought that only relatively weak earthquakes would occur.

For these reasons, it is presumed that Tangshan City did not have a disaster prevention plan for the earthquake. As a result, many of the buildings were made of bricks and lacked seismic strength, causing a lot of damage.

Tangshan was severely damaged, but experts from all over China made a restoration plan to transform the traditionally vulnerable metropolis with many tall buildings into low-rise buildings. Currently, it meets the earthquake resistance standards at a sufficiently high level. In fact, the seismic standard of Tangshan City has been set from seismic intensity 6 in 1976 to seismic intensity 8, similar to Beijing.

16.1.2.2 Sichuan Earthquake

The Sichuan earthquake was a direct earthquake with a magnitude of 7.9 that occurred on 12 May 2008 in Wenchuan County, Sichuan Province, China, and is said to have generated 30 times more energy than the Great Hanshin earthquake in Japan. The damage caused by the earthquake included 69,222 dead, a further 18,176 missing and presumed dead, 347,171 injured, 216,000 collapsed houses, 4.15 million damaged houses, and a direct economic loss of 852.3 billion yuan. Companies in each industry suffered serious economic losses from the quake.

According to statistics from Sichuan Province, 16,280 companies in all provinces were damaged by the Sichuan earthquake, and the direct economic loss reached 99.78 billion yuan. Of the 66 listed companies, one-third were affected by the earthquake. Due to the great destructive power of the Sichuan earthquake, 51,429 companies in the provinces around Sichuan, such as Sichuan, Gansu, and Chongqing, suffered damage, and the direct economic loss exceeded 20 billion yuan.

16.1.2.3 Yunnan Earthquake

An earthquake struck Yunnan Province on 3 August 2014 at 17:30 Japan time. The epicenter was 10 km underground and the scale was M6.2. There were 589 dead, nine missing and presumed dead, and 2401 injured. Similar to the Sichuan earthquake, the cause was that the Indo-Australian plate collided with the Eurasian plate. 170,000 homes were damaged, of which 29,000 were totally lost, 42,000 partially destroyed, and almost 100,000 partially lost.

16.1.3 Earthquake Insurance

As a general rule, life insurance and agricultural insurance were not exempt from earthquake liability, so even damage caused by an earthquake was paid in the same way as other natural disasters. However, in 1958, all insurance businesses were abolished nationwide in order to carry out socialist policies. Insurance business was resumed in 1980, and China's agricultural insurance, to cover the damage caused by the decrease in agricultural yield due to natural disasters, was reopened after the reform and opening up in 1982.

Agricultural insurance is currently supervised by the Ministry of Health and Welfare (equivalent to the Ministry of Health, Labor and Welfare of Japan) and the Ministry of Agriculture, and is sold by private insurance companies while providing subsidies. Most domestic life insurance companies include earthquakes in their insurance coverage. Life insurance that covers a person's body and life, including life insurance (term life insurance, whole life insurance, and so on), accident insurance, medical insurance, travel accident insurance, and so on, usually includes earthquake coverage.

On the other hand, from 1980 to 1996, when the establishment of a private non-life insurance company was approved, property insurance was held responsible for all natural disasters. However, since natural disasters occurred frequently and some insurance companies had a deficit in their insurance balance, property insurance was exempted from liability for natural disasters such as earthquakes and tsunamis. "Earthquake supplementary insurance" has been approved by the China Insurance Supervisory Commission since July 2000, but it is usually too risky for insurance companies to explain when selling insurance. In addition, since the insurance premiums for earthquake insurance are also high for policyholders, they were often excluded when taking out insurance. As a result, the existence of "earthquake supplementary insurance" was not recognized in the market for a long time.

In addition, the Chinese government, led by the China Insurance Supervision and Administration Committee, has since 2001 been conducting research on the earthquake insurance system, and has promoted the earthquake disaster insurance business including financial support in the wake of the 2008 Sichuan earthquake. Then, on 17 May 2016, it announced a plan to implement earthquake catastrophe insurance for residential residents in urban and rural areas of China. Based on this, 45 insurance companies were established as a joint insurance pool to provide coverage for earthquake risk.

This earthquake insurance covers the housing of urban and rural residents. In addition, this earthquake insurance is a flat-rate insurance plan, and the insurance amount is calculated based on the national standards set by the National Earthquake Bureau and the Ministry of Civil Affairs, taking into consideration the insurance payment method of rural housing insurance in each region. As a general rule, the insurance payment is mainly for the building itself and the attached equipment in the rooms that meet the building quality standards (including earthquake-resistance standards) set by the government. In addition, the main insurance liability covers destructive earthquake motions and secondary disasters such as tsunamis, fires, explosions, land subsidence, debris flows, and landslides caused by them. Table 16.1 lays out the content of residential earthquake giant disaster insurance.

Table 16.1 Residential earthquake giant disaster insurance

Classification	Contents	
Coverage	Insured house and indoor ancillary facilities (insurance decorations and signs, indoor property, attached buildings are exempt)	
Compensation liability	Tsunami, fire, volcanic eruption, explosion, and so on due to destructive earthquake vibration[a]	
Insurance amount Destruction grade: I: No compensation II: No compensation III: 50% of insurance amount (half loss) IV and V: 100% of insurance amount	Minimum amount: Castle Town Housing: 50,000 yuan Rural housing: 20,000 yuan	Maximum amount: Urban housing: one million yuan Rural housing: one million yuan
Insurance premium	At least four yuan Note: Insurance premium standards vary depending on the area, degree of risk, and structure of the building facility	

Source: Mitsui Sumitomo Insurance (China) Co Ltd.

[a]M4.7 grade or intensity VI and above earthquakes published by the National Earthquake Department

The basic insurance money for this earthquake insurance is 50,000 yuan per house for urban residents and 20,000 yuan per house for rural residents. This insurance amount was set for each city and rural area, taking into consideration each situation, such as the overall structure of the house, average reconstruction cost, and compensation/relief level after a disaster.

The insurance money for earthquake insurance is a flat-rate insurance plan to simplify the operation and spread it rapidly. In addition, the insurance money to be paid is calculated based on the insurance amount and with reference to the national standard set by the National Earthquake Bureau and the Ministry of Civil Affairs.

In addition, the insurance money will be adjusted according to the five levels set according to the degree of damage to the house. In other words, if the degree of damage is grade I and grade II, it is considered that there is almost no damage and no insurance money is paid. In the case of grade III (moderate damage), 50% of the insurance money will be paid. If the degree of damage is grade IV (serious damage) and grade V (total destruction), the insurance money will be paid in full. In addition to earthquakes, secondary disasters such as tsunamis, fires, explosions, land subsidence, and landslides are also covered.

16.2 Typhoon/Flood

16.2.1 Occurrence of Disaster

China is a country located in the east of the Eurasian continent and has the world's fourth largest land area of about 9.6 million km^2. Its vast land is about 5000 km east to west and about 4000 km north to south, so even within a country, the climate varies greatly from place to place.

Hainan Island at the southern end has a savanna climate, the southern part of the mainland has a mild winter temperate/humid climate, and the Seibu mountain range has a tundra climate. In addition, the Gobi Desert spreads out in the area adjacent to Mongolia, and it has a desert climate. Northeastern China has a subarctic winter climate with light rain. In the summer, the temperature rises and precipitation increases due to the influence of the monsoon. In addition, typhoons near the equator approach and may be exposed to storms. In addition, the coastal areas may be damaged by storm surges due to the effects of typhoons. On the other hand, although the northeastern part has a high latitude, it is dry, so heavy snowfall does not cause much damage.

First of all, regarding typhoons, the coastal areas of China may overlap with the course of typhoons, so they are often damaged by typhoons. In August 2009, heavy rain caused by a typhoon caused a debris flow, affecting about 8.8 million people in four provinces. Following that, typhoons landed continuously in 2018 and 2019, causing great damage. In particular in 2019, just as in 2009, heavy rains caused by typhoons caused debris flows and landslides, resulting in the evacuation of 1.2 million people.

Heavy rains have caused flood damage in China. In May 2015, a once in every 50 years flood occurred in Jiangxi Province. In 2016, heavy rain floods in Gangbuk province, killing 130 people throughout the province. In 2018, a torrential downpour flooded the Xinjiang Uygur Autonomous Region, killing 20 people with eight missing. In addition, part of the dam collapsed in the heavy rain.

In addition, floods caused by heavy rains that have continued since June 2020 in China caused flooding over a wide area of the Yangtze River basin. As a result, the embankment broke due to the muddy stream, houses were flooded, and many residents evacuated on boats and rafts. According to the Chinese government, heavy rains killed at least 141 people, and in July 2020 alone nearly 15 million people were forced to evacuate. Every year in the Yangtze River basin, floods occur due to summer rainfall and the melting of glaciers in the upstream Tibet Plateau. A list of recent typhoon and flood events is given in Table 16.2.

Table 16.2 Typhoons and floods in China

Date of occurrence	Damage
August 2009	Heavy rain caused by typhoon No 8 caused a debris flow in Zhejiang Province, China. In addition to the damage in this province, more than 6000 homes collapsed in Fujian, Jiangsu, and Anhui provinces. About 8.8 million people were affected
May 2015	Heavy rain caused a once every 50 years flood in Jiangxi province. Road floods, landslides, and debris flows also occurred in other provinces
August 2015	Large typhoon No 13 landed in Fujian Province, China. 14 people were killed, four were declared missing, and more than 180,000 were evacuated due to landslides and debris flows
July 2016	Heavy rains continued in Hebei Province, causing floods and landslides. 130 people died throughout the province
August 2018	Floods caused by torrential rains in the western Xinjiang Uygur Autonomous Region resulted in 20 dead, eight missing
September 2018	A large and strong typhoon No 22 landed in Guangdong Province, China, killing two people. About 2.45 million people have been evacuated in the ministry
August 2019	A large and extremely strong typhoon No 9 landed in Zhejiang Province on the coast of China, killing 32 people, with 16 people missing due to landslides and debris flows caused by heavy rain. 1.2 million people have been evacuated in Zhejiang, Shanghai, Jiangsu and Shandong
July 2020	Floods occurred in the upper reaches of the Yangtze River due to heavy rain. Heavy rains in Chongqing, Guizhou, Guangxi Zhuang Autonomous Region, Hubei, Hunan, Jiangxi, Anhui, and Jiangsu, resulted in high water levels

Source: Various materials

The Emergency Management Department is in charge of these "flood disasters" within the Chinese government. The department manages disasters in collaboration with local governments and, at the same time, supports relief activities for disaster-stricken areas and people.

16.2.2 Agricultural Disaster Insurance

Established in 1949, the Chinese People's Insurance Company has been providing livestock insurance for the first time in Shandong, Sichuan, and Beijing since 1950, targeting 1384 farm cattle. At that time, cattle for farming were the most important property of farmers. An insurance cooperation company was established to develop this livestock insurance, and farmers who voluntarily took out livestock insurance became employees of the cooperation company by paying a small amount of funds. The insurance cooperation company purchased reinsurance from the prefecture's accounting firm. In the event of a natural disaster or illness, insurance companies could borrow money from the people's insurance company if their income could not keep up with their spending. In some areas, the state-owned Agricultural Bank provided specialized loans to livestock insurance cooperation companies.[1]

From 1951, livestock insurance was tried one after another all over the country, and in 1952 14 million cattle were insured. Among them, 400,000 cows died and insurance money was paid to farmers. At that time, the insurance money for cattle per cow was set at 80% of the market price of cattle, and 20% was borne by the farmers themselves. After that, because there was an opinion that the insurance money paid was small, the insurance money was raised to 100% of the market price of cattle. However, due to a moral hazard in which farmers no longer value cattle, the insurance money was adjusted to 80% of the market price of cattle.

After that, agricultural disaster insurance was expanded to cotton, tobacco, paddy rice, corn, and so on, and was sometimes suspended. In 2007, Central Finance contributed 2.15 billion yuan to subsidize the first agricultural insurance premium. Insurance premiums for the trial project were subsidized in 3 units: the central government, provinces/autonomous regions, and cities/prefectures. The actual contributions of the participating farmers are only about 20% of the total contributions. The government has granted a business tax exemption to insurance companies that run agricultural disaster insurance. In 2012, the Agricultural Disaster Insurance Law, the Agricultural Insurance Ordinance, was promulgated.

Subsidies for agricultural disaster insurance were provided by the central, provincial, city/prefecture, farmers and other related departments at a "joint burden". The amount of subsidy for central finance is determined by item according to the importance of agricultural products related to the national economy and people's lives. Specifically, the subsidy amount for major agricultural products such as paddy rice, wheat, corn, cotton, and oil-extracted crops is about 35–68%, and the subsidy amount for major livestock such as breeding pigs and dairy cows is about 40–80%. Each province/municipality/autonomous region bears a subsidy of 25–50%, and the city/prefecture bears a subsidy of 15–40%. As a result, the premium borne by the farmers is equivalent to about 20% of the total amount.

[1]QIN Meng-ni, Study on the Spread Factors of Agricultural Disaster Insurance in China (Tohoku University, 2015).

There are various management models for the agricultural disaster insurance trial project all over the country, and the following five are typical.

First, as a government-sponsored model, a local government invests to establish a specialized agricultural insurance company—for example, Anshin Agricultural Insurance Co Ltd. in Shanghai.

Second, as a commercial insurance company model, a commercial insurance company manages agricultural disaster business insurance under the initiative of the government. Most provinces and autonomous regions, such as Beijing and Hebei, have adopted this type of management—for example, Beijing's Anhua Agricultural Insurance Co Ltd.

Thirdly, as a mutual company (mutual assistance) model, agricultural insurance cooperative companies established mainly by farmers form an agricultural accident insurance group at the town / prefecture level and manage agricultural accident insurance. It is a model in which a mutual insurance company is established at the city/provincial level to plan and coordinate agricultural disaster insurance operations—for example, Heilongjiang Province's Sunshine Agricultural Mutual Aid Insurance Company.

Fourth, as a joint insurance model, a management method is to establish an agricultural disaster insurance joint insurance body with the support of the government, instead of a specialized agricultural insurance company—for example, the Zhejiang joint insurance model can be mentioned.

Fifth, as a government-insurance company alliance model, an insurance company manages agricultural accident insurance together with the government—for example Guoyuan Agricultural Insurance Company in Anhui Province, which was founded in 2005 by 12 state-owned enterprises.

The agricultural disaster insurance system has the following characteristics. First, in most areas, agricultural disaster insurance employs cost rather than yield as the basis for its compensation. The cost standard basically covers only agricultural production costs such as seeds, fertilizers, and labor costs, regardless of the yield. The second is compulsory enrollment, depending on the type or region of grain. Crops are divided into important food crops (such as paddy rice, wheat and corn, which are closely related to the national economy and people's lives) and general crops. Forcibly enrolling these important food crops in insurance has contributed to the income of participating farmers and the stability of the national grain market. In addition, farmers in developed areas such as Beijing and Shanghai can join voluntarily, but provinces with relatively low economic power, such as Anhui Province, are compulsory joining all provinces. Third, farmers who have taken out agricultural disaster insurance are required to record and report on the crops and livestock covered by the insurance during the period of enrollment. For example, in the case of livestock insurance, for livestock raised in the area for 1 year or more, the presence or absence of illness, nutritional status, and so on within the scope of insurance liability are inoculated by the immune procedure of the prefecture-class quarantine department, and records and reports are required. Fourth, there is a cooperation staff system. A counselor is a person who cooperates with the agricultural disaster insurance business. Most of the counselors are village residents and, after being hired by an insurance company, they receive various trainings and cooperate for the smooth execution of agricultural disaster insurance services.

16.3 Cyber Risk

16.3.1 Overview

It has long been said that China has a lower level of security measures than Japan and Western countries. However, in recent years, the situation has improved, due to the success of the enactment of cybersecurity law and the strengthening of control by the authorities.

The threat trend changes every year, but the damage caused by targeted attacks, fraudulent e-mails, and ransomware is large. Attacks that exploit weaknesses in the supply chain are also increasing. This is a chain of risks caused by insufficient cyber security of the trading partner. The main kinds of cyber attacks are as follows.

16.3.1.1 Malware Infection

“Malware" is an abbreviation for “malicious software”. The following software and programs that are created with the intention of causing problems are generic names.

First, worms are a typical example of malicious malware. They increase the number of programs that cause malfunctions by self-proliferating rather than just being infected. Sometimes the system transforms existing programs.

Second, there is Trojan horse malware. At first glance, it looks like no problem, but it is in fact malware that, like its namesake in Greek mythology, disguises itself and, after a while, starts to behave harmfully. It is also characterized by no self-renewal function.

Third, there is malware known by the English term “backdoor”. It works by sending malware to a computer or smartphone as a virus that opens a back door that is easy to invade later, causing harm. Trojan horses are also known as backdoor-related malware.

Fourth, ransom is a word that ordinarily means the sum paid to recover a hostage. The feature is that the files and other data of the infected computer become hostages and cannot be read. It is called ransomware because it is a mechanism that requires money on condition that the data is restored.

16.3.1.2 Targeted Attack E-mail

Targeted attack-type e-mail is an attack method that targets a specific organization or individual mainly using e-mail and aims to steal important information related to that organization or individual. By opening an attached file that may be infected with malware, information in the computer may be stolen, and the security of the entire organization may be dangerously compromised. This includes junk e-mail files.

16.3.1.3 DoS/DDoS Attacks

A DoS, or denial of service, attack is one of the attack methods that targets computers and communication devices through a communication network, sending a lot of illegal data to drive the system of the other computer into a state where it cannot operate normally. Where this is performed from multiple locations at the same time, it is known as a DDoS, or distributed denial of service, attack.

16.3.1.4 Website Tampering

Website tampering is an attack in which the content or system of a legitimate website operated by an organization or an individual is tampered with by an attacker and changed to an unintended state.

16.3.1.5 List-Type Account Hacking

List-type account hacking is a method in which an attacker who obtains an ID and password of an organization or an individual by some means logs into any system or site by listing these IDs and passwords.

16.3.1.6 Watering Hole Attack

A watering hole attack is a method directed at websites frequently used by specific users who are the target of the attack. The attacker examines the websites that the attacked users often visit and puts a virus on the websites to infect the users who visit the sites.

16.3.2 Cybersecurity Law

The Cybersecurity Law was enacted on 1 June 2017, with the aim of ensuring corporate and individual rights, as well as China's sovereignty and security. First of all, China has its own concept of cyber security, which has a very different meaning from that of Japan, the United States, and Western countries. China's cybersecurity sees cyberspace as free, and the threat is a cyberattack on the national critical infrastructure that is the basis of people's lives. However, on the other hand, China and Russia regard cyberspace as something that the government should manage as much as possible, and the government judges whether it is information that threatens the domestic system and considers all that correspond to it as a threat. Other countries have criticized it for controlling the speech and ideas of the people, but China is increasing this tendency year by year.

The contents of the Cybersecurity Law include protection of personal information, storage of confidential information, and penalties for legal liability. In principle, data transfer to foreign countries was also prohibited. In addition, the target business operators of this Cybersecurity Law are defined as network operators. This applies even if the service of setting up a website outside the company is not provided, as long as information is exchanged via the network, both inside and outside the company. As a result, almost all companies in China will be covered. It was also stipulated that important information infrastructure operators should be under the close scrutiny of Chinese authorities. However, it is significant that this law provides clear guidance on corporate IT management responsibilities.

An outline of China's Cybersecurity Law is given in Table 16.3.

Table 16.3 Overview of China's Cybersecurity Law

Classification	Contents
Protection of personal information	Clarified requirements for collection, specifications, and protection of personal information in China
Network operator	It has been clarified that the business operator corresponding to this is responsible for security
Important information infrastructure operator	It has been clarified that businesses that fall under this category will be subject to strong control by the Chinese authorities in the name of protecting important information
Storage of confidential information	Personal information and data collected and generated in China are obliged to be stored in China
Data transfer abroad	It has been clarified that data transfer to foreign countries is prohibited in principle
Security product certification	Security certification by Chinese authorities is required for important cyber equipment and security products
Liability and penalties	The strong authority of the Chinese authorities in cyberspace has been stipulated, and it has been clarified that violators will be penalized, including with high fines

Source: Various materials

The operators subject to the Cybersecurity Law of China are the "network operators" and "important information infrastructure operators" in Table 16.3. The law defines a "system consisting of a system computer that collects, stores, exchanges, and processes information, other information terminals, and related equipment" as a "network". In addition, everyone who owns, manages, and provides this is defined as a "network operator".

When the term "network operator" is used in Japan and Western countries, it mainly refers to telecommunications carriers, wireless telecommunications carriers, and Internet service providers. However, China Cybersecurity Law also includes all organizations and companies that own and operate IT networks and information systems in China.

The following are stipulated as the main duties of the network operator. First, to meet the security requirements based on China's national standards and accept the audit of the authorities. Second, to require the user to register their real name. Third, to provide technical support for public security authorities to maintain national security and conduct criminal investigations.

And among the "network operators", those who are certified as "important information infrastructure operators" by the authorities are subject to even stricter requirements. The target of important information infrastructure operators is all businesses involved in public telecommunications, information services, energy, transportation, water resources, finance, public services, and electronic administration. It also includes businesses that could have a significant impact on national security, the national economy, and public interests if data is destroyed, or rendered non-functional or leaked.

If you are certified as an important information infrastructure operator, you are obliged to do the following in addition to the obligations of the network operator: to conduct background checks on important executives, to introduce network products and security equipment that have undergone security audits by the Chinese authorities, and to undergo security evaluations by the authorities when transferring personal information and important data to other countries. Under this standard, it is said that government agencies are not allowed to use Windows. The relationship between these two target businesses and their obligations are set out in Table 16.4.

Table 16.4 Operator obligations under the Cybersecurity Law of China

Classification	Duty of the operator
Network operator	• Meet security requirements based on Chinese national standards • Accept the audit of the authorities • Require the user to register their real name • Technically support public security authorities
Important information infrastructure operator	In addition to the above obligations • Conducti background checks on important managers • Introduce network products and security equipment that have undergone security audits • Receive a security evaluation by the authorities when transferring data • Implement regular inspections of the company's network

Source: Various materials

As well as tackling the threat of cyber attacks, the China Cybersecurity Law is also a risk management tool, in that it aims to avoid risks that are expected to occur in the future by imposing regulations and obligations on the target business operators. However, there are some criticisms of this law, and there are harsh opinions that strengthening the control of citizens' speech and ideas will lead to infringement of human rights.

16.3.3 Cyber Risk and Insurance

Prior to the enforcement of the Cybersecurity Law of China, Zurich China, AIG Mia Insurance and Allianz Insurance had launched insurance against cyber risk (see Table 16.5).

Table 16.5 Cyber security insurance of foreign-affiliated companies

Release year	Company	Insurance products	Compensation details	Other
2013	Zurich Insurance	Privacy protection comprehensive insurance	Trade secret leak, client information leak, employer personal information leak	–
2015	Allianz Insurance	Network security insurance and honor insurance	Internet fraud, information theft, cost of business suspension and equipment damage due to network security	Up to ten million euros in compensation
2015	AIG Property Insurance	Corporate network security insurance	Information leaks, internet viruses, malicious damage to data by employers, data theft, and so on	–

Source: Websites of each company

A foreign-affiliated insurance company had launched insurance against cyber risk, but all of its insurance products were sold as a special contract attached to property insurance.

Then, in May 2017, network security insurance,[2] the first comprehensive network information security insurance in China, was launched. In April 2018, network security insurance[3] was sold in collaboration with the Ministry of Public Security No 3 Research Institute of China and Heian Industrial Insurance (see Table 16.6).

Table 16.6 Domestic cyber security insurance in China

Release year	Company	Insurance products	Compensation details	Other
May 2017	An Heng Information and Zhong An Insurance Company[a]	Network security insurance	Malicious programming intrusions, cyber attacks, information destruction	Contractor classification: Class A: Government, business organizations, companies (state-owned and private) Class B: Private SMEs Insurance period: 1 year Minimum insurance premium: 20,000

(continued)

[2]www.dbappsecurity.com.cn/show-62-69-1.html.

[3]www.cnmstl.net/insurance/insurance?rel=2.

Table 16.6 (continued)

Release year	Company	Insurance products	Compensation details	Other
				yuan Maximum compensation amount: three million yuan Eligibility for purchase: Strictly limited by the number of employees and operating income
April 2018	An Heng Information and Zhong An Insurance Company The 3rd Research Institute of the Ministry of Public Security and Ping An Insurance Company[b]	Network security insurance	Cyber threats, data recovery costs, internet security and defense costs, pre-accident inspection costs, and so on	Contractor: Mainly SMEs Insurance premium: 50,000 yuan Compensation amount: 600,000 yuan

Source: Websites of each company

[a]Security Information Company: China Domestic Safety Service Company, ZhongAn Insurance: China's First Internet Insurance Company

[b]www.cnmstl.net/insurance/insurance?rel=2

In recent years, economic activities related to finance and online business such as electronic payment based on the Internet, e-Commerce, and Internet landing (P2P) have been spurred on in China. Foreign-affiliated companies are not seen in the cyber security insurance for financial and commercial services, but domestic companies are selling insurance (see Table 16.7).

Table 16.7 Cyber security insurance for financial and commercial services in China

Release year	Company	Insurance products	Compensation details	Other
December 2009	Linkage between China Pacific Insurance and Bank of Communications	Online bank account theft insurance	Loss due to online bank account theft	Insurance premium level: 5 yuan, 10 yuan, 50 yuan, 100 yuan Compensation amount: 50,000 yuan, 100,000 yuan, 500,000 yuan, one million yuan

(continued)

Table 16.7 (continued)

Release year	Company	Insurance products	Compensation details	Other
April 2014	Huatai Property Insurance and JD Finance	Personal account security insurance	Financial security risk for personal accounts on the internet	Maximum compensation: 500,000 yuan
2015	Ping An Property Insurance	Ping An Bank Card Theft Insurance	Note: Risk of theft of all bank cards and online bank accounts in the name of an individual	Insurance period: 1 year Insurance premium: 28–300 yuan Compensation amount: 50,000 to one million yuan
2016	Zhong An Insurance Company and Ari Baba	Data safety insurance	Data loss and information leakage due to cyber attacks	Maximum compensation amount: one million yuan Insurance eligibility: Limited to Alibaba cyber users

Source: Websites of each company

These insurances primarily cover damage caused by theft of personal accounts, cards, or data.

16.4 Pandemic

16.4.1 Pandemic History

Looking back on history, humankind has been exposed to pandemic horrors many times. The plague (also known as the Black Death) from 1346 to 1353 raged in Africa, Asia, and Europe. Scientists estimate that the pandemic killed 75 to 200 million people. In fact, a 2010 paper published in Nature Genetics by a research team led by Dr. Mark Achtman of the University College Cork in Ireland claimed that the three plagues that left a big mark on the world in the sixth, fourteenth, and nineteenth centuries could be attributed to China. According to the World Health Organization (WHO), scientists and others believe that plague caused by infection with Yersinia pestis is likely to have spread across continents through rat fleas that had invaded commercial ships.

The pandemics of the new influenza so far include the 1918 "Spanish flu", the 1957 "Asian flu", the 1968 "Hong Kong flu", and the 2009 swine flu pandemic. Of these, "Asian cold" and "Hong Kong cold" have been found to originate from China.

In addition, it is said that China is the source of infection of highly pathogenic avian influenza (H5N1, H7N9) in humans and SARS (severe acute respiratory syndrome).

The Spanish flu began in 1918, killing 20–50 million people, the worst plague in history. The Centers for Disease Control and Prevention (CDC) said that about 500 million people about 30% of the world's population at the time, worldwide had the Spanish flu. This number is higher than the death toll in World War I. There is also a theory that the catastrophe caused by this pandemic led to the end of World War I. At that time, information was controlled all over the world because it was in the midst of World War I, and the name was given after the epidemic in Spain, which was a neutral country, was fully reported. Scientists have disagreed about the origins of the Spanish flu epidemic in various places such as China, France, and the midwestern United States.

Asian cold is an influenza virus that appeared in the hinterland of mainland China in February 1957. The Asian cold has been reported to be epidemic from Singapore, Taiwan, and Manila. It was then transmitted to the densely populated Singapore and Hong Kong, where it was revealed that it had mutated into a new influenza virus. Less than 6 months later, cases were confirmed worldwide. This Asian cold has caused more than two million deaths worldwide. During the Asian flu, medical advances and knowledge about the influenza virus were rapidly advancing compared to 1918 when the Spanish flu was spreading. In addition, WHO's global influenza surveillance network had been in operation for 10 years, and infectious disease control had progressed. As a result, vaccines became available, but they were limited in number and could not be used worldwide. Avoiding crowds was the only way people could prevent a pandemic.

Hong Kong cold was discovered in 1968 in China (Hong Kong). Infections have been attributed to humans and pigs, and have also been mutually transmitted between humans and pigs. It had a slower epidemic spread than previous influenza virus pandemics, was mild, and had a low fatality rate. The number of deaths in the world was about one million.

SARS began with reports of atypical pneumonia in Guangdong Province, southern China, on 16 November 2002, and expanded to 32 regions and countries, centered on Asia, the east of India, and Canada in the northern hemisphere. Initially, 305 cases (five deaths) occurred in China, causing nosocomial infections in Hanoi, Vietnam and in Hong Kong through travelers in early March 2003. On 12 March 2003, WHO issued a global alert on the epidemic of atypical pneumonia, and a full-scale investigation was conducted. They named it "a global health threat" and announced unusual travel restrictions.

The 2009 swine flu pandemic (pandemic 2009H1N1) was a worldwide epidemic of the A (H1N1) pdm09 influenza virus, a pig-derived influenza virus, from spring 2009 to March 2010. The source is said to be the swine flu virus that was prevalent among pigs, and it is said that this virus directly transmitted from pigs to humans on farms and then spread among humans as a new virus.

Middle East respiratory syndrome (MERS) is a viral respiratory disease caused by the MERS coronavirus (MERS-CoV). It is an infectious disease caused by a new type of coronavirus discovered in a case of someone who had traveled to the Middle

East in 2012, and was discovered in London, England. MERS-CoV is a virus that causes cold symptoms in dromedary camels and is thought to cause severe pneumonia when infecting humans. It is said to have occurred in Saudi Arabia and the source of infection was dromedary.

A "viral pneumonia of unknown cause" was first confirmed in Wuhan City, Hubei Province, People's Republic of China on 22 November 2019. The infection then spread from Wuhan City to mainland China and spread to countries and regions other than China. The characteristics of the new coronavirus were thought to be similar to those of SARS and MERS. However, due to its unprecedented latency, the infection spread rapidly using human economic activities, and on 30 January 2020, the WHO announced a "public health emergency of international concern" (PHEIC), which was sixth on its list of "international concerns". The pandemic caused by this new coronavirus has not ended as of January 2021.

16.4.2 Infectious Diseases and Insurance

In China, infectious diseases are classified into class A, class B, and class C, based on the Infectious Disease Prevention and Treatment Law (revised 2004). It was announced that the new corona will be designated as a "class B infectious disease" similar to SARS, and that preventive and control measures will be at the same level as plague and cholera (class A). This has made it possible to forcibly perform isolation treatment for infected persons and isolation/follow-up of close contacts.

According to the Infectious Disease Prevention and Treatment Law, if the isolation treatment is refused or the treatment is abandoned without permission, the public security authorities will cooperate with the medical institution to perform forced isolation. In addition, at the local government level, it is possible to blockade entertainment facilities, limit or suspend the activities of residents, suspend classes, attendance, and corporate management activities, and block certain areas (provincial level). On the other hand, the national government (State Council) decides on the blockade of trunk roads and traffic that straddle large-scale, small- and medium-sized cities, provinces, and autonomous regions. On 23 January 2020, Wuhan City and its surrounding areas were closed.

The new coronavirus has been designated as a legally infectious disease, and the blockage of infected areas, restrictions on the activities and behaviors of residents, isolation treatment of infected persons and close contacts, and so on were implemented under the Infectious Disease Prevention and Treatment Law. In addition, along with the designation of a legally infectious disease, the government announced a public subsidy and, in response, Wuhan City announced that there would be no burden on the counter at hospitals. In other words, if a new corona is diagnosed and treated, the out-of-pocket portion of medical expenses will be subsidized at public expense.

Discussion Questions

1. Explain the characteristics of earthquakes in China and earthquake insurance.
2. Explain the cyber risk in China and the corresponding insurance.
3. Explain the response to the pandemic in China.

17 Risk Management in South Korea

Korea is a country with a population of about 51 million. The country is prone to natural disasters such as windstorms and floods, and there is a public and private insurance system to protect against such natural disasters. In addition, measures are being taken against cyber risks and pandemics. This chapter provides an overview of risk management in South Korea.

17.1 National Disaster Treatment

Article 3 (definition) of the Basic Law on Disaster and Safety Management enacted on 11 March 2004 stipulates as follows: "Disasters can damage people's lives, bodies, property and the nation, and can be divided into natural disasters and social disasters."

Natural disasters are "typhoons, floods, heavy rains, strong winds, waves, tsunamis, heavy snow, cold waves, lightning, droughts, heat waves, earthquakes, yellow sand, outbreaks of seaweeds, tides (tide water), volcanic activity, disasters caused by crashes and collisions of natural space objects such as asteroids or meteoroids, and other similar natural phenomena".

On the other hand, social disasters include the following that need to be dealt with by national or local governments: first, damage to human life or property due to fire, collapse, explosion, traffic accident (including aviation and marine accidents), chemical weapons accident, environmental pollution accident, and so on; second, the paralysis of national infrastructure such as energy, communications, transportation, financial medical care, and water services caused by them; third, the spread of infectious diseases covered by the Act on Prevention and Management of Infectious Diseases or the spread of infectious diseases among livestock under the Act on Prevention of Infectious Diseases of Livestock, and any damage caused that is covered by the Special Act on Reduction and Management of Fine Dust.

H. Lee, *Risk Management*, Springer Texts in Business and Economics,
https://doi.org/10.1007/978-981-16-3468-0_17

The Central Disaster and Safety Countermeasures Headquarters (CDSCHQ) has been established in the Ministry of the Interior and Safety to summarize and coordinate matters related to the response to and recovery from large-scale disasters in the Republic of Korea and to take necessary measures. The Minister of the Interior and Safety is the head of the CDSCHQ. However, in the case of a disaster that occurs overseas, the Minister of Foreign Affairs will exercise the authority of the Minister of Foreign Affairs and, in the case of a radioactive disaster, the chairman of the Nuclear Safety Commission, who is the head of the Central Radiological Disaster Countermeasures Headquarters, will exercise the authority of the head of the CDSCHQ.

Seismic observations using equipment in South Korea began on 24 March 1905, during the Japanese colonial era, when the governor-general of Korea set up an earthquake observatory in Incheon. Korea's own seismic stations were first set up in 1977 in Seoul and Gwangju. The 1978 Hong-seung earthquake (scale 5.0) highlighted the importance of seismic observation. After that, the Korea Meteorological Administration completed a system for producing high-quality seismic data and systematically notifying the occurrence of earthquakes through two projects to modernize seismic observation equipment in 1991 and 1999.

The Kobe and the Great Hanshin-Awaji earthquakes in Japan triggered the establishment in South Korea of the first earthquake-related legal provisions, which were added to the Natural Disaster Countermeasures Law in 1995. Further, the Earthquake Disaster Countermeasures Law was enacted in order to build a disaster prevention system for the 2009 earthquake disaster and protect the lives and property of the people and major core facilities from the earthquake. This law was renamed the Earthquake and Volcanic Disaster Countermeasures Law in 2013. This law obliges managers of major public facilities, such as bridges, dams, airports, gas facilities, and nuclear facilities, to install seismic acceleration measuring instruments, operated by the Ministry of the Interior and Safety, for the purpose of disaster prevention at those facilities.

In addition, seismic design of buildings has been carried out since 1988, and the government is required to "confirm the actual conditions of setting and operation of seismic design standards" based on the Earthquake and Volcanic Disaster Countermeasures Law.

17.2 Natural Disasters

17.2.1 Wind and Flood Damage

According to the Ministry of the Interior and Safety's Annual Disaster Report, in 2002 the damage from typhoon Lusa and others was 7989.1 billion won (equivalent to USD 7260 million). The average annual damage caused by natural disasters during the 10 years from 2008 to 2017 was 348.6 billion won (equivalent to USD 317 million), and the amount of damage caused by heavy rains and typhoons during the same period accounted for 88.4% of the total damage caused by natural disasters.

In other words, heavy rains and typhoons are the main natural disasters in South Korea, and disaster management policies focus on the prevention and recovery of damage caused thereby. However, the 2017 Gyeongju and Pohang earthquakes have spread the public perception that South Korea is not safe from earthquakes. In addition, a high concentration of fine dust continues for a certain period of time and, just as with other disasters, active response at national level is required. So, the external environment regarding disaster management policies has changed significantly, such as the inclusion of fine dust in social disasters.

17.2.2 Earthquakes

Records of earthquakes on the Korean peninsula date back to medieval times. According to the records, there have been about 40 earthquakes that have caused damage to human life and property. Since 1905, when the observation of earthquakes by equipment began, a total of six earthquakes have occurred, including the Pohang earthquake of magnitude 5.4 that occurred on 15 November 2017.

There were just three deaths in Tokai City and surrounding areas due to the tsunami caused by the Nihonkai-Chubu earthquake that occurred in Japan on 26 May 1983. The number of injured has amounted to fewer than 30 (23 people were injured in the Gyeongju earthquake). However, it should be pointed out that the fact that there were few earthquakes leading to death was the cause of neglecting earthquake countermeasures.

The difference between an earthquake and a typhoon, which is a typical natural disaster, is that it is unpredictable. In South Korea, seismic design standards for general buildings were established in 1988 and have been strengthened since then. In December 2017, seismic design was obligatory for buildings on the second floor and above.

In recent years, as an example of a large-scale earthquake in South Korea, a magnitude 5.4 earthquake occurred near Pohang in Gyeongsangbuk-do, southeastern South Korea, at around 2:30 p.m. on 15 November 2017. News media reported it as the second-largest earthquake in history. In Pohang, which is close to the epicenter, damage—such as buildings cracking and collapsing—was reported. In total, 123.5 billion won (about USD 110 million dollars) of damage to buildings such as public facilities, houses, and factories, was caused by the earthquake. Furthermore, it was found in March 2018 that this earthquake was caused by a geothermal power generation experiment conducted as a national research and development subject, and it became clear that it was an induced earthquake.

17.3 Wind and Flood Insurance

Natural disasters are generally exempt from fire insurance; these exempt risks are therefore covered by special contracts.

17.3.1 Disaster Support Money and Storm and Flood Damage Insurance

In South Korea, there was a disaster relief fund system for private property based on the Basic Law on Disaster and Safety Management. This disaster relief fund system is paid for the purpose of promptly stabilizing the livelihood of residents who have suffered damage to private facilities, such as housing and agricultural products, due to natural disasters.

However, since the amount of payment was only 30–35% of the amount actually required for recovery, the problem that disaster recovery could not be done with that amount was exposed. In addition, disaster relief funds were limited to agriculture, forestry and fisheries, and support for small and medium-sized enterprises was sought.

The target and amount of disaster relief funds (2019 standard) are as set out in Table 17.1.

Table 17.1 Target and amount of disaster relief funds (2019 standard)

Classification	Support target	Amount of money
Relief money	Family/disappeared bereaved family	10 million won
	Injured with disability grade 14 or higher	1–7 grade five million won, 8–14 grade 2.5 million won
Housing	Housing damage (totally destroyed, partially destroyed, etc.) Restoration costs	Completely destroyed 13 million won, partially destroyed 6.5 million won
	Relief of housing damage (totally destroyed, partially destroyed, flooded)	8000 won/day/person (60 days completely destroyed, 30 days partially destroyed)
Victim support	Damage of 50% or more of major livelihoods and agricultural and fishery facilities	1.19 million won (standard for a family of four)
Living expenses support	Damage of 50% or more of major livelihoods and agricultural and fishery facilities	730,000 won (Seoul standard)

Source: Korean National Assembly materials

National and local governments will bear 100% of the disaster relief funds (70% national government and 30% local governments). However, as the storm and flood damage insurance system described below is developed, the facilities that have taken out the insurance will be exempted from the disaster relief payment because the insurance premiums will be subsidized. However, even in that case, relief expenses and various donations other than disaster relief funds will be paid in accordance with the applicable conditions. In addition, the maximum amount of disaster relief money for facilities not covered by wind and flood insurance was unlimited until 2005, but it was gradually reduced from 2006 to 50 million won after 2010. In this way, the Korean government was trying to induce people to take responsibility for disasters and eliminate the moral hazard that makes them indifferent to disaster.

On the other hand, the MAEMI typhoon that occurred in 2003 caused 117 deaths, 13 disappearances, and total damage of 4781.0 billion won. Three years later, in 2006, a voluntary storm and flood insurance system was institutionalized as law, and 2 years later, in 2008, it was implemented.

This storm and flood damage insurance is an insurance that the government supports a part of the premium and compensates for property damage caused by storm and flood damage (typhoon, flood, heavy rain, strong wind, wave, storm surge, heavy snow) and earthquake disaster (earthquake, tsunami). This insurance is a policy insurance managed by the Ministry of the Interior and Safety and operated by a private insurance company.

The types of storm and flood insurance are set out in Table 17.2.

Table 17.2 Types of storm and flood insurance (2018 standard)

Classification		Contents	Insurance premium support
Fixed amount compensation	Housing/greenhouse wind and flood damage insurance	Individual compensation for housing (including movables) and greenhouses	Income classification (General) 52.5–92% (Intermediate) 75–92% (Welfare) 86.25–92%
	Group participation housing wind and flood damage insurance	Joined housing (including movables and lessees) through local governments	
Actual loss compensation	Actual loss compensation Housing wind and flood damage insurance	Compensation for housing in proportion to the scale of damage, enrolled individually or in groups	
	Actual loss compensation Greenhouse wind and flood damage insurance	Compensation for greenhouses in proportion to the scale of damage, individual subscription	
	Actual loss compensation Small business and industry wind and flood insurance	Individual compensation for housing (including movables) and greenhouses	34%

Source: Korean National Assembly materials

Facilities covered by storm and flood insurance are housing (including movables), greenhouses (including vinyl greenhouses), and shops and factories of small businessmen. In addition, the target risks are wind and flood damage (typhoons, floods, heavy rains, strong winds, waves, storm surges, heavy snow) and earthquake disasters (earthquakes, tsunamis). See further Fig. 17.1.

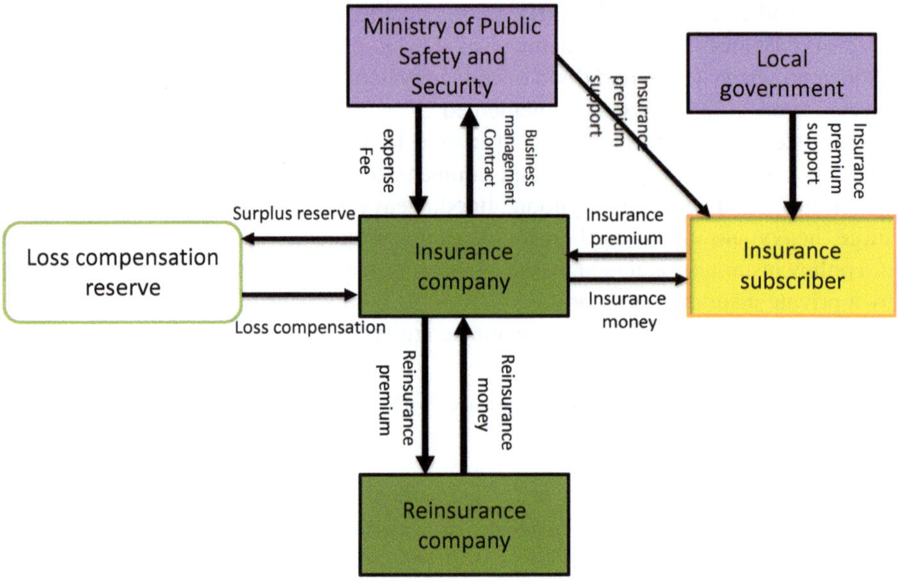

Fig. 17.1 Operation system of wind and flood insurance (*Source:* Korean government)

The premium for wind and flood insurance is supported by the national treasury. The insurance premium rate is calculated for each local government area by the Insurance Development Institute, which is a rate calculation organization in the insurance industry, and is undertaken by a private insurance company. There are two types of contract methods: a fixed-amount benefit type in which the insurance amount determined at the time of contract is paid, and an actual loss compensation method in which the amount of damage actually incurred is paid up to the insurance amount determined at the time of contract. The actual loss compensation method is a method in which the actual amount of damage is paid as insurance money, up to the amount of insurance specified by the contract. In addition, the insurance coverage rate can be selected from 50, 70, and 90%.

For subscribers with a general income category, the government will support 52.5–92% of the insurance premium, and the subscriber's burden will be 8–47.5%. In addition, 56.25–92% will be assisted to the welfare recipients, and the subscriber burden will be 8–43.75%. And there is a mechanism to recontract every year. Regarding reinsurance, each insurance company has its own contract with the reinsurance company for damages with a loss ratio of up to 180%.

17.3.2 Risk Diversification of Insurance System

Wind and flood insurance has financial risk diversification in its management. The primary risk diversification is carried out through reinsurance, which is commonly used in private insurance (Article 22 of the Wind and Flood Insurance Law). The amount of natural disasters varies greatly from year to year, and reinsurance is provided only for damages with a loss ratio of 200%. The reinsurance premium is determined by negotiation between the primary insurer and the reinsurer.

The second risk diversification is that insurance claims with a loss ratio of over 200% are provided by the extraordinary risk reserve and loss compensation reserves accumulated by the insurance company. Insurance companies are obliged to reserve extraordinary risk reserves and loss compensation reserves for the stability of insurance finances.

If the amount of insurance money exceeds the accumulated extraordinary risk reserve and loss compensation reserve after that, the excess amount will be supported by the national treasury (Article 21 of the Wind and Flood Insurance Law). See further Table 17.3.

Table 17.3 Diversification of financial risks in the management of wind and flood insurance

Damage classification	Risk taking	
Huge damage (loss ratio over 200%)	Government: compensate for excess of extraordinary risk reserve Primary Insurance Company: extraordinary risk reserve, loss compensation reserve	
Normal damage (loss ratio within 200%)	Primary insurance company (Retention)	Reinsurance company (Underwriting of reinsurance)

The disaster relief fund system still exists, but buildings and household goods that are covered by wind and flood insurance are not covered by the disaster relief fund.

17.4 Cyber Risks

17.4.1 Cyber Risks Trends

Cyber risk is also increasing in South Korea.

The main cyber risks that have occurred in recent years are shown in Table 17.4.

Table 17.4 Major cyber risks that have occurred in recent years

Year month	Organization	Type	Damage scale
January 2014	KB Kookmin Card, Lotte Card, NH Agricultural Cooperative	Personal information leakage	20 million people
March 2014	KT Corporation	Personal information leakage	12 million people
March 2014	SKT, LG U +, etc.	Personal information leakage	12.3 million people
March 2014	Ministry of Land, Infrastructure and Transport (Government)	Personal information leakage	20 million people

(continued)

Table 17.4 (continued)

Year month	Organization	Type	Damage scale
September 2015	Pump	Personal information leakage	2 million people
July 2016	INTERPARK	Personal information leakage	10.3 million
April 2017	Yapizon	Cryptocurrency outflow	5.5 billion won
June 2017	Bithumb	Personal information leakage	36,000 people
July 2017	20 companies including Eugene futures	Personal information leakage	33 million cases
September 2017	ESTsoft	Personal information leakage	130,000 cases
September 2017	Hana Tour	Personal information leakage	1 million
December 2017	Youbit (formerly Yapizon)	Cryptocurrency outflow	17.2 billion won
June 2018	Coin Rail	Cryptocurrency outflow	40 billion won
June 2018	Bithumb	Cryptocurrency outflow	35 billion won
April 2019	Naver	Personal information flow	About 2200 people
November 2019	Upbit	Cryptocurrency outflow	58 billion won

Source: Various materials

In the past, many cyber risks were aimed at information leakage or online shutdown, but in recent years many financial accidents, such as actually withdrawing funds, have been seen.

17.4.2 Cyber Risks and Insurance

Insurance against cyber risk includes corporate insurance and personal insurance. In the past, the coverage of cyber insurance for companies was limited to information leakage, but recently the coverage has been expanded and most cyber risks are comprehensively covered depending on the type of insurance. Then there are cases where individual contracts are made according to the demands of individual companies. This corporate cyber insurance covers reputational risks, such as recovery costs for data damage or theft, liability for information leaks, business interruption damages, and costs associated with cyber threats, and liability for officers.

In addition, as for personal insurance, there is no insurance that guarantees cyber risk on its own, and it is sold as a special contract of other insurance such as household comprehensive insurance.

On the other hand, the Credit Information Law, the Information and Communication Network Law, and the Electronic Financial Transaction Law provide financial resources for damages by purchasing insurance (mutual aid) against information leakage due to the occurrence of cyber risks.

The applicable targets for each law and the minimum insurance coverage amount for personal information liability insurance (cyber insurance) (mutual insurance) are as shown in Table 17.5.

Table 17.5 Applicable targets for each law and minimum insurance coverage for liability insurance (mutual insurance)

Classification	Targets of the law	Applicable minimum subscription amount (won)
Credit Information Law	Credit information concentration agencies, credit information companies, commercial banks, financial holding companies, Korea Industrial Bank, Korea Import/Export Bank, Agricultural Cooperative Bank, Korea Housing Corporation	2 billion
	Local banks, domestic branches of foreign banks, financial investors, securities finance companies, general financial companies, fund brokerage companies, transfer agency companies, insurance companies, credit specialist companies, technical guarantee funds, credit guarantee funds, Korea Trade Insurance Corporation, Deposit Insurance Corporation	1 billion
	Other	500 million
Direct information and communication facility operator	Businesses with sales of 10 billion won or more	1 billion
	Businesses with sales of 1 billion won or more and less than 10 billion won	100 million
	Businesses under 1 billion won	50 million
Electronic Financial Instruments and Exchange Act	Commercial banks, agricultural cooperative banks, industrial banks	2 billion
	Local banks, domestic branches of foreign banks, industrial banks, Suhyup Bank, post offices, credit specialist financial companies	1 billion
	Financial investors, securities finance companies, general financial companies	500 million

(continued)

Table 17.5 (continued)

Classification	Targets of the law		Applicable minimum subscription amount (won)
	Other financial companies		100 million
	Electronic fund transfer and debit electronic payment method issuance and management electronic financial companies		200 million
	Debit electronic payment method: an electronic financial company that stores information used during transactions such as credit cards and debit cards issued by electronic financial companies that issue and manage electronic payment methods		1 billion
	Other electronic finance companies		100 million
Information and Communication Network Law	Use for over one million people	Over 80 billion won in sales	1 billion
		Sales exceeded 5 billion won, less than 80 billion won	500 million
		Sales exceeded 50 million won, less than 5 billion won	200 million
	100,000 or more and one million or less	Over 80 billion won in sales	500 million
		Sales exceeded 5 billion won, less than 80 billion won	200 million
		Sales exceeded 50 million won, less than 5 billion won	100 million
	Used by 1000 or more and 100,000 or less	Over 80 billion won in sales	200 million
		Sales exceeded 5 billion won, less than 80 billion won	100 million
		Sales exceeded 50 million won, less than 5 billion won	50 million

Source: Various materials

Businesses that are obliged to take out insurance or mutual aid on information and communication networks are businesses that operate websites and the like for the purpose of profit on the Internet and hold customer information.

17.5 Pandemic

The South Korean government issued a de facto end of MERS declaration on 28 July 2015, with the first case—a man who had stayed in South Korea and returned to the Middle East—having occurred in May 2015. By then, 186 people had been infected in the country, 37 had died, and the number of quarantines had increased to more than 16,000. Most of the transmission routes were due to in-hospital infections, and the case fatality rate from MERS reached 20%. The government's information hiding was cited as one of the reasons for the outbreak and spread of MERS in South Korea.

Such infectious diseases were managed by the Korea Centers for Disease Control and Prevention (KCDC), which was established on 18 December 2003. It became the Korea Disease Control and Prevention Agency (KDCA) in September 2020 and manages infectious diseases.

In South Korea, measures against the new coronavirus (Covid-19) have been taken from an early stage, taking into account the government's inadequate measures against infectious diseases during the MERS epidemic. Therefore, the confusion of people due to the spread of the new coronavirus epidemic has been lessened in South Korea compared to other countries, and there have been few criticisms of the current government's measures.

Covid-19 triggered a revision of the Act on Prevention and Management of Infectious Diseases (the "Infectious Disease Prevention Law"), the Quarantine Law, and the Medical Care Law, which came into effect on 4 June 2020.There is no charge for treatment of infectious diseases, and medical insurance provided by the government regardless of nationality bears the medical expenses. However, if an infected person violates the above-mentioned laws such as hiding the movement route or giving an explanation that is different from the fact in the investigation to identify the contact person, he/she will be punished with criminal penalties. At the same time, infected persons who violate the law are required to pay damages for government expenses such as medical expenses once borne by the government.

International Standards for Diagnostic Testing of Infectious Diseases (such as Covid-19), proposed by South Korea to the ISO, were established on 2 December 2020. The international standard for diagnostic technology for infectious diseases such as Covid-19 is ISO 17822, "In vitro diagnostic test systems, Nucleic acid amplification-based examination procedures for detection and identification of microbial pathogens-Laboratory quality practice guide".

ISO 17822 was published after the "K-Epidemiological 3T (Test for diagnosis–Trace for epidemiological investigation–Treat for patient management) promotion strategy" announced by the Korean government in June 2020. This is an example of the international standardization of the K-epidemiological model. The aim is to prevent the spread of infectious diseases by taking measures faster than the rate of outbreaks. In particular, "K-Episode Prevention 3T" includes drive/walk-through sorting clinics, mobile sorting clinics, and living treatment centers in the international standard proposal stage. The three elements of the Korean-style epidemic prevention strategy (test, trace, treat) can be summarized as follows.

First, test means expansion of inspection capacity. Currently, South Korea uses the real-time RT-PCR test, which can test up to 40,000 cases a day. This is linked to the smooth supply of epidemic prevention supplies.

Second, trace means the rapid tracking of the movement of confirmed infectious diseases. The following data is used to track movements: mobile phone GPS records, mobile phone base station connection records, credit/debit card usage records, shopping receipt records, transportation card usage records, hospital consultation records (compulsory records, prescription records and so on), tickets for public transportation, city railroads, train tickets, intercity bus tickets, taxi usage records, QR code-based electronic entry / exit lists, CCTV records, and so on. Currently, EISS (the Epidemic Investigation Support System), which is a (semi-) automated movement tracking system for these data, is in operation.

Third, treat means rapid isolation treatment of confirmed infected individuals. Mild patients are isolated in a life care center, and moderate or higher patients are treated in a negative pressure isolation treatment bed.

Discussion Questions

1. Explain natural disasters and insurance in South Korea.
2. Explain the mechanism of wind and flood insurance and risk diversification in South Korea.
3. Explain the pandemic in South Korea and the response to it.

References

Japanese Literature, etc.

Cabinet Office. (2013). *Business continuity guidelines—Strategy and response to overcome all crisis events*, 3rd ed.

Hiyoshi, N. (2001). *Alternative risk transfer (ART).*

Kamei, K. (2011). *Basic theory and cases of risk management.* Kansai University Press.

Kamei, K. (2014). *Basic theory and cases of modern risk management.* Law Culture Co Ltd.

Kani, S. (2013). *Fusion of finance and insurance.* Financial and Financial Situation Study Group.

Kinsen Co Ltd. (2014). *Risk finance method in enterprises.*

Kobayashi, M., & Yasuda, Y. (2008). *Subprime problems and housing finance market.* Housing Shinposha.

Lee, H. (2019). *Principles of risk management* (in Japanese). Seibundou.

Lee, H. (2020a). *Principles of risk management* (in Chinese). Hakueisha.

Lee, H. (2020b). *Principles of risk management* (in Korean). Hakueisha.

Lee, H. (2021a). *Insurance theory* (in Japanese). Hakueisha.

Lee, H. (2021b). *Personnel risk management and insurance* (in Japanese). Hakueisha.

Ministry of Economy, Trade and Industry Risk Finance Study Group. (2006). Risk Finance Study Group report—toward the spread of risk finance.

Nakaide, S. (2016). *The essence of compensation for damage.* Seibundo.

Otani, K. (2012). *Insurance theory* (3rd ed.). Seibundo.

Qin, M. (2015). *Study on the spread factors of agricultural disaster insurance in China.* Tohoku University.

Suzuki, S. (2017). Changes brought by insurance linked securities (ILS)—Underwriting of insurance risks by capital markets. Sompo Japan Nipponkoa Research Institute Report.

Tada, O. (2012). Expectations for insurance link securities that have begun to flourish—Trends centered on CAT bonds. Sompo Japan Nipponkoa Research Institute Report.

Ueda, K. (2007). *Corporate value creation-type risk management, concepts and cases.* Hakuto Shobo.

Ueda, K. (2014a). *Introduction to risk management learned from case studies* (2nd ed.). Dobunkan.

Ueda, K. (2014b). *Management of corporate ethics risk.* Dobunkan.

Ueda, K. (Ed.). (2017). *Essence of risk management.* Dobunkan.

H. Lee, *Risk Management*, Springer Texts in Business and Economics,
https://doi.org/10.1007/978-981-16-3468-0

English Literature

Banks, E. (2004). *Alternative risk transfer*. John Wiley & Sons.

Ben Ammar, S., Braun, A., & Eling, M. (2015). *Alternative risk transfer and insurance-linked securities: Trends, challenges and new market opportunities*. Institute of Insurance Economics I.VW-HSG, University of St Gallen.

Business Accounting Council. (2007). *Standards for the evaluation and audit of internal control over financial reporting*.

COSO. (2004). *Enterprise risk management—Integrated framework*. Executive summary framework.

COSO. (2017). *Enterprise risk management—Integrating with strategy and performance*.

Culp, C. L. (2002). *The art of risk management*. John Wiley & Sons Inc.

Doherty, N. A. (2000). *Integrated risk management*.

Financial Services Agency. (n.d.) Financial inspection manual.

Fraser, J., & Simkins, B. J. (2010). *Enterprise risk management*. John Wiley & Sons, Inc.

Gallagher, R. B. (1956). Risk management: A new phase of cost control. *Harvard Business Review*.

Hull, J. C. (2018). *Risk management and financial institutions*. John Wiley & Sons Inc.

Internal Accounting Subcommittee, Corporate Accounting Council. (2005). *On standards for evaluation and audit of internal control over financial reporting*.

ISO, International Standard ISO 31010 (2009).

ISO, International Standard IEC/ISO 31000 (2018).

Lane, M. (2002). *Alternative risk strategies*. Risk Waters Group.

Ministry of Economy, Trade and Industry. (2003). *Internal control in the new era of risks: guidelines for internal control functioning together with risk management*. Study Group on Risk Management and Internal Control.

Ministry of Economy, Trade and Industry. (2005). *Business continuity planning guidelines*.

Moeller, R. R. (2007a). *COSO Enterprise risk management—Establishing effective governance, risk and compliance processes*. John Wiley & Sons Inc.

Moeller, R. R. (2007b). *COSO Enterprise risk management—Understanding the new integrated ERM framework*. John Wiley & Sons Inc.

Perin, M. (1999). Innovative weather bonds get cool reception from investors. *Houston Business Journal*. www.bizjournals.com/houston/stories/1999/11/22/story7.html.

Shrivastava, P., Mitroff, I. I., Miller, D., & Miglani, A. (1988). Understanding industrial crises. *Journal of Management Studies*.

Taleb, N. N. (2006). *The black Swan*.

Willet, A. H. (1951). *The economic theory of risk and insurance*.

Index

H. Lee, *Risk Management*, Springer Texts in Business and Economics,
https://doi.org/10.1007/978-981-16-3468-0

MIX
Papier aus verantwortungsvollen Quellen
Paper from responsible sources
FSC® C105338

If you have any concerns about our products,
you can contact us on
ProductSafety@springernature.com

In case Publisher is established outside the EU,
the EU authorized representative is:
Springer Nature Customer Service Center GmbH
Europaplatz 3, 69115 Heidelberg, Germany

Printed by Libri Plureos GmbH
in Hamburg, Germany